# TANK
# HUNTER

# TANK HUNTER
## WORLD WAR I

CRAIG MOORE

The
History
Press

## Artwork Disclaimer

All the illustrations in this book are an artist's impression of the tank, armoured fighting vehicle, artillery tractor or supply vehicle. They are not to be viewed as accurate engineering drawings. The camouflage livery patterns and colours used are the artist's best guess from studying black and white photographs and surviving tanks. The illustrations are by David Bocquelet.

## Acknowledgements

I would like to thank the following people who have helped provide information that was used in writing this book: Herbert Ackermans, Pierre-Oliver Buan, David Bocquelet, Mikhail Blinov, Rob Cogan, Len Dyer, Charles R. Lemons, Ed Francis, Andrew Hills, Marcus Hock, Doug Hone, Christophe Mialon, Sue Moore, Matt Newton, Nathaniel MacDonald, Pascale Mathieu, Steve Osfield, Ralf Raths, Lucian Stan, Yuri Pasholok, Clark Ward. Charlie Webb and Steven J. Zaloga.

*Front cover illustrations. Top:* Male Mark V★ tank, serial No. 9543, serving in 'B' Company, 15th Battalion, under Lt R.P. Foster, with identity number 037. Photographed on 8 August 1918 in a 'tank park' in the village of Villers-Bretonneux, France (AWM E0 5426). *Bottom:* Sturmpanzerwagen A7V tanks No. 543 'Hagen' (foreground), No. 505 'Baden I' (behind) and No. 503 'Faust' (far background) at Finkelberg Training Area near Saarburg on 1 October 1918 (AWM H1 3452).

First published 2017

The History Press
The Mill, Brimscombe Port
Stroud, Gloucestershire, GL5 2QG
www.thehistorypress.co.uk

© Craig Moore, 2017

The right of Craig Moore to be identified as the Author
of this work has been asserted in accordance with the
Copyright, Designs and Patents Act 1988.

British Library Cataloguing in Publication Data.
A catalogue record for this book is available from the British Library.

ISBN 978 0 7509 8246 7

Typesetting and origination by The History Press
Printed in Turkey

# CONTENTS

## THE BATTLES

THE BATTLES

# INTRODUCTION

The First World War lasted from 28 July 1914 to 11 November 1918. The first few years of fighting in north-west Europe was a stalemate with soldiers living in squalid conditions in defensive trenches, a few 100yd apart from the enemy. When the men went over the top to take part in an attack, modern machine guns slaughtered thousands within minutes, for very little ground captured.

Tanks revolutionised warfare. They could crush, cut and rip up the layers of barbed-wire fences in no-man's-land. The tank's weapons could silence German machine guns and fire into their trenches as they drove over and along them. Supporting infantry could then occupy and hold the captured territory as the tanks continued the push forward.

There were lots of problems that had to be solved. The tanks were mechanically unreliable; their crews fought in extreme heat and noise while breathing in poisonous exhaust gases from the engine. The caterpillar tracks could negotiate rough ground but they had their limits. Waterlogged, muddy, slippery tracts of land that had been pummelled by artillery bombardment were difficult for them to cross. Large numbers ditched and had to be left in deep craters. Any stationary tank became a target for German field guns and artillery.

This book will show you where you can go to see surviving First World War tanks. Please remember though, and this may sound strange, tanks move; they are often loaned to other museums as temporary exhibits. Some may not be on show because they have been moved to the workshop for restoration.

Before you visit a location or museum to see a particular tank, contact it first and check to see if the tank you want to see is still on public display.

The chapters at the beginning of the book concentrate on the history of early tank development and the different types used during the First World War. The later chapters cover some of the important battles of the war where tanks were used on the battlefield.

# THE
# TANKS

# 'LITTLE WILLIE'

The first tank prototype was designed under the auspices of the British Admiralty not the Army, which surprisingly had nothing to do with it. Winston Churchill, 1st Lord of the Admiralty at the time, had grown impatient at the way the war was going in France and was convinced there were better ways of conducting it. He formed the Landships Committee, which included Royal Navy engineers, and told it to come up with a solution. This is why lots of the terms used to describe tank components were those used in the Navy, such as decks, hatches, sponsons, cupolas, cabins and hull.

In February 1915 the committee granted William Foster & Co. of Lincoln the contract to build the first prototype British tank. Part of the requirement was to utilise an extended agricultural tractor crawler track system developed by Bullock Creeping Grip Tractor Company of Chicago, USA.

The task of designing the first Landship fighting vehicle was shared between William Tritton, the Managing Director of William Foster & Co., and Walter Wilson, a British Navy officer assigned to the company, who was also an engineer.

The first prototype, named by the company the 'Number One Lincoln Machine', was completed on 9 September 1915. It had a turret fixed to the top of a riveted steel box body and the front metal plates were angled to help the vehicle negotiate undulating terrain.

The American tracks were set back from the front of the vehicle; they were too short and not strong enough to cope with the 16-ton vehicle weight. Modifications were made but cross-country performance during tests was poor.

The 'Number One Lincoln Machine' tank prototype was designed to have a rotating turret on the top. During trials it was found that the tracks were too short at the front. It had difficulty getting out of ditches.

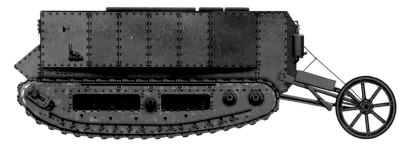

The 'Little Willie' tank prototype did not have a turret. The tracks had been lengthened at the front of the vehicle to help it climb out of ditches.

William Tritton and Walter Wilson worked on a solution to the track problem. They developed a new wider, longer and stronger system that ran the length of the vehicle.

A track frame was built, with a series of rollers mounted on the frame for the track to run on. To stop the tracks getting clogged with mud, openings were cut into the frame that acted as mud chutes.

The track drive sprocket wheel was at the rear. The track tension could be adjusted by repositioning the front idler wheel, one on each side. There was no suspension and hence the ride was very bumpy.

To enable the tracks to be fully tested the turret was removed and the circular hole in the roof was plated over. It was at this stage that the Number One Lincoln Machine was renamed. It was given the derogatory nickname 'Little Willie' after the German Kaiser Wilhelm II's eldest son, Crown Prince Wilhelm.

The Prince was causing some problems for the Kaiser. In an interview in October 1914 he stated, 'Undoubtedly this is the most stupid, senseless and

The 'Little Willie' prototype can be seen at The Tank Museum in Bovington.

The 'Little Willie' tank prototype. The driver sat on the right and the commander on the left. The hole in the middle was for mounting a machine gun. The tracks were wide to help disperse the weight of the vehicle on muddy, waterlogged ground.

unnecessary war of modern times …' It was hoped that this new fighting machine would also cause the Kaiser a few problems. (The second, bigger tank prototype that followed was called 'Big Willie', but this was later changed to 'Mother'.)

The engine was fitted at the rear of the vehicle. It was a British Daimler 13-litre straight-six petrol engine. That sounds extremely powerful but it could only produce 105hp at 1,000rpm. The transmission only had three options: first, second and reverse gears.

As this new armoured fighting vehicle did not have wheels, the design team had to work out how it was going to be steered. Agricultural tractors used steering brakes; to turn right the driver pulled the right lever and to turn left he applied the left track brake lever.

It was felt that the longer tracks on the tank needed the additional help of two large wheels, and these were placed on a frame that protruded from the rear of the hull on a hydraulic arm. It was hoped that this would act like a rudder fitted to the back of a boat. When going over very uneven ground the rear steering wheels could be raised.

# 'MOTHER'

The next prototype started to look like British tanks that fought in the First World War. Walter Wilson wanted to give the tank better cross-country performance and he enlarged the track frame used on the 'Little Willie' prototype, making it a rhomboid shape. He also fitted a lengthened track to go all around the outside of the frame that enabled the vehicle to cross enemy trenches.★ It still had the rear steering wheeled trailer that could be raised or lowered.

The prototype was finished by December 1915. At first it was known as the 'Wilson' in the factory, although officially it was designated 'His Majesty's Land Ship Centipede'. It was also known as 'Big Willie' because it was bigger than the 'Little Willie' prototype, and eventually, 'Mother', because from this design lots of other tanks were spawned. It was transported from William Foster & Co.'s factory in Lincoln to Hatfield Park in Hertfordshire, where it underwent trials.

The Royal Navy had a stock of 6-pounder cannons that were a 1915 modification of the French Hotchkiss 75mm gun. It had a muzzle velocity of 606yd/sec (544m/sec) and a maximum range of 4.26 miles (6.86km). The gun barrel length was 7ft 5in (2.28m).

However, fitting a 6-pounder gun in a turret was impractical. It would have been located above the very hot and noxious engine, which would have made working the cannon uncomfortable for the gun crew. The other major concern was that a turret would have raised the tank's centre of gravity too high and caused it to topple over when negotiating undulating landscapes found on battlefields caused by shell craters.

Eustace Tennyson d'Eyncourt, Director of British Naval Construction, suggested using side-mounted sponsons that gave each weapon a 110-degree traverse. A curved armoured gun shield was fitted to the cannon. When the gun was moved in the sponson's aperture the shield sealed off the crew compartment.

---

★ Edwin Wheelock of the US Pioneer Tractor Company claimed that he invented the Rhomboid-shaped track system, not Walter Wilson. He also claims that in a meeting in London in April 1915 with Col Sir Henry Capel-Lofft Holden, Director of Mechanical Transport, at the War Office in London, the company's representative, Francis J. Lowe, handed over the only blueprint copy of the design to Walter Wilson, who was also at the meeting, for further evaluation. The US Pioneer Tractor Company never received the blueprint back or any orders from the British government. No documentary proof has yet been found to substantiate this claim.

The gunner moved the weapon manually. He had a folding stock under his right arm that he moved to his left or right and up and down to elevate or depress the gun. He had a pistol grip with a trigger to fire the gun when it was on target. To find his target the gunner used a telescopic sight fitted to the gun mounting that looked through a small vertical slit.

Compared with modern tanks there appears to be a lot of room inside both 'Little' and 'Big Willie' but it has to be remembered that they were designed to have a crew of eight. The sponsons helped increase the space available slightly but they were fitted with bulky machine guns and cannons.

The same British Daimler straight-six 13-litre petrol engine, producing 105hp, which was fitted to 'Little Willie' was also used in its bigger brother. The engine was moved more towards the centre of the vehicle, while the radiator and cooling fan were mounted at the rear of the engine.

The engine had to cope with an increase in vehicle weight from 16 tons to 28 due to the addition of sponsons, weapons, ammunition, and the increased size of the track frame and track. Additional gearboxes were added to give four forward gears and two reverse gears.

The first cross-country trials took place in the grounds of Hatfield House on 29 January 1916 and they went well. These were repeated four days later in front of an audience of government officials and senior officers, including Field Marshal Kitchener. 'Mother' managed to successfully negotiate all the obstacles placed in her way: trenches, lines of barbed wire, hills, waterlogged ground and large holes dug to have the same characteristics of an artillery shell crater.

The Army Council placed an order for 100 tanks ten days after the last presentation. The contract was split between William Foster & Co. of Lincoln and the Metropolitan Carriage, Wagon and Finance Company of Birmingham. Seven may have been built by Robey and Company in Lincoln but this has not been confirmed by surviving documents. Unfortunately, 'Mother' was cut up for scrap metal after the war.

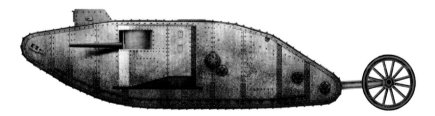

On 29 January 1916, the 'Mother' prototype successfully underwent cross-country trials in the grounds of Hatfield House, Hertfordshire.

# MARK I TANK

The first production tank was only given the designation 'Mark I' after new versions were built. The Metropolitan Carriage, Wagon and Finance Company of Birmingham had a large production capacity; it built seventy-five tanks of the original 100-tank order at its Oldham Railway Carriage & Wagon Company factory, while the remaining twenty-five tanks were built in William Foster & Co.'s factory in Lincoln.

The Mark I tank needed good quality armour plate to protect the crew, and the standard steel plate used on the 'Mother' prototype was not good enough. Two thicknesses were used: 10mm to cover important areas and 6mm for non-vital ones. The steel was cut and drilled in a soft state by the manufacturer and then hardened by heating and cooling rapidly while being pressed flat.

The War Office wanted to create six tank companies equipped with twenty-five tanks each, so it increased the initial order from 100 to 150. However, this caused a problem: there were not enough 6-pounder guns available to equip all the vehicles.

A decision was made to fit seventy-five with a pair of 0.303in (7.62mm) Vickers water-cooled machine guns in each sponson and the remaining seventy-five with a forward-facing 6-pounder (57mm) gun and a side-facing 0.303in (7.62mm) Hotchkiss air-cooled machine gun in each sponson. The machine gun-only tanks were called Mark I Female tanks and those armed with two 6-pounder guns and three machine guns were called Mark I Male tanks.

There was a gun port at the front of the tank situated between the driver and commander. It was covered with a movable armoured plate and was used to enable a 0.303in (7.62mm) Hotchkiss air-cooled machine gun to be fired forward.

To modern eyes it may seem strange to build a large tank armed only with machine guns. You have to remember that in 1915 the enemy did not possess any tanks, so they only had to deal with infantry and machine-gun nests. The Male tank's 6-pounder guns were intended to be used against enemy fortified positions.

Eight Mark I tanks fought in Gaza and they formed 'E' Company, Heavy Branch Machine Gun Corps (later renamed the Palestine Tank Detachment). They left England in January 1917 and were to be part of the British Egyptian Expeditionary Force that was going to attack the Turkish soldiers of the Ottoman Empire in what was then called Palestine.

After arriving in March 1917 they were transported to the British Army positions outside Gaza. The four Male gun tanks were called 'Sir Archibald',

'Otazel', 'Pincher' and 'Ole Luk Oie'. The four Female machine gun-only tanks were called 'War Baby', 'Kia Ora', 'Nutty' and 'Tiger'.

These were not deployed in a close group as a hammer to smash through enemy front lines. The senior officers disregarded the advice given to them by the young officers who commanded the tanks and instead they were used in pairs, spread apart.

The Turkish Army used artillery to stop the tanks, although the desert sand also helped the enemy. It got into the mechanical systems and the abrasive effect caused damage, hence breakdowns were common. The sand also caused the tracks to come off, which could be fatal on the battlefield as a stationary target was easier for the artillery to target. They were last used in combat in Palestine during the Third Battle of Gaza in November 1917 but had very little impact on the overall campaign because they were so few in number.

## SURVIVING MARK I TANKS

There is only one Mark I left and it is on display at The Tank Museum, Bovington, Dorset, UK. It was originally placed in Lord Salisbury's Hatfield Park in Hertfordshire on 8 May 1919 as a 'Presentation Tank' by the Army Council to commemorate the secret tank trials and inspection there by HM King George V in February 1916 of the first type of tank approved for use by the British Army in the war. After fifty years at Hatfield Park it was moved to the Royal Armoured Corps Tank Museum on 7 May 1969.

When it arrived it was fitted with the Mark IV Male tank short-barrelled 6-pounder gun rather than the early long-barrelled naval gun. The gun shield had been changed to fit the later gun. It was also missing the Mark I rear steering tail and hydraulic lifting and lowering apparatus. The tail hydraulics attached to the back came from a Mark II tank. These were all removed and replaced when the tank was restored.

The anti-hand grenade wood and wire mesh roof had to be newly fabricated. Some tanks had this roof mesh extended over the top of each sponson for added protection. Not all Mark Is had these roofs fitted.

Research has not been able to confirm its wartime identity or service history, although the museum believes it was used as a tank crew training vehicle.

The museum restoration workshop painted the vehicle in similar camouflage colours used on the Mark I Male tank No. 705 C19 called 'Clan Leslie', of 4 Section, 'C' Company, Heavy Section Machine Gun Corps, commanded by

Maj. Holford Walker. Mark I tanks took part in the Battle of Flers–Courcelette, as part of the Somme offensive on 15 September 1916, the first time tanks were deployed in battle.

## Specifications

| Dimensions | Length 26ft (7.92m)<br>Length with tail 32ft 6in (9.92m)<br>Width 8ft 4in (2.53m)<br>Width with sponsons 13ft 2in (4.03m)<br>Height 8ft (2.44m) |
| --- | --- |
| Total Weight | 27.5 (Female) 28.4 (Male) tons |
| Crew | 8 |
| Propulsion | British Foster-Daimler, Knight sleeve valve, water-cooled, straight-six, 13-litre petrol engine; 105hp at 1,000rpm |
| Road Speed | 3.7mph (5.95km/h) |
| Fuel Capacity | 50 gallons (226 litres) |
| Range | 28 miles (45km) |
| Trench-Crossing Ability | 11ft 6in (3.5m) |
| Armament Male Tank | 2 × Hotchkiss QF 6-pounder (57 mm) gun (1.4m-long barrel)<br>3 × 0.303in (7.62mm) Hotchkiss air-cooled machine guns |
| Armament Female Tank | 4 × 0.303in (7.62mm) Vickers water-cooled machine guns<br>1 × 0.303in (7.62mm) Hotchkiss air-cooled machine gun |
| Armour | 6–12mm (0.23–0.47in) |
| Total Production | 150 |

This is the only surviving Mark I Male tank. It is on display at The Tank Museum, Bovington.

A two-wheeled steering tail was attached to the rear of the Mark I. A wood and wire mesh roof was added to deflect German hand grenades.

The Mark I Male was armed with two long-barrelled 6-pounder cannon and three 0.303in (7.62mm) Hotchkiss air-cooled machine guns.

# MARK II TANK

The British Army needed a vehicle with which to train new crews to use the Mark IV tank so fifty Mark II training tanks were built to serve this purpose: twenty-five Males and twenty-five Females. The Males were constructed by the Metropolitan Carriage, Wagon and Finance Company of Birmingham, the Females by William Foster & Co. of Lincoln.

These tanks were not intended to go into battle; they constructed in mild, not hardened, steel and could not stop a rifle bullet. Some sponsons taken from recovered, battle-damaged Mark I tanks were fitted to Mark II tanks. They were made in hardened steel and gave the crew some protection. Amazingly, these death traps were used once in action at the Battle of Arras in April 1917 as not enough Mark IV tanks had been delivered to the front lines in France in time for the next attack.

They were very similar in design to the Mark I. Most were built as Males armed with the 6-pounder gun and three Hotchkiss 0.303in air-cooled machine guns. Female Mark II tank sponsons were armed with a pair of 0.303in (7.62mm) Vickers water-cooled machine guns in an armoured sleeve on each side and one Hotchkiss 0.303in (7.62mm) air-cooled machine gun in the front cabin. Some Mark II Female tanks, like Nos 578 and 593, had their sponson machine gun apertures modified to accept the smaller 0.303in (7.62mm) Lewis machine gun instead of the large Vickers machine gun used on the Mark I Female tank. A few that were built were used as testbeds for different transmission systems.

The steering tail wheels arrangement at the back of the tank and the hydraulic lifting equipment, fitted to Mark Is, were not a feature of the Mark II. At this stage in tank development they were considered unnecessary.

The only surviving Mark II is at The Tank Museum in Bovington and is a Female version. It is the only tank with an early First World War version of the double Vickers 0.303in water-cooled machine gun-armed Female sponson. Each machine gun was mounted in an armoured jacket and both weapons could sweep a total of 180 degrees on one side of the tank.

A major problem with this design was that the crew escape hatch at the rear of the sponson was reduced in height to accommodate a second machine gun. If the tank was hit and caught fire the men inside would have difficulty getting out quickly as the hatch was only 61cm long and 41cm wide. The Mark V Female had a hatch that was 145cm high and so was much easier for the crew to escape from.

During the restoration of the Mark II the number 'F53' and the words 'The Flying Scotsman' were discovered under the layers of paint. It served with 'C' or 'D' Company during the Battle of Arras and there are some battle damage holes caused by enemy shells still visible in the back of the vehicle.

The Mark II driver's and commander's cab is a little bit narrower than the Mark I's; this was to accommodate the fitting of wider tracks but these were never used.

The same British Foster-Daimler, Knight sleeve valve, water-cooled, straight-six, 13-litre, 105hp petrol engine and transmission system was used as on the Mark I. It still took four people to drive it.

Bovington Camp received its first batch of Mark II training tanks in December 1916. Not all the fifty delivered were used for training; five were employed on testing new gearboxes, petrol-electric drives used in trams and new hydraulic systems.

Later in the war the surviving Mark IIs were converted into unarmed, armoured, ammunition- and supply-carrying tracked vehicles.

You can spot the difference between a Mark II and a Mark I on photographs by looking for several identifying features. The Mark II tank has a slightly narrower cab and the row of eleven rivets across the front of it were not all the same distance apart, unlike those on the Mark I. The two outer rivets were much closer together.

The Mark II had a raised observation hatch shaped like a cheese dish on the roof. The rear of the Mark I has the tail wheel hydraulic jack fitted; this was not fitted to the rear of the Mark II tank. The shape of the track adjustment apertures at the front of the track horns on the Mark I tank are more rounded, the Mark II's more squared.

## SURVIVING MARK II TANKS

There is only one surviving Mark II tank. It is on display at The Tank Museum, Bovington. In April and May 1917 it took part in the Battle of Arras as a Male tank, No. 785, 'D' Battaltion D5 'Dahlia'. It was converted into a supply tank and served in 'F' Battalion, F53, 'The Flying Scotsman'. It is displayed with a Female sponson.

## Specifications

| | |
|---|---|
| Dimensions | Length 26ft (7.92m)<br>Width 8ft 4in (2.53m)<br>Width with sponsons 14ft 5in (4.39m)<br>Height 8ft (2.44m) |
| Total Weight | 27.5 (Female) 28.4 (Male) tons |
| Crew | 8 |
| Propulsion | British Foster-Daimler, Knight sleeve valve, water-cooled, straight-six, 13-litre petrol engine; 105hp at 1,000rpm |
| Road Speed | 3.7mph (5.95km/h) |
| Range | 28 miles (45km) |
| Trench-Crossing Ability | 11ft 6in (3.5m) |
| Armament Male Tank | 2 × Hotchkiss QF 6-pounder (57mm) gun (1.4m-long barrel)<br>3 × 0.303in (7.62mm) Hotchkiss air-cooled machine guns |
| Armament Female Tank | 4 × 0.303in (7.62mm) Vickers water-cooled machine guns<br>1 × 0.303in (7.62mm) Hotchkiss air-cooled machine gun<br>OR<br>5 × 0.303in (7.62mm) Lewis air-cooled machine guns |
| Armour | 6–15 mm (0.23–0.59in) |
| Total Production | 50 |

The only surviving Mark II Female, on display at The Tank Museum, Bovington.

The Mark I's two-wheeled steering tail and hydraulic lifting mechanism were deemed no longer necessary so they were not fitted to the rear of the Mark II.

The Mark II Female was armed with four 0.303in (7.62mm) Vickers water-cooled machine guns and one 0.303in (7.62mm) Hotchkiss air-cooled machine gun at the front.

# MARK III TANK

The Mark III tanks were designed as a tank crew training vehicle. Fifty were built by the Metropolitan Carriage, Wagon and Finance Company of Birmingham.

The steering tail wheels arrangement at the back and the hydraulic lifting equipment, fitted to Mark Is, were not a feature of the Mark III because by this stage in tank development they were considered unnecessary.

The driver and tank commander's cab was reduced in width to allow for wider tracks to be used. A smaller one-man cab with protected vision loopholes was fitted to the rear of the tank. It replaced the escape hatch on the roof and enabled a crewman to look around to see what was happening at the sides and rear.

The tanks were not intended to be used in combat so the metal used in their construction was not armoured: it did not undergo special heat treatment to make it stronger and therefore was unable to resist machine gun and rifle bullets.

A strange feature of the Mark III was that it was 1 ton heavier than the Mark I and II. Thicker metal, 12mm thick not 10mm, was used in its construction as part of an experiment by the team developing the Mark IV.

While being used for tank driver training, Mark III tanks had their two 6-pounder guns and machine guns removed. On hot days the sponson rear hatch and the roof hatch were fixed in the open position to increase ventilation.

One of the other skills taught at Bovington Camp to all students was tank maintenance; this included the officer in charge of each vehicle. Crews practised trying to extricate tanks that had driven into a trench or shell crater. Initially this involved using a 'torpedo spud', a rounded wooden beam with a central metal collar attached to a chain. The crew would fix the other end of the chain around the track and hope it dug into the earth to give the extra traction necessary for the tank to get itself unstuck. If this failed they had to use spades and get digging. Two were carried on the roof of the tank. Later, unditching rails and long beams would be added to the Mark IV.

Near the end of the course the students would participate in tactical training, which taught them how to attack a network of trenches. Finally they would go to the ranges and practice firing the guns. Officers had to attend additional courses: map reading, report writing, signalling and route-laying using white tape.

The Mark III was built at the time of the transition from 0.303in (7.62mm) Vickers water-cooled machine guns to 0.303in (7.62mm) Lewis air-cooled light machine guns. There are photographs of Mark III Female tanks with the old style Mark I tank long Female sponsons. They were also photographed with the newer short Female sponsons and crew hatches underneath. Being lighter, the Lewis machine gun did not require such a large sponson.

Mark III tanks never left Great Britain. Two Mark III Females with the smaller sponsons were given as presentation tanks to the people of Maidstone and Canterbury as a thank you for raising money under the National War Savings Committee scheme. Unfortunately they were not looked after and both were cut up for scrap metal.

# SURVIVING MARK III TANKS

There are no surviving Mark IIIs.

## Specifications

| | |
|---|---|
| Dimensions | Length 26ft (7.92m)<br>Length with tail 32ft 6in (9.92m)<br>Width 8ft 4in (2.53m)<br>Width with Sponsons 13ft 2in (4.03m)<br>Height 8ft (2.44m) |
| Total Weight | 28.5 (Female) 29.4 (Male) tons |
| Crew | 8 |
| Propulsion | British Foster-Daimler, Knight sleeve valve, water-cooled, straight-six, 13-litre petrol engine; 105hp at 1,000rpm |
| Road Speed | 3.7mph (5.95km/h) |
| Fuel Capacity | 50 gallons (226 litres) |
| Range | 28 miles (45km) |
| Trench-Crossing Ability | 11ft 6in (3.5m) |
| Armament Male Tank | 2 × Hotchkiss QF 6-pounder (57mm) gun (1.4m-long barrel)<br>3 × 0.303in (7.62mm) Hotchkiss air-cooled machine guns |
| Armament Female Tank | 4 × 0.303in (7.62mm) Vickers water-cooled machine guns<br>1 × 0.303in (7.62mm) Hotchkiss air-cooled machine gun<br>OR<br>5 × 0.303in (7.62mm) Lewis air-cooled machine guns |
| Total Production | 50 |

No Mark IIIs survived the scrap metal merchant's blowtorch. They were built as training tanks and not used in combat. This is a Male. They were armed with the long-barrelled 6-pounder gun but this was later replaced with the short-barrelled 6-pounder gun and they were also later fitted with the new style sponsons. Most were painted brown during the First World War.

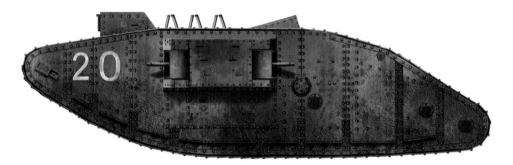

The Female Mark IIIs were also used as training tanks. They were armed with two 0.303in (7.62mm) Vickers water-cooled machine guns on either side in sponsons and a 0.303in (7.62mm) Hotchkiss air-cooled machine gun in the front. Later they were armed with five 0.303in (7.62mm) Lewis air-cooled machine guns. This example was later earmarked as a presentation tank and given to the people of Batley in Yorkshire to be used as a war memorial. It was the government's way of saying thank you for raising money to fund tank production.

# MARK IV TANK

The Mark IV was the first mass-produced tank. It was built at a number of different factories around Britain, not just in one place. Around 1,200 were built: 1,155 were used for combat or training; 205 were built as armoured supply tanks; 11 were used for testing and 54 were surplus reserve tanks. It is believed that 595 were built as machine gun-only Female tanks and 420 as 6-pounder gun- and machine gun-armed Male tanks.

The Mark IV is very similar to its predecessors. It has the same British Daimler-Benz engine and gearbox system, and still required four men to drive and change gears. Another four men were still needed to load and fire the guns in the two sponsons.

The armour on the Mark IV was slightly improved from earlier models. It could keep out rifle fire, machine gun bullets and now some anti-tank rifle bullets. It still could not protect the crew from artillery shells.

The other change was to the sponsons. These could now be pushed into the body of the tank rather than having to be unbolted and removed when the tank was transported by rail. The cab was narrower than the Mark I's to accommodate the fitting of wider tracks. Unfortunately these did not become available until late 1918.

The 6-pounder gun on the Mark I had a long barrel that got in the way during transportation and sometimes stuck in the mud. The Mark IV was now fitted with a short-barrelled 6-pounder (57mm) gun that could still pack the same punch. It was officially called the Ordnance Quick Firing 6-pounder six hundredweight Mark I gun. The gun barrel, measured from the sponson, was now only 65.6cm long.

A 0.303in (7.62mm) Lewis air-cooled light machine gun ball mount was fitted at the front of the cab between the two visors, as well as behind each 6-pounder gun on the Male tanks.

The way fuel was stored was also changed. On the Mark I there were two 25-gallon petrol tanks fitted to the front. This was an impractical location as this part of the tank received the most amount of enemy fire. If one of the fuel tanks was ruptured they could explode or ignite and burn the tank crew alive.

The engineers placed the new 70-gallon armoured fuel container on the outside of the tank, at the rear. The Mark IV tank no longer used the rear-wheeled steering trailer so there was enough room to mount the container. A device called an auto-vac sucked the fuel into the tank and then straight to the engine carburettor.

The larger 70-gallon (318 litre) fuel capacity compared with the previous 50 gallons (226 litre) carried by the Mark I gave the tank a longer operational range. The Mark IV had a fuel consumption rate of about half a mile per gallon so the tank could drive for an extra 10 miles (16km) before it needed to refuel. Spare fuel cans could be stowed on top of the tank at the back.

Sprung suspension was not fitted to any First World War British tanks. The rollers that ran along the track were sandwiched between the metal frames. Each roller was held in place by a static axle that could not move up or down as they were bolted to the tank frame. The rollers were now solid, not hollow, for extra strength. It was not a comfortable ride for the tank crew.

To cope with the muddy ground, track extenders, called 'torpedo spuds', were bolted on to every sixth or eighth track. They looked like the end of a spade and are today more commonly called 'grousers'. They did not work very well and were not used on the Mark V.

Even though a track is made of metal, it stretches and there is always a danger of it being thrown off the rollers. The crew have to adjust the tension of the track to take in any slack. In this case, at the front of the tank there was a large bolt. The crew had to loosen off the nut and move the idler wheel forward, then tighten the nut again with a very large spanner.

To help the Mark IV tanks cross wide trenches they were fitted with a large round bundle of wood called a 'fascine' on top of the roof. When they came to a trench, the commander and driver released the securing cables and let the fascine fall into the trench before driving over it. Fascines were only ever used at the Battle of Cambrai.

The Mark IV was also fitted with two unditching rails. These were fixed on top of the tank. The large wooden unditching beam was secured to the rails with chains. If the tank got stuck in the mud the crew would have to get out of the tank and chain the beam to the tank tracks. The beam would give the tank something more substantial to drive over.

Only the driver and commander had a seat. The rest of the crew were standing or crouching at their weapons or gearbox controls. The very hot engine was in the middle of the tank, giving off headache-inducing and stomach-churning noxious fumes. A new exhaust silencer system was added to help reduce engine noise and take some of the gases away from the crew.

From the early summer of 1917 to the end of the war, Mark IV tanks took part in every planned British offensive and assisted in stopping German attacks.

## SURVIVING MARK IV TANKS

Seven Mark IV tanks survived: two Males and five Females. The Mark IV Male 'Lodestar III' can be seen at the Royal Museum of the Armed Forces and Military History in Brussels, Belgium. 'Lodestar III' is believed to have been part of the 12th Battalion, Royal Tank Corps, that participated in the offensive on the Hindenburg Line near Cambrai in August and September 1918. It was a gift from the UK. The tank was unloaded from a train flat-back transport at Brussels Etterbeek station having been landed at the port of Antwerp. It served as a gate guardian in front of the Etterbeek Cavalry Barracks at the end of the First World War. Later it was driven the few miles from Etterbeek to the new Royal Museum of the Armed Forces and Military History, which was opened to the public in 1923.

The Mark IV Male tank No. 102, on display at The Tank Museum, Bovington, does not have the unditching rails fitted because it is believed it never saw action and was used only as a training vehicle in Britain. The tank is still in working order.

Mark IV Female tanks can be seen at the Australian War Memorial, Canberra, Australia; the National Armor and Cavalry Museum, Fort Benning, Georgia, USA; the war memorial in Flesquières, France; St George's Square, Ashford, Kent, England, and the Museum of Lincolnshire Life, Lincoln, England.

## Specifications

| Dimensions | Length 26ft 3in (8m)<br>Length with tail 32ft 6in (9.92m)<br>Width 8ft 4in (2.53m)<br>Width with Sponsons 13ft 7in (4.15m)<br>Height 8ft (2.44m) |
|---|---|
| Total Weight | 27.5 (Female) 28.4 (Male) tonnes |
| Crew | 8 |
| Propulsion | British Foster-Daimler, 6-cylinder, in-line, sleeve valve petrol engine; 105hp at 1,000rpm |
| Transmission | two-speed and reverse primary box with secondary two-speed selectors on the output shafts |
| Road Speed | 3.69mph (5.95km/h) |

| | |
|---|---|
| Fuel Capacity | 70 gallons (318 litres) |
| Fuel Consumption | 2.08 gallons per mile (5.6 litres/km) |
| Range | 35 miles (56km) |
| Trench-Crossing Ability | 11ft 6in (3.5m) |
| Armament Male Tank | 2 × OQF 6-pounder (57mm) short-barrelled guns<br>3 × 0.303in (7.62mm) Lewis air-cooled light machine guns |
| Armament Female Tank | 5 × 0.303in (7.62mm) Lewis air-cooled light machine guns |
| Muzzle Velocity (6-pounder) | 1,348ft/sec (411mps) |
| Max range (6-pounder) | 4.53 miles (7.3km) |
| Ammunition | High explosive, solid shot |
| Ammunition Stowage (Male) | 332 × 6-pounder shells, 6,272 × 0.303in rounds |
| Armour | 6–12mm |
| Total Production | 1,220 |

This British Mark IV Male heavy tank No. A347 called 'Lodestar III' participated in the offensive on the Hindenburg Line near Cambrai. It was hit by an artillery shell on 17 August 1918. It is on display at the Royal Army and Military History Museum, in Brussels, Belgium (Musée Royal de l'Armee et d'Histoire Militaire Bruxelles en Belgique).

To help the Mark IVs cross wide trenches they were fitted with a large round bundle of wood called a 'fascine' on the roof. This Mark IV Male is on display at The Tank Museum, Bovington. It is missing its unditching beam rails as this tank was used for training. Notice the 6-pounder gun has a short barrel.

Mark IV Males were armed with three 0.303in (7.62mm) Lewis air-cooled light machine guns and two Ordnance Quick Firing 6-pounder (57mm) guns.

# MARK V TANK

There were a lot of changes made to the Mark V even though it looked very similar to the Mark I.

A new, more powerful, Ricardo crosshead valve, water-cooled, straight-six, 19-litre, 150hp petrol engine was fitted. The Mark I to IV tanks had been fitted with a 105hp British Daimler engine.

One of the designers of the first tank, Walter Wilson, a British naval officer and engineer assigned to William Foster & Co., came up with the Epicyclic steering system that, for the first time, meant only one person was needed to drive the vehicle, unlike the four crew members necessary in the previous versions.

The driver could now operate all the gears using the new Wrigley Company four-speed gearbox with an independent reverse gear that had been designed for use on trains. The driver had to stop the tank to change gear. He had to select the correct gear for the type of terrain the tank was going to cross and try to stay in that gear for as long as he could without damaging the engine.

Both the new engine and steering system had to fit into the existing space in the Mark IV as it was hoped, at a later date in 1918, to upgrade the older machines with the new Mark V's features.

One thing that was a retrograde step was the way the engine was cooled. The new system sucked in cooler air from outside the tank, whereas prior to this the air was taken from inside the vehicle.

The older system circulated the noxious internal air, of which only some was forced out of the vehicle. This did not happen in the Mark V so there was still a problem of exhaust gas build-up making the crew feel sick and inflicting serious debilitating headaches upon them. There are a number of accounts of tank crew members becoming incapacitated through carbon monoxide poisoning. Additional vents were fitted later.

The driver's cabin on top of the tank was narrower than the one fitted to the Mark I because the designer intended that wider 26in tracks would eventually replace the 20in tracks fitted to the older tanks.

The driver's vision porthole was now a lot wider than the one on the left as he now had total control of the tank and needed to have better vision. A large escape hatch was built into the roof of the cab, replacing the two smaller hatches on earlier models. This larger hatch was fitted on late production Mark IV tanks. The crew member who sat on the left of the driver was now the front machine-gunner.

A rear cab was added to the Mark V along with a machine gun in a ball mount just below. This was the commander's cab, from where he could see what was happening on the battlefield. He could also send messages via the semaphore device fitted to the roof of the tank at the rear. He could talk to the driver via a speaking tube like those used on Royal Navy ships.

The sides of the rear cab were hinged. When the tank got stuck in the mud the crew were able to chain the underitching beam to the tracks without leaving the interior of the tank while under enemy fire.

The Mark V Male was still armed with the two Ordnance Quick Firing 6-pounder (57mm) six hundredweight Mark I guns but the Lewis guns were replaced with the slimmer 0.303in (7.62mm) Hotchkiss air-cooled machine guns.

An additional fuel tank was added to the Mark V, bringing its capacity up to 90 gallons (409 litres). They were all stored outside the tank in an armoured container at the rear. This meant the range of the tank was increased to 45 miles, 10 miles more than the Mark IV. A metal-framed tray was fitted to the roof just behind the rear cab. Additional fuel cans were often stored there along with other equipment.

William Foster & Co.'s factory in Lincoln was the birthplace of British tanks but it was not involved in building the new Mark V. This contract was given to the Metropolitan Carriage, Wagon and Finance Company of Birmingham, which produced the tanks at two of its subsidiary companies, one in Oldham, Lancashire, and the other in Saltley, Birmingham.

The Mark V, like the Mark IV, had rails fitted to the top to enable an underitching beam to be carried. If the tank got stuck in the mud the crew chained it to the tracks and it would travel under the tank, giving the track something firm to dig into.

## SURVIVING MARK V TANKS

Two Mark V Males have survived in the UK. One is kept at the Imperial War Museum, Lambeth Road, London. It saw action in the last year of the First World War at Hamel in July 1918 and played a vital role in the Battle of Amiens and the Hundred Days offensive that led to the Armistice in November 1918.

The other survivor is kept at The Tank Museum in Bovington. It saw action on 8 August 1918 at the Battle of Amiens, where its young commander, 2Lt Harold A. Whittenbury, was later awarded the Military Cross. It is shown in the Markings of 8th (H) Battalion Tank Corps.

The tank has the white and red identification markings (the colours of the English flag of St George) painted on the sides, front and roof of the cabin. This identifying feature was needed because in 1918 the German Army had captured some British tanks and was starting to use them against the Allies.

A surviving Mark V Female tank is exhibited in Arkhangelsk in north–west Russia. It was sent to the country to help the Royalist White Army fight the Bolshevik Red Army during the Civil War.

## Specifications

| | |
|---|---|
| Dimensions | Length 26ft 5in (8.05m)<br>Width 8ft 4in (2.53m)<br>Width with sponsons 13ft 7in (4.15m)<br>Height 8ft 8in (2.64m) |
| Total Weight | 27.5 (Female) 29 (Male) tons |
| Crew | 8 |
| Propulsion | Ricardo crosshead valve, water-cooled, straight-six, 19-litre petrol engine; 150hp at 1,250rpm |
| Transmission | Wrigley four-speed gearbox with independent reverse gear and Wilson two-speed epicyclics |
| Road Speed | 4.6mph (7.4km/h) |
| Fuel Capacity | 90 gallons (409 litres) |
| Fuel Consumption | 2.06 gallons per mile (5.5 litres/km) |
| Range | 45 miles (72.42km) |
| Trench-Crossing Ability | 10ft (3.04m) |
| Armament Male Tank | 2 × OQF 6-pounder (57mm) short-barrelled guns<br>4 × 0.303in (7.62mm) Hotchkiss air-cooled machine guns |
| Armament Female Tank | 6 × 0.303in (7.62mm) Hotchkiss air-cooled machine guns |
| Muzzle Velocity (6-pounder) | 1,348ft/sec (411mps) |
| Max Range (6-pounder) | 4.53 miles (7.3km) |
| Ammunition | High explosive, solid shot, case |
| Ammunition Stowage (Male) | 183 × 6-pounder shells, 24 case shot, 5,700 × 0.303in rounds |
| Armour | 6–12mm |
| Total Production | 400 (200 Male, 200 Female) |

Mark V Male at The Tank Museum, Bovington. It was in action at the Battle of Amiens, where its commander was awarded the Military Cross. Notice the new ventilation grille at the rear of the tank.

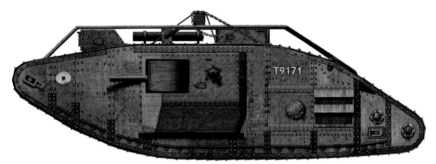

Mark V Male. In this version of the tank a machine gun was mounted at the rear. It also had a tank commander's observation cabin at the back. The tank was armed with two 6-pounder guns and four 0.303in (7.62mm) Hotchkiss air-cooled machine guns were fitted in ball mounts. They were also painted brown during the First World War.

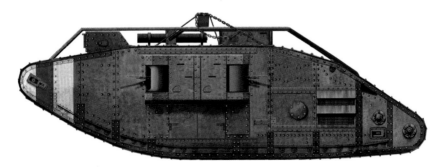

Mark V Female fitted with unditching beam and rails. It was armed with six 0.303in (7.62mm) Hotchkiss air-cooled machine guns: two each side in a sponson, one at the front and one at the rear. Red and white identification stripes were painted on the front of the tank after German-captured British tanks appeared on the battlefield. They were also painted brown.

# MARK V* TANK

After the shock of encountering British tanks on the battlefield for the first time, on 15 September 1916 the Germans started to research anti-tank precautions and weapons. After examining an abandoned Mark I they realised there was a limit to the gap the vehicle could cross so they started to widen their trenches in an effort to stop British tanks crossing their defensive lines. This was discovered by examination of Allied aircraft reconnaissance photographs of German trenches. The British Tank Corps HQ in France instructed the Army Central Tank Corps Workshops to develop a solution to counteract this anti-tank measure.

They built an extended Mark IV prototype. The body was cut in half just behind the sponson and extended by an extra 6ft (1.82m) with the addition of three extra panels. This tank did not enter production. It was not called the Mark IV★ tank, but some of its design features were used on the Mark V★ (pronounced Mark Five Star) tanks. The additional armour plate increased the weight of the tank by around 4 tons. This put more load on the tank's engine and reduced the already slow cross-country speed. Turning was also a problem as more track was in contact with the ground.

The new Mark V tank had a more powerful Ricardo crosshead valve, water-cooled straight-six 19-litre, 150hp petrol engine. It could cope with additional demands placed upon it when fitted to the Mark V★. The Royal Artillery used an asterisk to denote a modification to an existing design and this naming culture was adapted for tank development.

All the Mark V★ tanks were built by the Metropolitan Carriage, Wagon and Finance Company at its Birmingham workshops. They were 32ft 5in (9.88m) in length – 6ft (1.82m) longer than the standard Mark V tank. By the end of the First World War 579 had been built, with a further sixty-six built after the war. Unlike the extended Mark IV prototype that was built from an existing Mark IV tank, these were not modified Mark V tanks. They were built at the factory as Mark V★ tanks. A large door was put in the side just behind the sponson that enabled the crew and troops to easily get in and out.

The rear cabin was redesigned. It had a sloping front and rear with a machine gun ball mount on both panels. This was to enable the guns to be fired at enemy soldiers located in the second floor of houses in villages and towns. Both the front and rear cabins had large escape hatches in the roof. The rear cabin hatch allowed a member of the crew to attach the unditching beam to the tracks without exposing himself to enemy fire.

Unditching beams and rails were still fitted to most of the Mark V★ tanks to help them get out of deep shell craters and waterlogged, boggy ground. The Male version was armed with two 6-pounder (57mm) quick-firing guns mounted in side sponsons and eight 0.303in (7.62mm) Hotchkiss air-cooled machine guns. The Female version was armed with ten 0.303in (7.62mm) Hotchkiss air-cooled machine guns.

There was a bell at the rear of the tank for use by the infantry when they wanted to communicate with the tank crew. A rear hatch could be opened and a conversation could be had, with both parties protected from enemy fire by the armoured bulk of the tank.

The tank commander in the rear cabin could send messages using flags on a handheld pole. He could also raise the semaphore tower at the back of the tank. For longer distances he could tie a message to the leg of a carrier pigeon and release the bird through one of the loopholes.

The Mark V★ was fitted with the wider 26in tracks to spread the weight. The track edges stuck out proud from the body line so if the tank ran over a large rock there was a chance the track link could break along the exposed edge. This was a design flaw that was fixed in the Mark VIII.

They saw action during the Battle of Amiens, 8 August 1918, and during the many battles of the Hundred Days offensive that led to the Armistice of 11 November 1918. The British Army 'A' Battalion, Tank Corps, recorded that it had ten Mark V★ tanks and twenty-four Mark V tanks available for the first day of the Battle of Amiens.

The Canadian Corps, 4th Tank Brigade, was comprised of four tank battalions. The 1st Tank Battalion fielded thirty-six Mark V★ tanks. The 4th, 5th and 14th Tank Battalions each had thirty-six Mark V tanks for the Battle of Amiens.

The Australian Corps, 5th Tank Brigade, was comprised of four tank battalions. The 2nd, 8th and 13th Tank Battalions each had thirty-six Mark V tanks. The 15th Tank Battalion crewed thirty-six elongated Mark V★ tanks.

The Mark V★ tanks could be used for troop carrying. Tanks could attack and silence enemy machine-gun posts in German-held trenches and buildings but they could not hold and occupy the ground; infantry were required to carry out this task. In theory the new Mark V★ tanks could carry eight men in full kit, carrying additional supplies, ammunition and machine guns, across no-man's-land in relative safety from small arms fire. The men could then get out of the tank and occupy the now empty enemy trenches and strongpoints.

There are a few entries in war diaries that discuss the number of men that could be carried in the back of a Mark V★. One claims that it was possible to cram in two Lewis guns, each with a two-man crew; two Vickers guns, each with a four-man crew; an infantry scout; and one officer – a total of fourteen men in addition to the regular crew.

In reality conditions were so bad inside the tank that the machine gun squads and infantry carried in the back were often too ill to fight due to the heat and the noxious fumes from the engines and guns. Unlike in the Mark IX armoured personnel carrier, the Ricardo engine was still situated in the middle of the tank near the crew and troops.

The men could not sit down. They had to hold on tight as the tank violently went up and down over the rough battlefield terrain. Some would have been injured if they lost their grip and fell to the floor. If they smashed their head hard on the armour plate hull or internal girder beam they could suffer a serious injury or be knocked unconscious.

Five-gallon water containers were added to this tank so that the crew and passengers had something to drink to keep them hydrated in the very hot conditions. It was strategically placed next to the ammunition stowage area to provide additional protection from fire.

# SURVIVING MARK V* TANKS

The only surviving Mark V★ Male tank, No. 9591, is now at the National Armour and Cavalry Museum, Fort Benning, Georgia, USA. It was assigned to 1st Platoon, 'A' Company of the 301st Battalion, US Tank Corps.

On 29 September 1918, it was on the far left of 'A' Company's attack line and under the command of 2Lt Harry A. Hobbs. As the tank advanced it was hit by a 57mm round on its right gun sponson and knocked out of action. It was mechanically disabled to the point that it was not fit for combat at any stage during the rest of the war.

Sgt Mechanic Martin J. Doyle and Pte Walter F. Wiegand, a gunner, were killed. The rest of the tank crew came under machine-gun fire while they were trying to get out and find their way back to their own lines.

No. 9591 was recovered and shipped back to the USA for testing and evaluation at the US Army Ordnance Aberdeen proving grounds. It was then moved to the tank school at Fort Benning, where it was used as a training aid and a backdrop for many class photographs. In 1949 it was moved again to the Patton Museum, Kentucky. In 1974 it returned to Fort Benning.

# THE TANKS

The tank is now a memorial to those early American tankers who did not return from 'over there'. Today, it is the oldest-known surviving tank used by Americans in combat.

## Specifications

| | |
|---|---|
| Dimensions | Length 32ft 5in (9.88m)<br>Width 8ft 4in (2.53m)<br>Width with sponsons 13ft 7in (4.15m)<br>Height 8ft 8in (2.64m) |
| Total Weight | 30+ tons |
| Crew | 8 |
| Propulsion | Ricardo crosshead valve, water-cooled, straight-six, petrol engine; 150hp at 1,250rpm |
| Road Speed | 5mph |
| Range | 45 miles (72.42km) |
| Trench-Crossing Ability | 10ft (3.04m) |
| Armament Male Tank | 2 × OQF 6-pounder (57mm) short-barrelled guns<br>8 × 0.303in (7.62mm) Hotchkiss air-cooled machine guns |
| Armament Female Tank | 10 × 0.303in (7.62mm) Hotchkiss air-cooled machine guns |
| Armour | 8–16mm |
| Total Production | 579 (+66 after the First World War) |

The Mark V* Male chassis was longer than the Mark V by an extra 6ft. A large hatch was added behind the sponson. They were also painted brown.

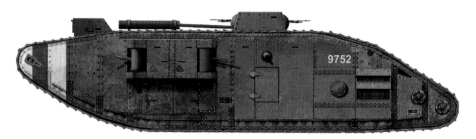

The Mark V* Female was armed with ten 0.303in (7.62mm) Hotchkiss air-cooled machine guns.

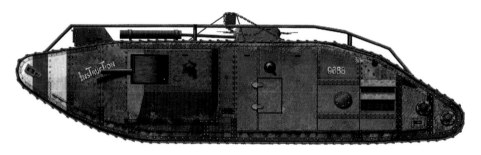

Mark V* Male tank No. 9688 'Instruction' in French Army service with underditching rail and beam fitted.

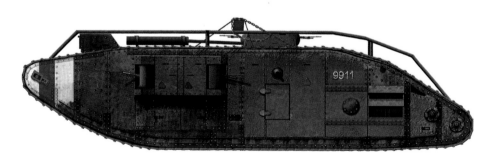

Female Mark V* No. 9911 in service with the 301st Battalion, US Tank Corps. It was later shipped to America. Mark V* tanks were also painted brown.

# MARK V** TANK

Under the Army asterisk system the correct way to pronounce 'Mark V★★' was 'Mark five two-star'. The version entered production very late in the war and only entered service in 1919. It did not see action in the First World War.

The Mark V★★ was also designed to cross the wider trenches that had been dug by the Germans as a defence against tank attacks. It was another stretched version of the standard Mark V tank. At 32ft 5in (9.88m), it was the same length as the Mark V★ tank, but it had a few improvements over the latter. Placing the engine further back improved the centre of gravity. This helped the tank cross trenches by allowing more of the front of the tank to cross the gap before sinking downwards. It improved the chances of the leading section of tracks digging into the far bank of the trench rather than sinking to the bottom.

The tank's tracks were widened to 25½in (64.77cm). The shape of the track rails was changed: it had a greater curve to reduce the amount of track in contact with the ground. These last two features helped reduce ground pressure and improved the tank's turning circle.

Unditching beams were not considered necessary as the length of the tank would enable it to cope with large shell craters and wide trenches. It could also act as an armoured personnel carrier.

Taller hatches were fitted to the sides of the tank to enable the crew and soldiers to get in and out more easily. As the engine had been relocated to the rear of the tank, there was extra space to carry more soldiers and equipment than could be carried on Mark V★ tanks. The engine was not in its own sealed-off compartment, meaning the intense heat and fumes made the crew and passengers feel sick. Some of the infantrymen would have been so ill by the time they reached the enemy trenches that they would not have been in a fit condition to capture and hold the trenches breached by the tanks.

The Mark V★★ at 35 tons was slightly heavier than the Mark V★. To cope with the additional weight a more powerful engine was used, the rebored 225bhp Ricardo 6-cylinder engine. It was slightly faster than the Mark V★ because of the more powerful engine.

As with the Mark V★, the edges of the tracks did stick out proud from the body line and could be damaged when driven over large stones – a design flaw fixed in the Mark VIII.

The Male version was armed with two 6-pounder (57mm) quick-firing guns mounted in side sponsons and five 0.303in (7.62mm) Hotchkiss air-cooled machine guns. Each sponson was armed with a machine gun. One was fitted in the front cabin facing forward and there was one in each crew door behind the sponson. A Mark V rear machine gun mount was not fitted to the Mark V★★. The Female version was armed with seven 0.303in (7.62mm) Hotchkiss air-cooled machine guns.

The Female's machine gun-only tank had a much smaller sponson than previous versions. It had two doors beneath the sponson to enable the crew to escape from the tank in a hurry if it was hit.

Just like the earlier Mark IV tank, the Mark V★★ had its fuel tanks repositioned to the rear of the vehicle to try and improve survivability, but here they were placed within the track frames away from the crew and passenger areas.

Out of an initial order of 700 (550 Males and 150 Female tanks), only twenty-five were built: five Female machine gun-only tanks and twenty Male gun tanks. Only one was completed by the end of 1918.

## SURVIVING MARK V** TANKS

There is only one Mark V★★ left and the only reason No. 10704, now at The Tank Museum in Bovington, survived was because it was used for trials at the Experimental Bridging Establishment (EBE) at Christchurch. It was fitted with a hydraulic crane at the front that was powered by the tank's engine.

The crane was used to transport a 20ft girder bridge that was capable of bridging a standard European canal lock. During the Battle of Cambrai it was found that there was a need to be able to bridge canals to enable cavalry, infantry and medium tanks, such as the Whippet, to cross and exploit the initial breakthrough of the enemy defences.

The crane was also used for testing rolling anti-mine sweeping devices. It was adapted to place and detonate demolition charges, as well as act as a normal crane. It was an early attempt to create one of the first Royal Engineers RE tanks but the project was not taken further.

# THE TANKS

## Specifications

| Dimensions | Length 32ft 5in (9.88m)<br>Width 8ft 4in (2.53m)<br>Width with sponsons 13ft 7in (4.15m)<br>Height 8ft 8in (2.64m) |
| --- | --- |
| Total Weight | 35 tons |
| Crew | 8 |
| Propulsion | Rebored Ricardo crosshead valve, water-cooled, straight-six petrol engine; 225hp |
| Road Speed | 4.6mph (7.4km/h) |
| Range | 45 miles (72.42km) |
| Trench-Crossing Ability | 12ft 5in (3.8m) |
| Armament Male Tank | 2 × OQF 6-pounder (57mm) short-barrelled guns<br>5 × 0.303in (7.62mm) Hotchkiss air-cooled machine guns |
| Armament Female Tank | 7 × 0.303in (7.62mm) Hotchkiss air-cooled machine guns |
| Armour | 8–16mm |
| Total Production | 25 |

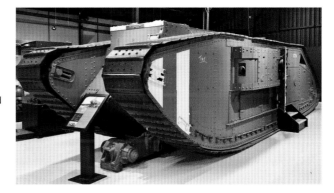

The only surviving Mark V** Female tank can be seen at The Tank Museum, Bovington. It was armed with seven 0.303in (7.62mm) Hotchkiss air-cooled machine guns.

The two side doors on the Mark V** were larger than those on the Mark V* tank. There was space for more than fifteen soldiers in the back. It could act as a troop carrier but was primarily a fighting tank. Notice the machine gun mount in the door.

To cope with the additional weight a more powerful engine was used, the rebored 225bhp Ricardo 6-cylinder engine. The crew and infantry inside the tank were not shielded from the heat, noise and poisonous fumes it generated. There was no engine cover and the exhaust and ventilation system was inadequate.

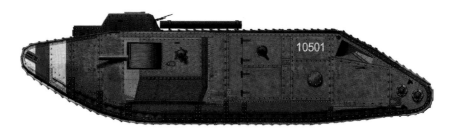

Mark V** Male. Out of an initial order of 700 (550 Males and 150 Females) Mark V** tanks, only 25 were built: five Female machine gun-only tanks and twenty Male gun tanks. Only one was completed by the end of 1918. They were also painted brown.

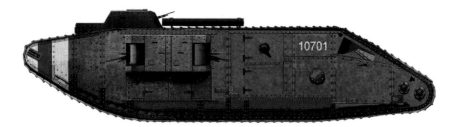

The Female Mark V** tanks were armed with seven 0.303in (7.62mm) Hotchkiss air-cooled machine guns, three each side and one at the front. There was only a 'pistol port' at the back. They were also painted brown.

# MARK V COMPOSITE

The Mark V Composite tank had a Male sponson on one side of the vehicle armed with a 6-pounder QF gun and one 0.303in (7.62mm) Hotchkiss air-cooled machine gun. On the other side it had a Female sponson armed with two 0.303in (7.62mm) Hotchkiss air-cooled machine guns.

After the shock of the first tank-on-tank battle on 24 April 1918 near the town of Villers-Bretonneux and the subsequent appearance of captured Mark IV tanks that were being driven by German tank crews on the battlefield, it became apparent that the machine gun-only Mark V Females were vulnerable. They could not knock out a German A7V or Mark IV *Beutepanzer* (trophy tank).

To deal with this problem Female tanks would be supported by Male tanks but a problem arose if the Male tank broke down, ditched or was knocked out. Then the Female machine gun-only tanks were left vulnerable again.

A stopgap solution was to add a Male sponson to a Female tank, armed with a 6-pounder gun. This modified tank was given the name Mark V 'Composite tank'. Later Male tanks had a Female sponson added.

The machine gun was still the most useful weapon on the tank as it could engage with enemy machine-gun posts and silence them. It was also the best weapon to fire into and down the length of enemy trenches. Tank-on-tank combat was rare.

There was no standardisation as to which side of the tank would have the Male 6-pounder gun sponson. As this tank had both Male and Female specifications the Mark V Composite is also known as the 'Hermaphrodite' Tank.

The job of converting standard Male or Female Mark Vs into Composite tanks was not as simple as just adding different sponsons; ammunition stowage racks inside the tank had to be changed.

Some British Tank Corps battalions were equipped with Composite tanks in 1918. The American 301st Battalion used fifteen Mark V Composites when it went into battle for the first time on 29 September 1918, 20km south of Cambrai (it also used Mark V and Mark V★ tanks).

The Composite had the same features as the Mark V and was powered by the more powerful (150hp) Ricardo engine. The tank could now be driven by only one member of the crew rather than four as in the earlier versions as it had an improved steering mechanism and epicyclical transmission. It had a second cupola fitted towards the rear of the tank so that a member of the crew could attach the unditching beam without leaving the relative safety of the vehicle.

At the end of the First World War, Mark V Composite tanks were shipped by the British, via Persia (Iran/Iraq) and up the Volga to Volgograd. Their purpose was to support the White Russian armies in the Civil War and they were used in battle in eastern Ukraine. Many were captured by the Red Army and used for a number of years until they were abandoned.

# SURVIVING MARK V COMPOSITE TANKS

Four Mark V Composite tanks survived. Three are in Ukraine: there are two on public display at Lugansk and one at Kharkov. The fourth is exhibited inside the Tank Museum in Kubinka, Russia. After the First World War all were sent to the Royalist White Army during the Russian Civil War but they were captured by the Bolshevik Red Army.

## Specifications

| | |
|---|---|
| Dimensions | Length 26ft 5in (8.05m)<br>Width 8ft 4in (2.53m)<br>Width with sponsons 13ft 7in (4.15m)<br>Height 8ft 8in (2.64m) |
| Total Weight | 28 tons |
| Crew | 8 |
| Propulsion | Ricardo crosshead valve, water-cooled, straight-six, 19-litre petrol engine; 150hp at 1,250rpm<br>Wrigley four-speed gearbox with independent revers and Wilson two-speed epicyclics |
| Road Speed | 4.6mph (7.4km/h) |
| Fuel Capacity | 90 gallons (409 litres) |
| Fuel Consumption | 2.06 gallons per mile (5.5 litres/km) |
| Range | 45 miles (72.42km) |
| Trench-Crossing Ability | 10ft (3.04m) |
| Armament Tank | 1 × OQF 6-pounder (57mm) short-barrelled guns<br>5 × 0.303in (7.62mm) Hotchkiss air-cooled machine guns |
| Muzzle Velocity (6-pounder) | 1,348ft/sec (411mps) |
| Max Range (6-pounder) | 4.53 miles (7.3km) |
| Ammunition | High explosive, solid shot, case |
| Armour | 6–12 mm |
| Production figure | Not known |

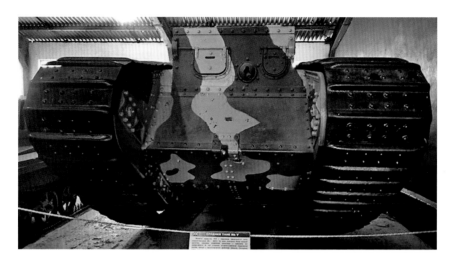

This preserved Russian Mark V Composite 'Hermaphrodite' tank can be found in the Tank Museum, Kubinka, Russia. The camouflage pattern may seem wrong but it is historically correct for the Russian Civil War. Notice the gap between the sides of the driver's cabin and the tracks. This was to enable wider tracks to be fitted at a later date but this never happened.

This is the Female side of the Mark V Composite with the machine gun-only smaller sponson.

This is the Male side of the Mark V Composite tank with the larger sponson mounting the 6-pounder gun.

10th Battalion, 'B' Company, Mark V Composite No. 9376 J19 was commanded by 2Lt G.A. Price on 8 August 1918. Official records show that it engaged the enemy but was damaged. It managed to return back to Allied lines and rallied. On 23 August 1918 it saw action again, commanded by 2Lt Price. On 2 September 1918 it was handed over to 'C' Company, 301st Battalion, American Expeditionary Force Tank Corps. It went into action again under command of Lt Vernon. It ditched in a trench in no-man's-land just prior to reaching the German trenches of the Hindenburg Line. Mark V Composite tanks were also painted brown.

# MARK VI TANK

On 16 June 1917, a conference was held at the 2nd Brigade Headquarters to discuss what had happened at the Battle of Arras. All the battalion and brigade commanders were present and features of the Mark VI tank were discussed. They were all asked the question: 'Is the Male tank of more assistance to the infantry than the Female?'

The group answer to that question, in note form, was: 'Female Tanks will kill more of the enemy – Males frighten them more. Agreed that one type of tank with 6-pounder gun in front will probably be the best pattern. Though the 6-pounder gun will have a small arc of fire, it should be capable of being used effectively with an improved pattern of tank. The tank must be more mobile for this. The tank will be lighter and this is considered worth doing so as to ensure being able to close with the enemy, and having a tank not so liable to be ditched.'

This report would have been submitted to the British High Command. The troops wanted a tank designed like the Mark VI. What they did not realise was that it had already been designed and a wooden mock-up built back in England.

It was going to be an improved Mark V with greater speed, lighter loading and more ease of control. The most radical design feature was that the Mark VI had one 6-pounder gun in the front, instead of two in sponsons on the side of the tank.

All-around defence was provided by six Hotchkiss machine guns with 10,000 rounds of ammo among them. The Ricardo engine was moved to the side, and the crew compartment was raised, allowing for a compact crew space.

What is interesting about the design is that it featured a new raised cabin that would eventually be used on the Mark VIII. There were four machine guns in ball swivel mounts: two to the side at the front and two to the rear. On the front of each side of the hull, two small machine gun sponsons were fitted. The tracks were to be widened to 29.5in (750mm).

An order for 600 Mark VI tanks was placed, to become a part of the recently formed American Tank Corps. The order was cancelled when the Mark VIII was chosen instead. The nearest the Mark VI got to being built was the mock-up.

On 23 June and 13 July 1917, this was shown to the military and members of the British War Department along with two other wooden mock-ups: the Mark V and the Gun Carriage Tank. The Mark V entered production but, like the Mark VI prototype, the Gun Carriage was not proceeded with.

During the winter of 1916–17, the British Army future tank design requirements were mainly to increase armour protection and armament. As the

Army gained more experience in the deployment of tanks on the battlefield, the calls for more technical improvements in performance became more pressing. Lt Col Stern, from the Ministry of Munitions, was more concerned with the production of as many tanks as possible and getting them transported to France.

Walter Wilson, as Director of Engineering, was looking towards the next improved versions of the tank. In the winter of 1916–17 he started work designing two new tanks, the Mark V and the Mark VI. His eagerness to show off these new designs would bring him into conflict with Stern, whose view was: 'Any tank is better than no tank.'

The two main performance issues with the earlier tanks were the lack of power of the engine and how it steered. The Mark I to Mark IV tanks needed four people to work the driving and gear changing mechanism correctly. In the Mark V and Mark VI, only one person would be needed to change gear and drive. With an epicyclic gearbox, the driver alone could control the tank and the commander was freed from the duty of working the steering brakes.

The proposed new Ricardo crosshead valve, water-cooled straight-six, 19-litre petrol engine would supply 150hp. It was more powerful than the Foster-Daimler, 6-cylinder, in-line sleeve valve, 105hp petrol engine fitted in the early tanks. This new engine was going to be used to power the Mark VI.

The Mark VI was Wilson's idea. Side sponsons caused problems when tanks were transported by rail and the early tanks had their sponsons unbolted for train travel. On later versions, the sponsons could be pushed inwards. His new design did away with bulky side sponsons, thus making transportation to the battlefront easier.

The new Mark VI would have a single 6-pounder gun firing straight forward between the 'horns' while the rest of the crew would work in an elevated structure in the middle of the tank firing machine guns.

One of the reasons the Mark VI did not enter production was the fact that the factories would have to be 'rejigged' as the engine position would have to be shifted from the middle to one side. The time needed to do this work and the cost were not looked on favourably.

## SURVIVING MARK VI TANKS

The Mark VI tank prototype did not survive. None entered into production.

# THE TANKS

## Specifications

| Dimensions | Length 26ft 5in (8.05m)<br>Width 8ft 4in (2.53m)<br>Height 8ft 8in (2.64m) |
|---|---|
| Total Weight | 28 (Male) tons |
| Crew | 8 |
| Propulsion | Ricardo crosshead valve, water-cooled, straight-six, 19-litre petrol engine; 150hp at 1,250rpm |
| Transmission | Wrigley four-speed gearbox with independent reverse gear and Wilson two-speed epicyclics |
| Road Speed | 4.6mph (7.4km/h) |
| Fuel Capacity | 90 gallons (409 litres) |
| Fuel Consumption | 2.06 gallons per mile (5.5 litres/km) |
| Range | 45 miles (72.42km) |
| Trench-crossing Ability | 10ft (3.04m) |
| Armament Tank | 1 × OQF 6-pounder (57mm) short-barrelled guns<br>6 × 0.303in (7.62mm) Hotchkiss air-cooled machine guns |
| Muzzle Velocity (6-pounder) | 1,348ft/sec (411mps) |
| Max Range (6-pounder) | 4.53 miles (7.3km) |
| Ammunition | High explosive, solid shot, case |
| Armour | 6–12 mm |
| Total Production | One wooden mock-up |

The Mark VI design wooden mock-up. It was very different from previous British tanks as it only had one 6-pounder gun, mounted at the front of the tank. It had a larger central cabin armed with four 0.303in (7.62mm) Hotchkiss air-cooled machine guns. There were two additional machine guns in small side sponsons. (Imperial War Museum Q14521)

# MARK VII TANK

The Mark VII tank was not used operationally or for training. It was a test bed for new ideas. An order for seventy-five was placed, but only three were built. In July 1918, construction of the three Mark VIIs commenced at the Brown Brothers plant in Edinburgh.

A new type of gearbox was fitted to the tank called a Williams-Janney hydrostatic transmission. This name was shortened to the hydraulic 'Janney clutch'. It had been used on Royal Navy ships as a turret-turning speed control mechanism.

The engine powered two hydraulic pumps using reduction gears. Two hydromotors were attached to each side of the tank controlled by one of the pumps. A shaft out of the rear of the hydromotor transferred the power to the final drive at the back of the tank.

It was easier to operate but not as efficient, susceptible to wear and more expensive. The transmission oil required cooling and another radiator had to be fitted. This required grates to be fitted on the roof of the tank to reduce the risk of dirt and dust affecting the running of the radiator. It was fitted with an electric starter, something that was not present on the early versions of the British heavy tanks.

Ventilation cupolas were installed in the hull and the fighting compartment. This was in response to the criticism from tank crews of the extreme heat and poisonous gases from the engine that filled the inside of the tank.

The rear tracks were extended to improve the tank's ability to cross widened trenches. It was of the 'tadpole' tail configuration similar to what had been previously tested on a few Mark IV and Mark V tanks.

Armament consisted of two 6-pounder (57mm) cannons and four 0.303in (7.62mm) Hotchkiss air-cooled machine guns but they were rarely actually fitted.

The tank's operational range was increased to around 50 miles (80.5km) and the fuel tank capacity was increased to 454 litres.

## THE DAIMLER ENGINE - TANK TRIALS

On 3 March 1917 a Mark VII tank took part in experimental demonstration trials at Oldbury, near Birmingham. It was fitted with a Daimler engine and the Janney clutch. The following was taken from a pamphlet marked 'secret' printed by Lt Col A.G. Stern, Director-General of WMSD (Ministry of Munitions). The information given was for all senior Army and government officials at the trials:

This machine is fitted with the Williams-Janney hydraulic transmission, in which the working fluid is oil. The pumps and motors work on the same principle, being of rotary type with cylinders parallel to the axis of rotation. Reciprocating motion is given to the pistons by means of a disc whose perpendicular axis may be inclined to the shaft. By varying the inclination of this disc to the shaft, the stroke and consequently the delivery of the pumps may be altered as occasion demands. The stroke of the motors is invariable.

*Power Unit.* – The power unit consists of single six-cylinder 105 bhp. Daimler engine.

*Transmission.* – This is hydraulic. The two pumps are arranged side by side and are driven from the engine by means of a reduction gear, giving a four-to-one reduction. The two motors transmit the drive through bevel gear and a single spur reduction gear to a wide gear wheel arranged in between the track-driving sprockets.

*Speed Control.* – The speed control is infinitely variable and is carried out by varying the inclination of the discs in the pumps.

*Steering.* – The steering is carried out by increasing the stroke of the pump on the side opposite to that to which it is desired to turn.

*Estimated Speed.* – The speed is infinitely variable from zero to four miles per hour.

The Mark V tank was cheaper to build and the production line was already working reliably. There are always teething problems when a new design is introduced into a factory and this reduces capacity. The British Army needed as many tanks as it could get in France as soon as possible so its order for seventy-five tanks was cancelled.

# SURVIVING MARK VII TANKS

None of the three Mark VII tanks survived.

## Specifications

| Dimensions | Length 32ft 5in (9.88m)<br>Width 8ft 4in (2.53m)<br>Height 8ft 8in (2.64m) |
| --- | --- |
| Total Weight | 28 (Male) tons |
| Crew | 8 |
| Propulsion | Daimler single 6-cylinder, 105hp petrol engine |
| Transmission | Williams-Janney hydrostatic transmission |
| Road Speed | 4mph (6.43km/h) |
| Fuel Capacity | 99 gallons (454 litres) |
| Fuel Consumption | 2.06 gallons per mile (5.5 litres/km) |
| Range | 50 miles (80.5km) |
| Trench-Crossing Ability | 10ft (3.04m) |
| Armament | 2 × 6-pounder (57mm) short-barrelled guns<br>4 × 0.303in (7.62mm) Hotchkiss air-cooled machine guns |
| Max Range (6-pounder) | 4.53 miles (7.3km) at 1,348ft/sec (411mps) |
| Ammunition | High explosive, solid shot, case |
| Armour | 2–12 mm |
| Total Production | Three |

The Mark VII Male tank was used as a testbed for different engines and transmissions. It used the elongated trench-crossing 'tadpole tail' that had been experimented on in earlier versions. Unlike previous 'tadpole' tails fitted to the Mark IVs, this one was strong enough to cope with the weight of the vehicle.

Only three Mark VIIs were built and they did not leave England. One or two were also fitted with unditching rails and beams.

# MARK VIII TANK

The Mark VIII International tank was designed and built at the end of the First World War as a joint project between Britain and the USA.

In Britain they were constructed at the North British Locomotive company in Glasgow. The company produced thirteen tanks, six of which entered service with the British Army.

Plans were under way to build a big factory in France so the Mark VIII tanks could be used in the planned offensives of 1919. The end of the war on 11 November 1919 stopped that project.

A new, more powerful engine was used in the Mark VIII. It could produce 300hp whereas the engine used in the Mark I could only produce 105hp. At first the British versions had a Rolls-Royce engine but then Two Ricardo engines were merged to make a V-12 petrol engine.

The Mark VIII tanks made in America were fitted with a US-built 300hp Liberty Aero petrol engine. For a short time the American-built machines were known as Mark VIII Liberty tanks.

Revolutionary in this tank's design was that for the first time on a heavy, large tank the engine was at the back of the vehicle in its own compartment away from the crew. This reduced the amount of heat and poisonous fumes to which they were exposed.

The transmission had only two forward gears and two reverse gears. The Mark VIII, like the Mark V★ and V★★, was built longer to get over wide trenches.

It was the first British heavy tank not to have a Male and Female version. The sponsons folded in from the back for when it was being transported by rail.

The tank was armed with the same short-barrelled Ordnance Quick Firing 6-pounder (57mm) gun as used on the Mark IV and V tanks, with one on either side. There was a machine gun mounted in the door on each side of the tank. For the first time, a machine gun was not mounted in a Male tank sponson. The elongated cabin on the roof had five machine gun mounts: two facing forward, two facing sideways and one covering the rear of the tank. The British used 0.303in (7.62mm) Hotchkiss air-cooled machine guns. The Americans fitted M1917 Browning machine guns.

The driver sat centrally in his armoured cab, high up to give him maximum vision of where he was going and what obstacles were in his way.

The tracks were a lot wider than those on earlier tanks: 26in (67cm) wide compared with the 20in (52mm) wide tracks on the Mark I. A wider track decreased ground pressure.

Wide tracks of this size had been used on the Mark V★★ but they stuck out proud from the body and were often damaged as a result. The width of the supporting frames was increased to take the wider tracks and as a result they were sturdier.

The Mark VIII had the normal crew of eight men. Like the Mark V, it only required one man to steer and drive. There was a gunner and loader on each side to operate the 6-pounder guns. The commander had a raised cab on top so he could see what was happening on the battlefield. There were enough machine guns mounted around the tank to give a 360-degree field of fire.

The Rock Island Arsenal in Illinois built 100 Mark VIIIs in 1919.

# SURVIVING MARK VIII TANKS

Two Mark VIIIs survive in the USA: one is at Fort Mead, Maryland, and the other at the National Armor and Cavalry Museum, Fort Benning, Georgia. There is only one Mark VIII in Europe, in The Tank Museum, Bovington.

This example was used as a training tank at Bovington Army Camp.

## Specifications

| Dimensions | Length 34ft 2in (10.42m)<br>Width 8ft 5in (2.57m)<br>Width with sponsons 12ft 10in (3.92m)<br>Height 10ft 3in (3.13m) |
| --- | --- |
| Total Weight | 38 tonnes |
| Crew | 10 US, 12 British |
| Propulsion | V12 Liberty or Ricardo crosshead valve, water-cooled, straight-six petrol engine; 150hp at 1,250rpm |
| Road Speed | 5.25mph (8.45km/h) |
| Range | 50 miles (80km) |
| Trench-Crossing Ability | 15ft 9in (4.8m) |
| Armament | 2 × OQF 6-pounder (57mm) short-barrelled guns<br>7 × 0.303in (7.62mm) Hotchkiss air-cooled machine guns or<br>7 × M1917 Browning machine guns |
| Armour | Max 16mm |
| Total Production | 125 |

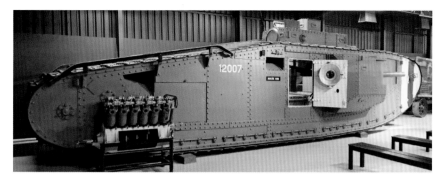

This surviving Mark VII can be seen at The Tank Museum, Bovington. It had a machine gun mount in the side door on both sides and a rear-facing machine gun in the roof cabin, although on this example that position has been blanked off.

This is the front view of the roof cabin on the Mark VIII. It had two forward-facing machine guns in ball mounts, one on each side and one covering the rear of the vehicle.

The British version was called the Mark VIII International tank. Those fitted with 300hp Liberty Aero petrol engines in America were known as Mark VIII Liberty tanks.

# MARK IX INFANTRY CARRIER

The Mark IX is not a tank. It looks very similar to other First World War British tanks but it was designed as a supply carrier and a personnel carrier, which is why it has the large doors on the side and no jutting out sponsons mounting machine guns or 6-pounder howitzers. It was built late in the First World War and did not see active service.

The British Army High Command realised that tanks were vulnerable without infantry support. Discussions went on to find a solution that would allow infantry to safely follow tank formations and deal with enemy soldiers. The first option was to increase the length of a tank so it could carry up to eight fully armed soldiers as well as the tank crew. This was the Mark V★. The heat and fumes from the engine in the middle of the tank made the men unfit to fight.

The next design, the Mark IX, moved away from the idea of carrying men in a fighting tank. To give the vehicle a large hold to store 10 tons of supplies or thirty soldiers, the engine was moved to the front of the vehicle. It had an electric starter motor as well as an internal crank handle. The gearbox was kept at the rear. The open propshaft, which took the power of the engine down to the gearbox, had to go down inside the length of the vehicle. Passengers had to make sure they did not get any equipment or clothing entangled with the mechanism.

Using the Mark IX as an armoured resupply vehicle that could keep pace with the new armoured columns would negate the need for British tanks to pull out of the front line and return to the lines to obtain more ammunition and fuel. The Mark IX could also tow metal sledges that would be packed with additional supplies.

The vehicle received the nickname 'Pig'; it is not known if this is because of what it looked like, the low front track silhouette that gave a snout-like appearance, or how difficult it was to drive. Unlike the earlier British tanks where the commander sat next to the driver in a protected armoured cab, the Mark IX had an armoured hatch with a vision slit for the driver on the left of the vehicle, who had access to a 0.303 Hotchkiss machine gun mounted to his right. There was an additional armoured cab above the driver with vision slits all around to enable the commander to see what was happening on the battlefield.

Although the Mark IX could carry thirty infantry soldiers the vehicle only had a crew of three: the commander, driver and rear gunner who manned the

0.303in (7.62mm) Hotchkiss air-cooled machine gun. Sometimes a fourth crew member joined the tank as a mechanic. The passengers had to stand; there were no seats or benches provided. Some had access to 'pistol ports': holes in the side armour from which revolvers or rifles could be fired at the enemy. When not in use, an armoured cover could be swung down to seal the hole.

The Mark IXs were constructed by a company that had not been one of those awarded the contract to build First World War tanks. Armstrong Whitworth & Co. Ltd of Elswick, Newcastle, built the two prototypes, but the production Mark IX APCs were built by Marshall Sons & Co., Gainsborough, Lincolnshire. It is believed that thirty-four were built.

The British Mark IX Infantry Carrier was designed so that it could be retrofitted with forward-facing cannons. This was a practical consideration in case there was a need for more main battle tanks that could fire high-explosive shells.

The British Mark IX Infantry Carrier could only just keep up with the main battle tanks. Its single Ricardo 6-cylinder gasoline petrol engine of 150bhp gave the vehicle a top speed of only 3.5mph on a good flat road. Cross-country speeds were a lot slower. It may have been slow but the 10mm armour plating would have kept the troops safe from enemy small arms fire. It would have enabled troops to be carried across no-man's-land in relative safety. This was something unthinkable in the first two years of the First World War.

## SURVIVING MARK IX INFANTRY CARRIER

There is only one Mark IX Infantry Carrier left, on display at The Tank Museum, Bovington. It is painted at the front with the letters IC followed by the number 15. The letters IC stood for Infantry Carrier.

## Specifications

| Dimensions | Length 31ft 11in (9.07m)<br>Width 8ft (2.44m)<br>Height 8ft 8in (2.64m) |
|---|---|
| Total Weight | 37 tons |
| Crew | 4 + 30 infantry men |
| Propulsion | Ricardo crosshead valve, water-cooled, straight-six petrol engine; 150hp at 1,250rpm |
| Road Speed | 4mph (6.4km/h) |
| Range | 45 miles (72.42km) |
| Trench-Crossing Ability | 12ft 5in (3.8m) |
| Armament | 2 × 0.303in (7.62mm) Hotchkiss air-cooled machine guns |
| Armour | Max 10mm |
| Total Production | 34 |

This surviving Mark IX Infantry Carrier can be seen at The Tank Museum, Bovington. It was armed with a forward-facing 0.303in (7.62mm) Hotchkiss air-cooled machine gun.

Unditching beams and rails were fitted to the roof of the Mark IX Infantry Carrier. A machine gun covered the rear of the tank. A 0.303in (7.62mm) Hotchkiss air-cooled machine gun was slotted into a ball mount.

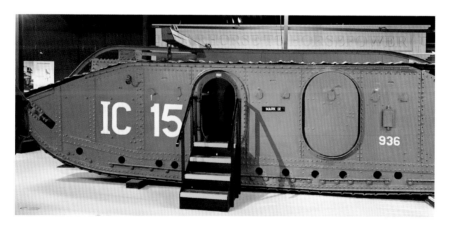

Two large doors were fitted to both sides of the vehicle to enable the infantry to get in and out quickly. Each side had eight 'pistol ports' through which the infantry could poke their rifles and shoot at the enemy.

# MEDIUM MARK A WHIPPET TANK

William Tritton was one of the engineers at William Foster & Co. based in Lincoln who had developed the first British heavy tanks. After visiting the battlefields of the Somme, where tanks had been used for the first time, he started work on a lighter tank that would eventually become the Medium Mark A Whippet.

Design work started on 10 November 1916, followed by the commencement of construction of the first prototype on 21 December 1916. It moved under its own power for the first time on 3 February 1917 and started trials on 11 February 1917.

The prototype was named the Tritton Chaser. It had a tall, circular tower fitted in the middle of the vehicle but offset to the left side. On top of the tower was a rotating turret that was fitted with one 0.303 Lewis machine gun. The driver's armoured cab was positioned next to the tower on the right.

On 3 March 1917 the tank took part in a demonstration of its abilities at Oldbury near Birmingham. It had a top speed of 8mph, which was double the speed of the current heavy tanks. A nickname, 'Whippet', was painted on the front because it was fast. The next time it took part in a demonstration the tank no longer had a turret.

It is believed that the two-man crew found it difficult to work in the confined space. A rigid, angular, fixed fighting compartment replaced the tower and turret. There was space for a third crewman who could move from one of the four Hotchkiss 0.303 air-cooled machine guns to the next as targets presented themselves. This relieved some of the pressure on the commander.

The driver needed to steer the vehicle on his own. A pair of 7,720cc Taylor JB4 4-cylinder London bus petrol engines were installed. They produced 45hp at 1,200rpm. Each engine had its own four-speed, one reverse transmission gearbox and they powered the rear track drive sprockets.

The Whippet was very hard to drive because the driver had to control two clutch pedals and two sets of gearbox controls, two handbrake levers, the limited slip differential lock and the steering wheel.

To start the engines a hand crank was inserted into a hole outside the tank at the back and then turned. If the engines stopped on the battlefield there was a secondary hand crank position inside the vehicle but this needed two men to turn the handle.

Each gearbox had its own clutch pedal and separate gear selector levers. The driver had both hands and both feet occupied when changing gears. He had no hand for the steering wheel when performing that operation. It is interesting to note that the steering wheel was used to control the left and right tracks rather than two levers as found on later tanks.

The Whippets were not pleasant vehicles to operate. The heat and fumes coming back off the two engines was very unpleasant, and the driver, gunner and commander were exhausted and in many cases nauseous after completing an operation. It was found essential that tank crews were rotated to stop the men becoming too debilitated and unable to operate the machine and its weapons.

In the summer heat of August 1918 some tanks found their Hotchkiss 0.303 machine guns would not work. The extreme heat of the cabin would make the metal of the guns too hot to handle. Bullets would expand inside the chamber and jam. In some cases they exploded.

One tank crew would man the vehicle on the first day and then be rested on the following day as a second crew would take over. The first crew would take the tank back out on the third day while the second crew rested.

The tracks had no suspension, so the ride was very bumpy. The track road wheels took the weight. In between the top and bottom tracks were five large openings in the armour plating. These were mud shoots, designed to stop the tracks being caked in mud as they crossed the battlefield.

Only the driver had a seat; the commander and gunner had to stand. There was very little room inside to stow personal items so the crews would strap their kit to the roof of the tank and pack it in boxes on the side. The fuel tank was at the front of the vehicle encased in protective armour plate. Spare fuel cans were often strapped to the top to increase the vehicle's range.

If one of the two engines failed the driver could lock the limited slip differential so that both tracks moved together. However, the Whippet would only be able to drive slowly back to the safety of British lines to be repaired.

During an assault on the Hindenburg Line, a Whippet tank commander, Maj. W.H.L. Watson, reported the loss of some of his unit's tanks because of problems with the clutch slipping. This had the effect of stalling the tank and making it stationary. It then became an easy target for the German artillery. When this happened and the driver was unable to get the engine back into gear the only option was for the crew to abandon the vehicle and find cover in a trench or shell hole.

The initial idea behind constructing lighter tanks was so they could work with the horse-mounted cavalry. In reality putting the tank and horses together just did not work. Horses would stampede, rear up, throw their riders and gallop off if the Whippet's engine backfired. Also, the tank could never keep up with a unit of charging horses.

What the British Army's senior officers failed to realise was that the Whippet tank was a new form of cavalry, not an alternative to or support for horse cavalry.

The British 3rd Tank Brigade was issued with ninety-six Mark A Whippets, which it divided between the 3rd and 6th Tank Battalions. Each battalion had forty-eight, which fought alongside Mark IVs and Vs.

During the Battle of Amiens on 8 August 1918 the 3rd Tank Battalion's Mark A Whippets broke through the German lines. They were finally able to operate doing the job they had been designed to do.

One Whippet, No. 344 of 6th Tank Battalion, named 'Musical Box' by its crew, famously drove so far into the enemy's rear that it found itself cut off from friendly forces. It was commanded by Lt C.B. Arnold, the gunner was C. Ribbans and the driver was W.J. Carney. For nine hours it just went hunting for targets. These included destroying an observation balloon unit, an artillery battery, a transport supply column of the German 225th Division and the HQ camp of an infantry battalion they found between Bayonvillers and Harbonnières. 'Musical Box' caused heavy casualties with its mobile heavy machine guns.

The crew had to wear gas masks to continue fighting when small arms fire ruptured spare cans of petrol carried on the roof of their tank. The petrol seeped into the crew compartment and the fumes were nauseating. If it caught fire they would all be burnt to death in an inferno. Knowing the risk, they still kept on fighting until a German gun crew managed to hit their tank with a round that disabled it. As the crew abandoned their Whippet they came under fire. Carney was shot dead and the other two were taken prisoner.

There were no variations of the Whippet. The 200 that were produced saw service in the last years of the First World War and also during the Russian Civil War, where they served with the White Russian Army fighting the Red Army. The White Russians lost that war and the twelve surviving Whippets were used by the victorious Soviet Army up until the 1930s. They called the tank the Tyeilor after the name they found on the tank's engine block.

It is believed that six Whippets were exported to Japan, where they were used in China up until the 1930s. The German Army had captured around fifteen Whippets that had been abandoned by their crew due to mechanical failure or because they had run out of fuel. After the war a few saw action again with the Freikorps in the German Revolution of 1918–19. They were called *Beutepanzer* A.

# THE WHIPPET'S FIRST BATTLE

On 24 April 1918 an RAF plane on a reconnaissance patrol spotted German troops moving towards the village of Cachy. He dropped a warning message to the British troops held in reserve behind the Cachy Switch trenches by the Bois l'Abbé woods north of the village of Cachy.

Two Sturmpanzerwagen A7V tanks of the 2nd Sturm-Panzerkraftwagen Abteilung (tank battalion), 'Siegfried' II No. 525 commanded by Lt Friedrich-Wilhelm Bitter and 'Schnuck' No. 504 commanded by Lt Albert Müller, were driving towards the British trenches in front of the village of Cachy in support of the advancing infantry.

At around 12.20 p.m. seven British Medium Mark A Whippets of 'X' Company, 3rd Battalion, 3rd Tank Brigade, armed only with 0.303 calibre Hotchkiss machine guns, moved towards the advancing German infantry, which they managed to halt and in some areas turn back.

The German Infantry commander contacted Lt Bitter and directed him towards the Whippets. Lt Müller's tank was too far south at that stage.

Caught out in the flat, open farmers' fields with a German heavily armed tank aiming its 57mm gun at them, the Whippet tank commanders soon realised the perilous situation they were in: they had no weapon that could knock out the enemy tank and so they tried to escape. The German Sturmpanzerwagen A7V tank's quick-firing 57mm cannon could fire high-explosive and canister shot shells at soft-skinned vehicles, artillery field guns and troops. For armoured targets such as the Whippet it could fire armour-piercing Panzerkampf shells.

Lt Bitter's gunner's first shot missed 2Lt Harry Dale's Whippet No. A256 but his second shot, at a range of 200m, set the tank on fire. The German gunner then fired at 2Lt D.M. Robert's Whippet No. A255 at a longer range of around 700m. Again his first shot missed but he hit his target with his second shell, knocking it out of action.

The firing pin's striker springs broke under stress so Lt Bitter's tank no longer had a 57mm gun with which to fire at the enemy tanks. Unlike British Mark IV Male tanks that were armed with two cannons, one on each side in a sponson, German tanks only had one main gun.

Lt Bitter engaged a third British Medium A Whippet with machine guns. No. A244 was commanded by 2Lt George Richie. It was damaged and could not move, and further machine-gun fire hit either the fuel tanks or ammunition and set it on fire.

The four remaining Whippets started to withdraw from the battlefield towards the protection of the woods. As they went they continually fired their machine guns at the German infantry. Lt Albert Müller's tank No. 504 'Schnuck' emerged through the mist near the village of Cachy and fired at the British tanks. 2Lt Thomas Oldham's Whippet No. A236 'Crawick' was knocked out and caught fire. The other three tanks, 'Crustacean' No. A286, 'Centaur III' No. A277 and 'Crossmichael' No. A233, made it back safely to British lines at 3.30 p.m.

The Whippets had done the job to which they were assigned: they had stopped the German infantry capturing the village of Cachy. The Germans were forced to dig trenches 500m–1km to the east of the British trenches and the village.

On 16 April 1918 British crews were ordered to paint distinctive white-red-white national identification stripes to the side, cabin roof and front of their tanks to distinguish them from those captured examples, known as *Beutepanzern*, now being used by the Germans. These modifications had not yet been implemented on the British Mark IVs and Whippets involved in the fighting at Villers-Bretonneux during the first tank *v.* tank battles on 24 April 1918.

## SURVIVING MEDIUM A WHIPPET TANKS

There are five surviving Whippets. They can be found at: the Army College, Pretoria in South Africa; Canadian Forces Base, Borden, Canada; US Army Center for Military History, Anniston, Alabama, USA; The Royal Museum of the Armed Forces, Brussels, Belgium and The Tank Museum, Bovington.

The Whippet on display at Bovington, called 'Caesar II', went into battle on 29 August 1918 at Fremicourt, France. Its commander, Lt Cecil Sewell, was in charge of a section of Medium Mark A Whippets. He noticed that one of his Whippets, A259 under the command of Lt O.L. Rees-Williams, had slipped into a shell crater and turned upside down. The crew escape hatch at the rear could not be opened as it was jammed against the side of the crater. A fire had started and the crew were in danger of being burnt alive.

Lt Sewell jumped out of his tank to rescue them and, having grabbed a shovel, he managed to dig away enough earth to allow the door to be opened wide enough for the trapped crew to escape.

Looking back at his Whippet he saw his driver, W. Knox, taking shelter at the rear. He had been wounded when he tried to follow his commander. Running back to help him, Sewell was injured by enemy fire. He managed to reach his colleague and started to administer first aid. A few minutes later he was hit again, this time fatally. Driver Knox was also killed.

Lt Sewell was awarded the Victoria Cross for his outstanding bravery. It is the highest military honour that can be awarded to British and Commonwealth forces.

Lt Sewell had been educated at Dulwich College between 1907 and 1910. He had been a tank commander at the Battle of Cambrai in November 1917 and held the rank of a lieutenant in the Queen's Own Royal West Kent Regiment, attached to 3rd (Light) Battalion, Tank Corps, when he died, aged 23.

## Specifications

| | |
|---|---|
| Dimensions | Length 20ft (6.09m)<br>Width 8ft 4in (2.54m)<br>Height 9ft (2.74m) |
| Total Weight, Battle Ready | 14 tons |
| Crew | 3 |
| Propulsion | Twin Tylor 4-cylinder, water-cooled, side valve, JB4 petrol engine<br>2 × 45bhp at 1,250rpm (90bhp in all) |
| Transmission | Cone clutch to four-speed and reverse gearbox to worm reduction and bevel drive, chain loop to drive sprocket, one for each track |
| Speed | 13.4km/h (8.3mph) |
| Range | 43.49 miles (70km) |
| Trench-Crossing Ability | 10ft (3.04m) |
| Armament | 4 × 0.303in (7.62mm) Hotchkiss air-cooled machine-guns |
| Ammunition Stowage | 5,400 0.303in (7.62mm) rounds |
| Armour | Max 14mm |
| Total Production | 200 |

This Mark A Medium Whippet nicknamed 'Caesar II' can be found at The Tank Museum, Bovington. It did not have a rotating turret. Notice the four mud shoots under the top part of the track.

The Whippet was armed with four 0.303in (7.62mm) Hotchkiss air-cooled machine-guns

This Mark A Whippet, named 'Firefly', can be found at the Royal Army and Military History Museum in Brussels in Belgium (Musée Royal de l'Armée et d'Histoire Militaire Bruxelles en Belgique). It stands next to a Mark IV Male named 'Lodestar III'.

# FRENCH SCHNEIDER CA TANK

In 1915 the French Army had experimented with using armoured cars and agricultural tractors to attack German trenches. Both experiments were failures. They realised they needed a fully tracked vehicle to cope with the undulating, muddy, shell hole-riddled ground conditions of First World War battlefields. They needed a vehicle that could overcome lines of barbed wire, cross trenches and neutralise machine-gun posts.

Schneider-Creusot was a French iron and steel company that developed into a shipbuilding, railway and armaments manufacturer. In 1914 it imported some American Baby Holt 45hp agricultural caterpillar tractors. The company's chief engineer, Eugène Brillié, had plans to construct an armoured box around the tractor with machine guns mounted on the sides and front.

Col Jean-Baptiste Estienne was an artillery commander in Gen. Philippe Pétain's 6è Division d'Infanterie. He watched a display of different armoured tractors in November 1915 and had the idea of mounting a gun in the front of the vehicle. He submitted a proposal to the French Army GQC (headquarters) and was given permission to visit arms manufacturers and seek their advice and interest.

He had a meeting at Schneider-Creuso, which agreed to produce a prototype tank. Brillié started designing the new vehicle on 27 December 1915. After a successful trial, on 25 February 1916 the company was awarded the contract to build 400 tanks. The construction work was given to its subsidiary company, Société d'Outillage Mécanique et d'Usinage Atillerie (SOMUA), in St-Ouen near Paris.

During the planning and construction stage, these new weapons were given the factory code name 'Tracteurs Estienne' but later had the official designation of Schneider CA. The letters CA are a factory product code. They are not an abbreviation for 'char d'assault' (assault tank). It was only called the Schneider CA.1 after designs for the prototype Schneider CA.2 were submitted.

The design used a lengthened Baby Holt suspension and caterpillar track. The front of the tank was shaped like the front of a ship, the idea being that this feature would help free the tank from the side of a muddy trench wall. A metal tail was fitted at the rear of the vehicle to help it cross wide trenches.

It was armed with a short-barrelled Canon de 75 court modèle 1916 Schneider gun, more commonly called the Schneider 75mm BS gun. The letters

BS were the abbreviation for Blockhaus Schneider. It was mounted on the right side of the tank in a ball mount. Two Hotchkiss 8mm air-cooled machine guns were fitted in swivel mounts, one on each side.

On 16 April 1917, at the start of the Nivelle offensive on Chemin des Dames, 208 Schneider CA tanks had been delivered to the French Army. These new tanks were under the control of the Artillerie Spéciale (AS). Four tanks formed an artillery battery, while three batteries comprised an artillery *groupe*. These seventeen Schneider groups were named AS 1 to AS 17.

On 15 September 1916 the British launched the first attack using tanks. The element of surprise had been lost and the French now feared that the Germans would move up 37mm light field guns to deal with the tank threat and widen their trenches. They started to add additional spaced armour to the front of the Schneiders that were being built at the factory and also to those already delivered to the front line for extra protection.

During the first battle, many Schneiders were destroyed by artillery fire. Others had to be abandoned owing to mechanical failure or because they became stuck in the mud. It was found that the tracks were not long enough and the engine needed more power to allow the tracks to get a proper grip on the muddy ground in order to extract the front from trench and shell crater walls.

The early Schneider CAs had their fuel tanks in the front of the vehicle. These were easily ruptured by enemy artillery fire with devastating results; tanks exploded and men were burnt to death. New 75-litre fuel tanks were mounted on the rear of the vehicle, one either side of the rear hatch. Another, bigger crew escape hatch was added to the left side of tanks on the production line.

Spain used six Schneider CA tanks in the Rif war in Morocco in the early 1920s, and they also saw limited combat in the Spanish Civil War in 1936–37.

## SURVIVING SCHNEIDER CA TANKS

There is only one surviving French Schneider CA Tank. It is on display at the Musée des Blindés (French Tank Museum) in Saumur, France. It was shipped on loan to America after the war for evaluation and testing, ending up in the US Army Ordnance Corps Museum, Aberdeen Proving Grounds, in Maryland. In 1985 it was given back to France along with a First World War Saint-Chamond and a Renault FT following a request by the government. Its war record is not known.

## Specifications

| Dimensions | Length 20ft 9in (6.32m)<br>Width 7ft 6in (2.30m)<br>Height 6ft 9in (2.05m) |
|---|---|
| Total Weight | 13.6 tons |
| Crew | 6 |
| Propulsion | Schneider 4-cylinder petrol engine; 60hp (45Kw) |
| Road Speed | 5mph (8km/h) |
| Operational Range, Road | 50 miles (80km) |
| Operational Range, Off Road | 19 miles (30km) |
| Armament | 1 × 75mm blockhaus Schneider BS gun<br>2 × 8mm Hotchkiss M1914 machine guns |
| Armour | 11mm + 5.5mm spaced |
| Total Production | 400 |

This is the only surviving French Schneider CA, which is on display at the French Tank Museum (Musée des Blindés) in Saumur, France. Notice the additional spaced armour on the front and sides of the tank.

The Schneider CA Tank was armed with a 75mm Blockhaus Schneider BS gun on the right side of the vehicle.

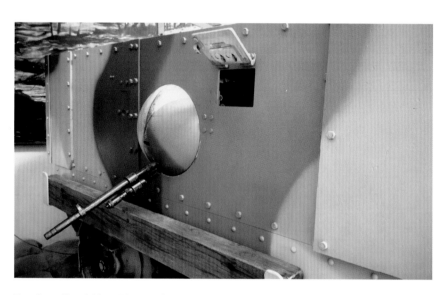

Two 8mm Hotchkiss M1914 machine guns were fixed in large ball mounting, one on each side of the vehicle.

# FRENCH SAINT-CHAMOND TANK

French Gen. Mourret was in charge of the Army Direction du Service Automobile (DSA) and wanted to build a better tank than the Schneider CA.

His team designed a tank armed with a long-barrelled Saint-Chamond 75mm TR field gun (TR was an abbreviation for *tir rapide* or rapid fire) and four 8mm Hotchkiss M1914 machine guns. The last batch of 190 tanks were armed with the more commonly available 'Canon de 75 modèle 1897' 75mm M1897 field gun.

The Holt track system was elongated with eight road wheels per side. It looked a more impressive vehicle but the designers had not taken into account all the difficulties of crossing a shell hole-riddled, muddy and waterlogged battlefield.

The prototype was demonstrated in autumn 1916, when a number of problems became apparent. The track width had to be increased from 324mm to 500mm to stop it sinking in the mud. A set of roller wheels had to be added to the protruding front of the tank and the rear to help it get out of trenches and shell craters.

The Panhard-Levassor 4-cylinder petrol engine produced 80hp and powered a Crochat-Collardeau electrical powertrain that drove the two electrical motors which turned the track drive sprocket wheel on each side of the vehicle. This arrangement did not need a manual gearbox and was therefore easier to drive than the Schneider CA tank, but it was more expensive and difficult to fix.

The company Forges et Aciéries de la Marine et d'Homécourt (FAMH) steelworks in Saint-Chamond was awarded the contract to build 400 tanks, forty-eight of which would be *chars caissons*, armoured supply tanks without a main gun or machine guns fitted.

The British had constructed wooden-framed, wire mesh-covered pitched roofs on top of some of their Mark I tanks to prevent German infantry throwing grenades and satchel bombs on to the top of the tank. In the light of this, before the Saint-Chamond had entered service the French Army demanded some changes. All tanks built after number 150 had a pitched roof rather than a flat one.

The Saint-Chamond tanks were under the control of the Artillerie Spéciale (AS). Four tanks formed an artillery battery; three batteries comprised an artillery *groupe*. The first Saint-Chamond group, AS 31, was formed in February 1917.

# SURVIVING SAINT-CHAMOND TANKS

There is only one French Saint–Chamond tank left and it is on display at the Musée des Blindés (French Tank Museum) in Saumur. It was shipped to America after the war, on loan, for evaluation and testing. It ended up in the US Army Ordnance Corps Museum, Aberdeen Proving Grounds in Maryland. It was given back to the French government following a request for the return of its tanks in 1985 along with a Schneider CA and a Renault FT. Its war record is not known.

## Specifications

| Dimensions | Length 29ft 2in (8.9m)<br>Width 8ft 10in (2.70m)<br>Height 7ft 10in (2.40m) |
|---|---|
| Total Weight | 23 tons |
| Crew | 8 (commander–driver, gunner–loader, assistant gunner, four machine-gunners, mechanic) |
| Main Armament | Saint-Chamond 75mm TR long-barrelled field gun or 75mm M1897 long-barrelled field gun |
| Secondary Armament | 4 × 8mm Hotchkiss M1914 machine guns |
| Propulsion | Panhard-Levassor 4-cylinder petrol engine; 80hp |
| Gearbox | Crochat-Colardeau electric transmission |
| Road Speed | 8mph (12km/h) |
| Operational Range, Road | 37.3 miles (60km) |
| Operational Range, Off Road | 18.6 miles (30km) |
| Armour | 11–19mm |
| Total Production | 400 |

This is the only surviving French Saint-Chamond, which is on display at the French Tank Museum (Musée des Blindés) in Saumur, France. It has been restored to a running condition.

The initial design of the Saint-Chamond had a grounding fault: it would get stuck trying to climb out of shell craters. Later production examples had added support rollers underneath.

Inside view of the 75mm long-barrelled field gun mounting inside the Saint-Chamond French heavy tank. It was also armed with four 8mm Hotchkiss M1914 machine guns.

# FRENCH RENAULT FT TANK

Col Jean-Baptiste Estienne was an artillery commander in Gen. Philippe Pétain's 6è Division d'Infanterie. He was instrumental in the development of the French Army heavy tank, the Schneider CA. However, many of the skilled factory workers had enlisted in the Army and supplies of the correct materials were in short supply so French industry was finding it difficult to produce large heavy tanks with powerful engines in the numbers required.

Estienne started looking for a solution. He came up with the idea of using a two-man, cheap to build, small light tank, armed only with a machine gun that could be built within the manufacturing restrictions of wartime French industrial capabilities.

Renault took on the challenge of designing the tank. The lead engineer was Charles-Edmond Serre. Within the Renault factory the tank was called the *char mitrailleur* (machine gun tank) and given the next production project code, 'FT'.

On 30 December 1916, after seeing a full-scale mock-up of the tank, the French Consultative Committee of the Assault Artillery voted to approve the production of the first batch of 100. It was given the official designation of *char léger* Renault FT modèle 1917 (Renault FT model 1917 light tank), which is often abbreviated to Renault FT or incorrectly to Renault FT-17.

In February 1917 the initial order was increased to 150 tanks and in April 1917 this order was increased by another 1,000. The first official trial of the prototype was on 21 April 1917 at Marly, France. After further demonstrations it was decided that 500 of the 1,150 tanks would be armed with the Hotchkiss 8mm air-cooled modèle 1914 machine gun and carry 4,800 8mm rounds. The remaining 650 would be fitted with a redesigned turret that was capable of mounting a Puteaux 37mm SA modèle 1918 gun. These tanks were known as Renault FT Char Canon and were capable of carrying 237 37mm rounds.

Many books and websites state that the Renault FT armoured fighting vehicle was the first to use a turret that traversed 360 degrees, but this is not true. Before and during the early part of the war, turrets were used on armoured cars and the British Number One Lincoln Machine tank prototype was designed to be fitted with a turret. However, the Renault FT was the first mass-produced tank with a turret that traversed 360 degrees to see action on the battlefield.

Col Estienne believed in the battlefield tactic of a 'bee swarm' of light tanks. Five Renault FT tanks could be built for the same cost as one Saint-Chamond heavy tank, and multiple fast targets would be harder for the enemy to deal with than one large, slow-moving tank. He put forward his suggestion on how the tank should be used and Gen. Philippe Pétain agreed and continued to increase the order for Renault FT tanks.

The French infantry mutiny of 1917 meant that no new offensives were conducted by the French Army; it waited until 1918 when sufficient numbers of Renault FT tanks were available for a massive spring assault.

Initially the tank's turret was made of cast metal. This was changed to a simpler polygon-shaped 'omnibus' turret made of sheet armour plate that could mount either the 8mm machine gun or the 37mm cannon. Later, a round metal turret was used.

German artillery, anti-tank mines, field guns and anti-tank trenches stopped a number of Renault FT tanks but poor-quality fan belts and air filters caused more to be put out of action due to mechanical breakdowns than enemy action. These design faults were not corrected until after the end of the First World War.

In one of the first actions involving Renault FT tanks they proved their worth by being able to negotiate small paths inside the wooded area of the Fôret de Retz that would have been impassable for larger tanks.

This working French Renault FT-17 is on display at the French Tank Museum (Musée des Blindés) in Saumur, France. It was recovered by French special forces in Afghanistan and brought back for restoration in 2007.

By September 1917 there were twenty-one French and two American FT battalions. Attack tactics changed and large-scale artillery bombardment no longer preceded an attack. This was necessary to minimise the number of shell holes the tanks would have to negotiate. The tank 'bee swarms' were able to neutralise enemy machine-gun posts, allowing the infantry to advance and attack in strength.

# SURVIVING RENAULT FT TANKS

There are more than fifty-five surviving Renault FT tanks in different museums around the world.

## Specifications

| | |
|---|---|
| Dimensions | Length 16ft 5in (8m)<br>Width 5ft 7in (1.74m)<br>Height 7ft (2.14m) |
| Total Weight | 6.48 tonnes |
| Crew | 2 (commander/gunner and driver) |
| Main Armament | Puteaux 37mm SA modèle 1918 gun or Hotchkiss 8mm air-cooled modèle 1914 machine gun |
| Propulsion | Renault 18CV, 35hp petrol engine |
| Road Speed | 4.8mph (17.5km/h) |
| Operational Range, Road | 25 miles (35km) |
| Armour | 8–22mm |
| Trench-Crossing Ability | 6ft (1.8m) |
| Total Production | more than 4,500 |

Each Renault FT-17 was fitted with a rear skid to help it cross wide trenches. This tank only had a two-man crew. It was more comfortable for the commander to sit on the rear of the tank when not involved in combat.

This Renault FT is armed with a Puteaux 37mm SA modèle 1918 gun. It is on display at the Royal Army and Military History Museum, in Brussels, Belgium (Musée Royal de l'Armée et d'Histoire Militaire Bruxelles en Belgique).

# STURMPANZERWAGEN A7V TANK

## THE GERMAN FIRST WORLD WAR HEAVY TANK

The situation in 1915–16 was dire as Germany, Britain and France had settled into a stalemate. In order to solve the 'bloody equation' formed by the artillery, barbed wire and machine gun combination, both Britain and France began development of a vehicle that had the ability to cross trenches with ease and be able to withstand enemy machine-gun fire. This tracked vehicle would eventually revolutionise the battlefield; thus the tank was born.

Although the tanks suffered from mechanical failures and inadequate crew training they had a major psychological impact on the German soldiers. German intelligence subsequently submitted reports to the Oberste Heeresleitung (German supreme command, or OHL), which then lobbied the war ministry for an equivalent machine. However, some of the senior officers of the time were more focused on artillery and infantry tactics rather than the development of the tank or similar armoured vehicles.

The acronym A7V stands for the committee of the Abteilung 7 Verkhrswesen (Department 7 Transport) of the Prussian War Office. It is commonly used in error to describe the German First World War heavy tank, whose correct name is the Sturmpanzerwagen (armoured assault vehicle). The A7V committee authorised the development of a tracked suspension system that became known as the A7V chassis. A number of different vehicles were built using that chassis, including the Sturmpanzerwagen A7V tank.

The committee, headed by chief designer Joseph Vollmer, rejected the trench-crossing rhomboid-shape track system as used on the British tanks because it wanted to build a chassis that could be used on a tank and a 'prime mover' heavy artillery gun tractor. This approach led to problems.

Two Caterpillar-Holt tractors were obtained and adapted to build a working prototype. It had a better speed than the very slow British tanks but its trench-crossing abilities were not as good. Eventually, the Heeresleitung received some funding from the war ministry to make an equivalent. After months of testing and building, it came up with the Sturmpanzerwagen A7V tank. The OHL ordered 100 chassis to be built. The rest were used to develop several A7V variants including the Überlandwagen tracked rough-terrain supply vehicle and an anti-aircraft version, called the Flakpanzer A7V.

British tanks had been knocked out by German artillery field guns firing directly at them. In the light of this, the Prussian War Office and the OHL ordered that the Sturmpanzerwagen's armour be increased to 30mm. This made the tank too heavy so only the front armour plates were 30mm thick. The rest, covering less vulnerable areas, were kept to 15mm thick. The additional weight at the front of the tank made it nose heavy, causing manoeuvrability problems when crossing trenches and uneven ground.

Vollmer chose to fit a British-made cannon into the Sturmpanzerwagen. A number of 57mm Maxim-Nordfeldt quick-firing, QF fortress casement guns had been captured by German forces in Belgium and from the Russians on the eastern front. The gun fired solid shot and high-explosive shells that could penetrate the armour on British and French tanks and was an efficient weapon.

The prototype A7V tracked chassis was put through a number of battlefield simulation trials. In May 1917 the A7V committee confirmed an order for ten A7V chassis-based tanks with a further ten to be built as reserves. The total order would be increased to 100 if they proved their worth at the front line. This order was approved by the German War Ministry on 28 June 1917.

The first completed Sturmpanzerwagen tank was a machine gun-only vehicle that the British Army would have called a 'Female tank'. It was given the number 501 and the nickname 'Gretchen' and rolled out the factory gates at the end of October 1917. It was later armed with a 57mm gun.

The German tank's quick-firing 57mm Maxim-Nordfeldt QF cannon could fire high-explosive and canister shot shells at soft-skinned vehicles, artillery field guns and troops. For armoured targets such as the Mark IV and Whippet tanks it could fire armour-piercing Panzerkampf shells.

The tank was issued to Sturm Panzerkraftwagen Abteilung 1 (1st Tank Battalion) and on 21 March 1918 five Sturmpanzerwagens took part in the spring offensive 'Michael'. Three of them broke down before they reached the front line and only 501 'Gretchen' and 506 'Mephisto' were involved in the action.

The two battalions Abteilung 1 and 2 were assigned five tanks each. A third battalion, Abteilung 3, was formed on 6 November 1917.

The British Mark V tank could cross a trench 10ft (3.04m) wide, whereas the Sturmpanzerwagen A7V tanks could only cross a 6ft 6in (2m) trench. Unlike the British tanks, all gunners as well as the driver and tank commander had somewhere to sit.

Officially the crew strength of the tank was eighteen men but extra crew members sometimes brought this total to twenty-four. They were needed to help dig the tank out when it got stuck in the mud, remove obstructions or act as 'runners', taking hand-delivered messages to other tanks or infantry units.

Like the British tanks, conditions inside the Sturmpanzerwagen were horrendous. The engine was situated in the middle of the vehicle and could raise the internal temperature to 140°F (60°C). In addition, poisonous carbon monoxide exhaust fumes mixed with the discharge gases from the weapons.

Crew members became physically sick if they worked too long inside the vehicle. Commanders had to regularly stop and open all the hatches to allow clean air to circulate and for the crew to cool down.

The forward 57mm gunner found it difficult to hit a target if the vehicle was moving. The gun's periscope for aiming was small, and the field of vision moved violently when the tank was crossing open fields. The tank had to be stationary to fire accurately and hit a target.

It suffered from mechanical problems. The unmodified Holt tractor suspension and tracks resulted in a front idler wheel that was too small and low down. This and the fact that the front of the tank was near to the ground hindered cross-country movement.

The problem with ground clearance was not helped by the large gearbox being in a low position. The weak frame had a habit of becoming distorted under a load and needed strengthening.

Also, the engines often overheated because airflow to cool the radiator was not effective. The vehicle's cooling system was overtaxed and could not cope with the generated heat.

The commander found it difficult to give orders to the tank crew from within the tank as only the commander and gunner had a signal light system. If the tank commander wanted to send instructions to other crew members he needed a 'runner', a spare crewman, who could take the new orders to the right person as it was too noisy for him to shout his instructions. This was not an efficient method of command and control of a fighting vehicle.

On 21 March 1918, Abteilung 1 (Battalion 1) fought at St-Quentin. Tanks 501, 502 and 506 'Mephisto' were returned to Charleroi for repair after the battle.

On 24 April 1918 Sturmpanzerwagen A7V tank 506 'Mephisto' was involved in an attack on Villers-Bretonneux. It is now considered the first German tank force success as Allied troops were pushed back. Two A7V tanks had to be abandoned on the battlefield; A7V tank 542 'Elfriede' had turned over in a sandpit and tank 506 'Mephisto' became stuck in a shell crater.

Later that night the Australian Imperial Force took part in a counter-attack and helped retake most of the captured ground. This included the two abandoned

Sturmpanzerwagens. Tank 542 'Elfriede' was recovered by the French on 15 May 1918. The 26th Australian Infantry Battalion captured Tank 506 'Mephisto'. With the aid of the 1st Gun Carrier Company, 5th Tank Brigade, armoured supply tank, it was dragged out of no-man's-land on 14 July 1918. 'Mephisto' was shipped to Australia after the war ended.

Germany only produced twenty Sturmpanzerwagen A7V tanks in the First World War, while Britain and France built more than 8,000 tanks in 1916–18. Indeed, in the battles of 1918 the German Army used more captured British tanks than it did tanks built in Germany.

# SURVIVING A7V TANKS

'Mephisto' is the only surviving First World War German Sturmpanzerwagen A7V heavy tank out of the twenty that were built. It is on display in the Queensland Museum, Brisbane, Australia.

The Sturmpanzerwagen A7V tank replica at The Tank Museum in Bovington was built by Bob Grundy. Having a running replica gives the public a chance to see what a First World War German heavy tank looked like on the move. Having it in the same arena next to the working British Mark IV replica allows the museum to recreate the first tank-on-tank engagement. There is another Sturmpanzerwagen replica at the German Tank Museum (Deutsches Panzermuseum) in Münster.

## Specifications

| | |
|---|---|
| Dimensions | Length 24ft 1in (7.35m)<br>Width 10ft (3.06m)<br>Height 10ft 11in (3.35m) |
| Total Weight | 33 tons |
| Crew | 18–24 |
| Propulsion | 2 × German Daimler 165-204 4-cylinder, 100hp petrol engine with sliding gear |
| Road Speed | 10 mph (16km/h) |
| Fuel Capacity | 90 gallons (409 litres) |
| Fuel Consumption | 2.06 gallons per mile (5.5 litres/km) |
| Range | 43 miles (70km) |
| Trench-Crossing Ability | 6ft 6in (2m) |
| Armament | 1 × 57mm Maxim-Nordfeldt Model 1888 quick-firing QF fortress casement gun<br>6 × 7.9mm Maschinegewehr 08 machine guns |

| Muzzle Velocity (57mm) | 1,597ft/sec (487m/s) |
|---|---|
| Max Range (57mm) | 4 miles (6.4km) |
| Ammunition | 50 × high-explosive HE shells<br>30 × armour-piercing rounds<br>20 × grapeshot<br>10,000–15,000 7.9mm rounds |
| Front Armour | 30mm |
| Side Armour | 15mm |
| Rear Armour | 15mm |
| Roof Armour | 6mm |
| Total Production | 20 |

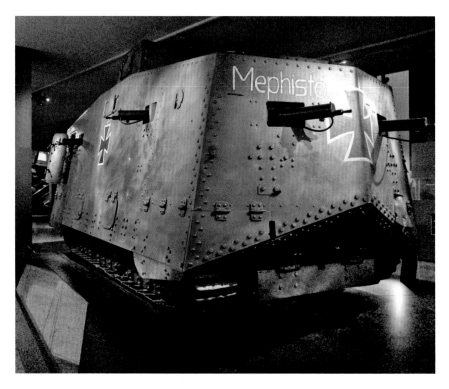

This, No. 506, is the only surviving German Sturmpanzerwagen A7V out of the twenty built. This tank, called 'Mephisto', was photographed at the Australian War Memorial in Canberra. This is the rear view. It is normally on display at the Queensland Museum in Brisbane.

This is a replica of the German Sturmpanzerwagen A7V tank, No. 535 'Wotan', on display at the Deutsches Panzermuseum (German Tank Museum) in Münster. (www.daspanzermuseum.de)

This working Sturmpanzerwagen A7V tank is a replica of No. 504 'Schuuck' and is kept at The Tank Museum, Bovington. The original vehicle was armed with one 57mm Maxim-Nordfeldt Model 1888 quick-firing (QF) fortress casement gun. (www.tankmuseum.org)

# GERMAN LK II LIGHT TANK

By the end of the First World War the German Army realised that it needed a smaller, lighter and faster break-out armoured vehicle as its large, heavy Sturmpanzerwagen A7V was too slow and cumbersome. It was also expensive to build and took a long time to manufacture, and it required a crew of eighteen as a minimum.

The A7V tank was ideal for smashing through the Allied defensive lines of barbed wire and trench systems but once the breach had been made the Germans needed a vehicle to take the role of the cavalry. They wanted a vehicle that could find enemy supply depots and artillery battalions situated behind enemy lines and then destroy them.

This was, in fact, what a British Whippet armoured tank of the 3rd Tank Brigade actually managed to do on 8 August 1918. It broke through German lines and caused havoc for nine hours. It hunted any enemy target it could find, including a German HQ post, a transport supply column, an artillery battery and an observation balloon. This capability was what the German High Command was looking for when it ordered the production of the Leichte Kampfwagen II (LKII) light tank.

The German engineers used a commercially available Daimler chassis as the basis of their new weapon. They retrofitted it with armour plating and added a caterpillar tracked system to the wheels. As this light tank was based on a production vehicle, the engine was in the front and the fighting compartment had to be built in the rear. This gave some additional protection for the crew as the engine block was between them and any incoming anti-tank shell.

Initially the Leichte Kampfwagen LK II was going to be armed with a 57mm cannon situated in the 360-degree turret and a 7.93mm machine gun in the hull. The gun in the turret was tested on 29 August 1918 but it was found to be too powerful as it had a strong destructive effect on the armoured chassis. For this reason the 57mm cannon was replaced with a smaller 37mm Krupp gun.

By June 1918 only two prototypes had been produced; an order for 580 tanks was placed but it was not completed.

The massed supply of German front-line troops with Leichte Kampfwagen LK II light tanks with the aim of overrunning the Allied trench defensive lines never happened. The First World War ended before they could be tested properly under battlefield conditions and they never became involved in a tank-on-tank action.

The Germans were banned from owning armoured vehicles under the terms of the Armistice and sold their Leichte Kampfwagen LK IIs to Hungary and Sweden. They were dismantled and boxed up for shipping, with the labels on the outside stating the boxes contained agricultural tractor parts.

# SURVIVING LEICHTE KAMPFWAGEN LK II LIGHT TANKS

There are four surviving German–built LKIIs, although only one survives in the original 1918 specifications. It is on display at the Arsenalen Tank Museum, 645 91 Strängnäs, Sweden. The Swedish Army called it the Stridsvagn m/21 Tank. The other three surviving LKIIs were upgraded and redesignated Stridsvagn m/21-29. Two are at the Arsenalen Tank Museum; the third is on display at the Deutsches Panzermuseum, Münster, Germany.

## Specifications

| | |
|---|---|
| Dimensions | Length 16ft 9in (5.1m)<br>Width 6ft 3in (1.9m)<br>Height 8ft 2in (2.5m) |
| Total Weight, Battle Ready | 8.75 tonnes |
| Crew | 3 |
| Propulsion | German Daimler-Benz Model 1910 4-cylinder 60hp petrol engine |
| Transmission | Cone clutch to four-speed and reverse gearbox to worm reduction and bevel drive, chain loop to drive sprocket, one for each track |
| Speed | 11mph (18km/h) |
| Range | Around 43.5 miles (70km) |
| Trench-Crossing Ability | 10ft (3.04m) |
| Armament | 37mm Krupp gun |
| Ammunition Stowage | 5,400 0.303in (7.62mm) rounds |
| Armour | 8-14mm |
| Total Production | 200 |

The only surviving 1918 original configuration LKII tank can be found at the Arsenalen Tank Museum near Stockholm. (www.arsenalen.se)

The Swedish Army called the 1918 German-built LKII the Stridsvagn m/21. It was armed with a 37mm Krupp gun.

A Swedish Army-modified Leichte Kampfwagen LK II (Stridsvagn m/21-39) was sent to the Deutsches Panzermuseum (German Tank Museum) Münster. It has sloped frontal armour designed to help it get up ditches, not deflect enemy shells. The two pear-shaped discs on the front of the LK protect two headlights.

It looks similar to the British Whippet but the Leichte Kampfwagen LKII had a rotating turret armed with a 37mm Krupp gun. The Germans were banned from owning armoured vehicles under the terms of the Armistice after 1919. They sold their Leichte Kampfwagen LK II light tanks to Hungary and Sweden.

# A7V FLAKPANZER
# ANTI-AIRCRAFT TANK

In the First World War, the Germans used the A7V tank chassis as a starting point in the development of several other variations. Although most would be used for the A7V Überlandwagen rough-terrain tracked supply vehicle, others were used to create unique vehicles, such as a trench-digging machine and the anti-aircraft version known as the A7V Flakpanzer.

Plans were also made to produce an A7V Funkpanzer wireless communication tank fitted with a Graben-Funkstation 16 radio transmitter and large circling antenna positioned on the roof.

In order to combat the ever more numerous aircraft in the skies, the German Army needed something that could fend off the enemy aviators, but also relocate to a more defensible position if necessary. Little is known about this mysterious A7V Flakpanzer – the earliest recorded tracked anti-aircraft vehicle – save for a few photographs. Three prototypes were being tested in the closing stages of the First World War.

The fate of these machines is unknown; it is possible that they were captured by the Allies and scrapped, or dismantled and the parts used for other things.

The guns themselves were positioned at each end of the platform. Ammo boxes were placed around the driving position and just under the guns. The Flakpanzer A7V was very similar to the Überlandwagen, which also had the A7V chassis and suspension, with the engines mounted centrally. The driving compartment was placed above them and was open and unarmoured, but had a tarpaulin cover to be used in bad weather.

The cargo bays were extended well over the front and rear of the vehicle, making the Flakpanzer longer. Each of these bays held an anti-aircraft gun mounted on a pedestal. These guns could traverse 360 degrees and could also elevate to fire at enemy planes.

Also present were two elevated guard rails, which seem to have had a double purpose. They could keep the crew from falling off the vehicle and serve as sitting places when moving. Under them were the ammunition compartments, which could be accessed from the outside of the vehicle when the wooden side panels were lowered.

The crew consisted of around ten men, with four needed to service each gun. There was also a driver and a commander, although it is not clear if these positions were somehow amalgamated.

## THE ARMAMENT

There is no verified information on the armament used by the Flakpanzer. However, it is believed that two of the prototypes were equipped with captured Russian M1902/30 76.2mm (3in) field guns. They were mounted on a new trunnion and elevation assembly to enable high elevation.

The Germans had captured copious numbers of such guns from the Tsarist Empire and pressed them into service; they even manufactured the ammunition for them.

The third prototype A7V Flakpanzer was equipped with a German Krupp-manufactured gun. It is believed that it was a 7.7cm (3.03in) German leichte Feld Kanone (l.F.K.) 1896 n/a (7.7cm light field cannon). Only one gun was fitted to this vehicle.

Whether these guns were effective against their intended targets remains a mystery as no paperwork related to their use has been found.

## SURVIVING A7V FLAKPANZERS

No A7V Flakpanzers have survived.

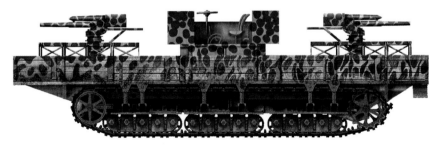

The A7V Flakpanzer anti-aircraft tank had two Russian M1902/30 76.2mm (3in) field guns mounted on each end.

# A7V ÜBERLANDWAGEN

## THE NEED FOR A TRACKED SUPPLY VEHICLE

The battlefield conditions during the First World War were horrendous. The muddy, crater-filled terrain proved too difficult and at times dangerous for both men and animals carrying supplies to the front. The German Army felt a need to come up with a way of moving these vital supplies quickly but also safely.

In February 1918 the initial modified order for 100 A7V tanks was changed to just twenty finished units. The remaining A7V production chassis were diverted into making anti-aircraft vehicles and prime movers: tracked supply vehicles that could also tow guns and broken-down tanks, armoured cars and lorries.

The 'prime mover' supply vehicle based on the A7V chassis had a number of different names as the Germans made distinctions between *Strassenwagen* (road vehicles). This vehicle crossed rough undulating ground and was called three different names: A7V Geländewagen (Terrain vehicle), A7V Raupenlastwagen (Caterpillar vehicle) and A7V Überlandwagen (Overland vehicle).

The first eight A7V Geländewagen vehicles (chassis numbers 508–515) were completed by September 1917.

In November 1917 they were in use with the German Armee Kraftwagen Kolonne (Raupe) III (AKK(R)111, 111th Tracked Army Motor Vehicle Column) in northern France. By September 1918 thirty were in service, with the AKK(R)111 and the AKK(R)112 Army transport columns.

The A7V Überlandwagen's carrying capacity was approximately 3–4 tons (2.7–3.6 tonnes). Although it was able to deal with the muddy terrain, it had limited success due its slow speed, poor rough-terrain handling and lack of protection for the crew.

Those that did make trips to the front were well received by the soldiers, as the vital supplies that the Überlandwagen brought to men on the front line arrived intact. These supplies included clothes, medicine, munitions and, at times, food.

The fate of most of these A7V Überlandwagens after the war is unknown; it is possible they were used for a while before being broken up and scrapped. A few were shipped to Aldershot in England for testing and evaluation before being cut up for scrap metal.

The twin Daimler 100hp engines were mounted side-by-side in the centre of the driving compartment, arranged to drive in either direction, placed on a platform above the engines. The driver did not have an armoured cab.

There was a canopy above the driver's head. In some vehicles rails were added to support a tarpaulin cover over the load spaces. These rails went from the top of the canopy down to the four corners of the vehicle.

The walls of the driver's cab were only about 2ft (0.6m) tall. It had four large open windows without glass. In bad weather canvas sheeting was unrolled from the top of the canopy and secured to the bottom of the window opening to give the driver and crew some protection from the elements. However, the driver and the crew were very vulnerable.

Unlike the British armoured tanks, which were used as supply vehicles that could travel right up to the front line under enemy fire, the German A7V Überlandwagen supply vehicles had to stay out of range of Allied rifles and machine guns.

The suspension was derived from the American Holt tractor, which had also provided the early inspiration for British and French tanks. The A7V–Überlandwagen had a front and rear cargo bay, with wooden panels on the side. Later versions had taller panels. For ease of loading and unloading the wooden panels could be unhitched and swung down on their hinges.

Two tow hooks were fitted to the front and back, and used to attach wheeled vehicles and guns. They were also intended to be used to help tow broken down, knocked out or stuck tanks back to safety.

## VEHICLE FAULTS

Early reports were favourable but the A7V Überlandwagens suffered from the same mechanical and design problems as the A7V tanks: they had poor cross-country performance and low ground clearance. Radiators and backboards were damaged if the load that was being carried was not sufficiently tied down. When the vehicle traversed very undulating ground the heavy load would slide around at fast speeds and hit the sides of the cargo areas, causing damage.

The front and back of the cargo area extended past the tracks. This was problematic if the vehicle descended into a big shell crater or trench as the nose got stuck in the mud wall on the other side because the tracks could not get a proper grip to drive up the wall.

Fuel consumption was another big issue, especially in 1918 when supplies were low. The A7V Überlandwagen required 10 litres of petrol/gasoline to travel 1km. A wheeled truck only required 3 litres of fuel to cover the same distance and as a result they were not heavily used.

# SURVIVING A7V ÜBERLANDWAGEN

No A7V Überlandwagen have survived.

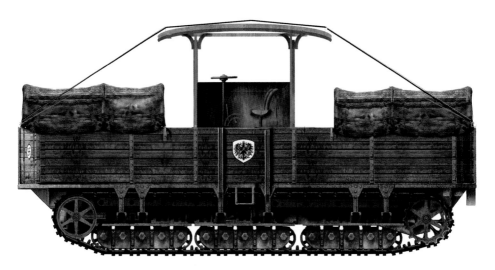

The A7V Überlandwagen was a rough-terrain supply vehicle that used the German Sturmpanzerwagen A7V heavy tank chassis.

# BRITISH SUPPLY TANKS

Armoured supply tanks were deployed as part of the British offensives of 1917 and 1918. It was impractical for a supply lorry to follow the tanks on to the battlefield as it would get shot at by enemy machine guns and rifles. The crew would be killed or wounded and any fuel or ammunition being carried would explode or catch fire.

The Army needed a method of resupplying the tanks on the battlefield and the simplest option was to build new tanks or convert old ones into supply vehicles. The armoured hull would protect the crew and the stores the tank was transporting. As it was a tracked vehicle it could cross the same terrain that the battle tanks were driving across.

In order to increase the amount of load the supply tanks could carry, boxes of stores were strapped securely to the roof. To enable even more stores to be transported to the front a large metal and wood sledge was built. It did not use wheels but instead had large skids, that looked like giant skis, fixed to the bottom. This was then attached to the back of the supply tanks by chains or strong rope and dragged over the bumpy terrain.

The sledges were not made in Britain as this task was given to the Central Workshops in France. Wood was used to build a lightweight upright 'fence' panel around the four sides of the sledge.

The boxes of fuel, ammunition, food and water had to be tied down very securely to stop them falling off. Speed was not a problem as the tanks very rarely went faster than walking speed. It was the bumps and dips in the rough ground the vehicles had to cross that could be problematic.

There is a photograph of a Mark IV Male supply tank near Bapaume in September 1918 pulling two fully loaded supply sledges down a road lined with an avenue of trees.

In the side sponsons, the holes where the guns would have been mounted were blanked off with metal plates. Internally wire mesh screens were used to stop boxes of stores falling out of the sponsons and on to the crew or the hot engine in the middle of the tank.

Loading the supply tanks was difficult because of the small crew hatches. When loaded there was limited space, which made it difficult for the driver and commander to move around. Therefore, a new large hatch was fitted to the front cabin roof. It still needed a minimum of four crew members to steer, operate the track brakes and change gear.

On the side of the vehicle in very large white letters the word 'Supply' would be painted. Very often this was painted on the front of the tank as well. Sometimes the word 'Baggage' would be painted on the side instead of 'Supply'.

Each Mark IV supply tank could carry 5 tons of stores internally; this meant that one supply tank could re-supply five battle tanks. The problem with all the First World War British heavy tanks was that they were prone to mechanical breakdowns and ditching; supply tanks suffered these same deficiencies.

If a supply tank got stuck in a shell crater and could not get out or it broke down early on in the battle then those tanks that were reliant on being able to refuel and load up with more ammunition halfway through the day were in trouble.

There are a number of regimental battle diary entries that report tanks having to return back to the start line because they were low on fuel or had ran out of machine gun ammunition. This left the infantry in the front line vulnerable.

Out of an initial order of 1,400 Mark IV tanks, 950 were Male and Female fighting tanks but 205 were built as supply tanks. (Eleven were used for experiments, fifty-four were surplus and 180 were cancelled once the Mark V entered production.)

Each Mark IV supply tank could carry 5 tons of stores internally. This meant that one supply tank could re-supply five battle tanks. They could also tow two sledges stacked with stores. They were also painted brown.

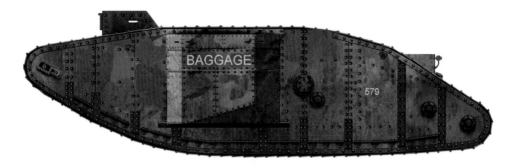

BAGGAGE

579

Older Mark II tanks were also turned into supply tanks. Some had the word 'baggage' painted on the side rather than the word 'supply'.

A few supply tanks were based on the now obsolete Gun Carrier tanks. They had two large oval doors in the back of the vehicle, which made loading boxes of stores inside the vehicle easier than on the Mark IV supply tank. The open section that used to be the gun crew fighting compartment was now used to stack up crates of food and water. Containers of fuel and ammunition that needed protection from small arms fire were put inside the rear armoured section of the tank.

Some of the older tanks were converted into supply tanks. At the Battle of Messines on 7 June 1917, twelve Mark Is and IIs were used as supply carriers. They were converted at the British Central Workshops in France. Queen Mary was photographed inspecting a modified Mark II supply tank when she visited the Tank Corps at Neuve-Eglise in July 1917. The Gun Carrier Mark I was also converted into a supply tank, but more about that in the next chapter.

## SURVIVING BRITISH SUPPLY TANKS

No supply tanks have survived.

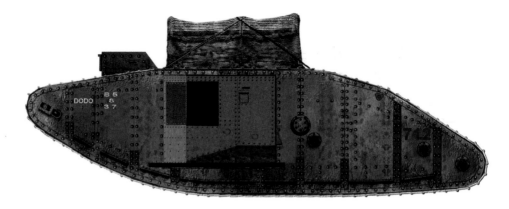

Some Mark I Males were used as supply tanks. This is tank No. 712, called 'Dodo', of B battalion, 5 Company, 8 Section, B37. It was photographed on 7 June 1917 at Messines. This was the first time old Mark I tanks were used as supply vehicles. This tank was later renamed 'Badger' and presumably remained with 'B' Battalion until the Mark I and II supply tanks were withdrawn.

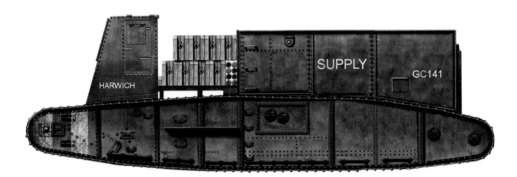

During the latter part of the war more Gun Carrier Mark I vehicles were used as supply tanks rather than as artillery gun transporters. When no gun was carried it left a large empty space to carry food and water. The armoured crew compartment was used to carry fuel cans and stack boxes of ammunition – explosive.

# SCHNEIDER CD SUPPLY VEHICLE

This tracked French First World War vehicle is called the Schneider CD Artillery tractor, also known as the Schneider Char de Dépannage. The French phrase *camion de dépannage* translates to 'tow truck'. The Schneider CD used the same Holt chassis as the Schneider CA tank and was fitted with a winch. The letters CD were a Schneider factory code, not an abbreviation for *char de dépannage*.

During the planning and construction stage of the Schneider assault tank, it was given the factory code name 'Tracteur Estienne' after the project leader, Col Jean-Baptiste Estienne, but later had the official designation 'Schneider CA'. The letters CA do not stand for *char d'assaut* (assault tank). They were also a Schneider factory code.

By 1915, some of the French First World War offensives had managed to breach the German front lines. The infantry attack across no-man's-land had been preceded by days of artillery bombardment to 'soften up' resistance. This had turned the battlefield into a churned-up lunar landscape covered in muddy shell craters. To support the breakthrough, the French artillery needed to be able to move their gun batteries, otherwise they would be out of range. Artillery barrages were needed to disrupt and hopefully stop German counter-attacks.

Most French artillery guns were drawn by a team of up to six horses. However, the terrain was just too difficult for them to move across and a new answer had to be found. The French Army looked towards an agricultural solution. For a number of years, French farmers had been using tracked steam-driven tractors and tracked tractors powered by petrol engines. They were purchased by the Army and put to use towing howitzers to the front lines.

Agricultural tractors including the early Holt-built tractor were slow and found it difficult to tow the heavier artillery howitzers. They also did not have any on-board storage so they had to tow trailers to deliver artillery ammunition and supplies. The French Army needed a heavier, more powerful vehicle to move and service the heavy guns adequately. Once the guns were in position, the Army wanted the same vehicle to be able to transport ammunition from the supply dump to the battery's new location.

The French Renault EG and Latil TAR large four-wheel-drive trucks were capable of carrying the heavy artillery shells, which ranged from 40kg to 100kg, along the muddy roads to the front lines. However, they could not cross the churned-up battlefield. The proposed tracked artillery tractor had to be capable of collecting these shells from just behind French lines and take them across the scarred landscape without getting stuck in the mud.

The French manufacturer Renault submitted a design for a fully tracked artillery tractor but decided to build a vehicle that could carry the gun rather than just tow one. This 'en portée' vehicle would only be able to carry light field howitzers and not the heavier guns. The small size of the flat wooden deck at the rear of the vehicle limited the size of weapon it could transport. The prototype was given the factory code Renault FB: the letters FB were not an abbreviation. This design did not meet the French Army's requirements.

The Schneider CD was built using a Schneider CA *char d'assaut* tank's lower chassis. It had a large storage area behind the driver's cabin. The design used a lengthened Baby Holt tractor suspension and caterpillar track and the front of the tank was shaped like the front of a ship. The idea was that this feature would help free the tank from the side of a muddy trench wall. This design was replaced by a driver's cabin at the front with a strong curved metal lower shield 'skid' that could slide up muddy embankments and the sides of shell craters. The rear metal 'skid' used on the tank was not fitted to the Schneider CD, but the tractor used the same engine and transmission.

There was room for a crew of four in the driver's cabin but there were only seats for two of them. The two in the back would have to sit on boxes of supplies. It would not have been a pleasant vehicle to operate in cold and wet weather conditions as the only protection the crew had was a canvas hood; there were no side doors or front windscreen. The heat from the engine would help keep them warm but they would be at the mercy of the biting winds, rain and snow. In the summer, the canvas hood could be folded back.

At the back of the driver's cabin, a large cable stowage reel was mounted. It had a handle attached to the side for manually winding up the towing cable. A powered revolving cylinder with a vertical axis was fitted to the rear of the vehicle and used for winding up and letting out the towing cable. This capstan winch was powered by the engine.

After a successful demonstration of the prototype, Schneider received an initial order for fifty vehicles. In October 1916, that order was increased to 500. In December 1916, Gen. Robert Georges Nivelle, a French artillery officer, became commander-in-chief. Priorities changed and Schneider was told to put all efforts into completing the order for the artillery tractor and supply vehicle at the expense of meeting the Schneider CA tank production targets.

In August 1917, the first production Schneider CD artillery tractor was completed. Only twenty vehicles had been delivered to the French Army by the end of December 1917; this averaged a production figure of five vehicles a month. In 1918, this figure rose to an average of eight vehicles a month. By the end of the war Schneider had only delivered 110 Schneider CD artillery tractors.

## POST-FIRST WORLD WAR SERVICE

The French Army continued to receive Schneider CD tracked tractors after the war but deliveries stopped after the 200th vehicle was delivered. Schneider manufactured a further 130 vehicles for civilian use on farms, by civil engineers and by forestry workers. The Schneider CD was still in French Army service when the German Army attacked in May 1940.

Many were captured and used by the German Wehrmacht as towing and supply vehicles. The rear capstan winch and cable reel behind the driver's cabin were removed on some vehicles. A few were used after the Second World War but only one is known to have been saved from the scrap heap; it was used by the company Barthez until the 1950s. It was rescued and restored by a private collector, and can occasionally be seen at exhibitions of classic vehicles in France.

## THE SCHNEIDER CD3 CHAR DE DÉPANNAGE

In December 1917, the French Army also issued a requirement for a tracked artillery tractor that was capable of towing the very heavy 9-ton howitzer. Schneider built a prototype CA.3 tank that used an extended Schneider CA chassis. It also had a slightly more powerful engine.

To improve weight distribution on soft ground, the track width was increased to 45cm rather than the original 36cm. The initial order for 200 tanks was cancelled in favour of building a tank fleet of lighter, more agile Renault FT tanks. The extended chassis design was used for Schneider CD.3.

The crew cabin canvas cover was removed and a long metal arm was extended, at an angle, over the front of the engine. It was held in place by an 'A'-shaped metal support. At the end of the metal boom there was a pulley, over which ran the powered winch tow cable. On the left side of the vehicle, Schneider fitted a small crane. This was used to hoist up the trail legs of the guns over the back of the vehicle.

Development took a long time and the prototype finally underwent trials in October 1918. Different artillery pieces such as the 7.45-tonne, 220mm

TR Schneider howitzer and the 3.3-tonne, 155mm L mle 1917 Schneider field gun were attached to the rear of the vehicle and driven across the undulating proving ground course. It successfully completed these tests. Although not designed to transport heavier guns, it was found that it could tow the 13-tonne Canon de 155mm Grande Puissance Filloux (GPF) mle 1917 howitzer.

# SURVIVING SCHNEIDER CD SUPPLY VEHICLE

Only one Schneider CD artillery tractor has survived. It has been restored by a private collector in France.

## Specifications

| Dimensions | Length 20ft 9in (6.32m)<br>Width 7ft 6in (2.30m)<br>Height 6ft 9in (2.05m) |
|---|---|
| Total Weight | 13.6 tons |
| Crew | 2 |
| Propulsion | Schneider 4-cylinder petrol, 60hp (45Kw) |
| Speed | 5mph (8km/h) |
| Range On/Off Road | 50/19 miles (80/30km) |
| Load Capacity | 3,000kg |
| Total Production | 330 |

The French Army used the Schneider CA tank chassis to build an artillery tractor that could tow field guns and be used as supply vehicle over rough ground. It was called the Schneider CD.

At the back of the driver's cabin, a large cable stowage bobbin reel was fixed. There was an engine-powered winch at the back of the vehicle.

The French Army was still using Schneider CDs when the German Army invaded in May 1940. Some Schneider CD artillery tractors were captured and used by the Germans as supply and towing vehicles. The winch and rear cable bobbin were removed.

# GUN CARRIER MARK I

The Gun Carrier tank was one of the world's first self-propelled artillery gun designs. On 15 September 1916 tanks went into battle for the first time on an attack front between the villages of Flers and Courcelette. An artillery barrage was used to rain down shells on the German infantry, who were waiting in their trenches to defend against the attacking British and Commonwealth troops. The tanks managed to break through the rows of barbed wire and cross the German trenches, silencing enemy machine-gun posts as they went.

The tanks then continued on to the next objective. The depth of the breakthrough meant that the artillery could no longer fire shells ahead of the advancing front line as they were now out of range so it had to saddle up and cross no-man's-land. Each gun required six horses to pull it and a nine-man crew, and the ground was so riddled with shell holes that this task was extremely difficult. They then had the problem of how to cross the captured enemy trenches.

Maj. Gregg, a British Army engineer attached to the tank building company Metropolitan Carriage, Wagon and Finances Ltd based in Birmingham, came up with a solution. He suggested building a modified tank chassis that could carry a large artillery howitzer across rough ground, ditches, shell craters and trenches. His design gave the gun team two options: to fire the weapon from the tracked vehicle or to attach the gun carriage wheels back on to the gun and wheel it off the vehicle so that it could be fired in the normal way.

This would enable the artillery to follow and keep up with the advancing tanks after a breakthrough had been achieved in the enemy's defences. They would be able to provide artillery support over the heads of the attacking infantry as they moved further inland.

On 5 July 1916, the production of a prototype was approved. On 3 March 1917, the Gun Carrier tank prototype took part in the secret Tank Trials Day at the Oldbury proving grounds near Birmingham. High-ranking Army officers and members of the government watched new experimental weapons put through their paces. The Gun Carrier tank impressed the influential crowd and an order for fifty was placed. The construction contract was awarded to Kitson & Company, a locomotive manufacturer based in Leeds.

The track system used on the Gun Carrier was very different from the rhomboid shape of the Mark I tank: instead of high and angled tracks, they were low, almost flat. It was also longer than the Mark I tank. The Gun Carrier's length, without the wheeled steering tail, was 30ft (9.1m) whereas the Mark I was only 26ft (7.92m).

The Gun Carrier was powered by a British Foster-Daimler, Knight sleeve valve, water-cooled, straight-six, 13-litre petrol engine that produced 105hp at 1,000rpm. This was the same engine used in the Mark I. It was housed at the rear, not in the middle of the tank, to provide room for the howitzer at the front. To keep the engine, transmission and crew safe from small arms fire, an armoured superstructure was built at the back. It was slow, only moving at a walking pace of 4mph (6km/h).

The vehicle needed four crew to drive it: the driver, two gearsmen and a brakesman. This was the same arrangement as the Mark I tank. The double-wheeled steering tail fitted to the rear of the Mark I was also used on the Gun Carrier but later discarded.

A lieutenant commanded the vehicle and the sixth member of the crew was the mechanic. The driver and brakesman sat in the two narrow armoured compartments at the front of the vehicle, either side of the gun barrel. The gun crew were carried on the vehicle.

The Gun Carrier could transport two different artillery pieces, but not at the same time. The wheels of the gun carriage were removed from the gun and strapped to the side of the vehicle. The 6in howitzer could be fired from the Gun Carrier's central platform. The vehicle was pointed in the direction of the target and the crew sheltered behind the gun shield as they worked out elevation, range and charge before loading the shell and propellant.

The larger BL 60-pounder (5in) gun could not be fired from inside the Gun Carrier. The wheels had to be reattached to the gun carriage and manhandled off the vehicle. The 6in 26cwt howitzer could also be taken off the Gun Carrier, enabling firing in the normal way.

The Gun Carrier's platform, which jutted out at the front of the vehicle, could be tilted down to assist in the loading and unloading of howitzers. Once the wheels had been removed from the howitzer's gun carriage it was laid down on to a trolley. This trolley was then winched inside the Gun Carrier with the gun on top of it. The Daimler engine provided the power for the winch. The platform was then returned to the horizontal position.

The Gun Carrier entered service in the latter part of 1917. They were organised into two Gun Carrier companies, part of XVIII Corps, with twenty-four machines in each. They were then shipped to France just before the Third

Battle of Ypres, which ran from 31 July to 10 November 1917, but were not used. The Gun Carrier companies did take part in the Battle of Pilckem Ridge, which began on 31 July 1917 and finished on 2 August.

They were mainly used as 'beasts of burden', not self-propelled guns, and they were tasked with transporting a lot of artillery guns and ammunition to battery positions. There are no records of them being used as mobile artillery in the Battle of Cambrai on 20 November 1917. Seven were shown on regimental records as available for deployment but they did not follow the Mark IV tanks following their breakthrough behind the German front lines. They were never allowed to function as a gun carrier, following the advancing infantry and tanks, on the battlefield.

The Gun Carriers were converted into supply tanks and also used as troop carriers. At the beginning of June 1918 both Gun Carrier companies were converted into supply companies. For the attack on 8 August 1918, day one of the Battle of Amiens, twenty-two Gun Carrier supply vehicles were allocated for use by the Australian Corps. Unfortunately sixteen were damaged beyond repair when one of them carrying explosives exploded on the night of 6–7 August 1918 near Villers-Bretonneux.

Experiments were conducted on some of the remaining Gun Carriers to see if a crane could be fitted so they could be used by engineers to recover broken-down and knocked-out tanks.

## GUN CARRIER MARK II PROTOTYPE

A wooden prototype mock-up of the next generation of the Gun Carrier was built and called the Mark II. The gun was winched up on top of the tank at the rear. The vehicle had the appearance of an elongated Mark V★ tank with a long thin 'tadpole' tail. Side sponsons were not fitted and were replaced by large doors.

It was not intended to fire the gun from the top of the Gun Carrier. The vehicle was designed to be a method of transporting artillery pieces over the rough, undulating ground of the battlefield. There was a ramp fixed to the back of the tank that could be raised or lowered. The winch was powered by the engine. Its cables passed through the roof and attached to a pulley mechanism situated just behind the driver's cab. A second pulley was fixed to a tripod frame and the winch cable was attached to the towing ring of the gun. The space inside the vehicle was used to store ammunition and supplies. Its armoured hull protected the shells and crew from small arms fire.

They never went into production, but as a result of this new design the original Gun Carrier was redesignated Gun Carrier Mark I and the wooden mock-up called the Gun Carrier Mark II.

## SURVIVING GUN CARRIERS

No British Gun Carriers have survived.

### Specifications

| | |
|---|---|
| Dimensions | Length 30ft (9.1m), 43ft (13m) with tail<br>Width 11.6ft (3.5m)<br>Height 7.9ft (2.41m) |
| Total Weight | 27 long tons unloaded, 34 long tons maximum |
| Crew | 6+ gun crew |
| Main Armament | 60-pounder gun or 6in, 26cwt howitzer |
| Engine | British Foster-Daimler, Knight sleeve valve, water-cooled, straight-six, 13-litre petrol engine; 105hp at 1,000rpm |
| Suspension | Unsprung |
| Operational Range | 23.5 miles (37.8km) |
| Speed | 3.70mph (5.95km/h) |

This is the Gun Carrier Mark I. The gun carriage wheels were chained to the side of the vehicle. The piece of metal jutting forward below the gun barrel is the loading ramp for the gun. When the gun was unloaded the wheels were reattached to the gun carriage.

Gun Carrier Mark II prototype wooden mock-up showing the gun being winched on to the back of the tank. (Imperial War Museum Q14524)

Gun Carrier Mark II prototype wooden mock-up showing the gun on the back of the tank with the rear ramps in the raised position. (Imperial War Museum Q14523)

# US HOLT GAS-ELECTRIC TANK

The US-designed Holt Gas-Electric Tank was of a very similar appearance to the British 'Little Willie' tank prototype. Both were armoured boxes built on top of an agricultural tractor tracked system.

US troops in the First World War did not ship over to Europe with American-built tanks as when the USA entered the war it did not have any. US Army senior officers read about the British use of tanks on the battlefield in 1916 and 1917 and were eager that their infantry benefit from the advantages of having tank-led assaults.

The 301st Battalion, US Tank Corps, trained at Bovington Camp in England on Mark IVs before being issued with Mark V, Mark V★ and Mark V Composite tanks in France. However, the US Army wanted its own tanks, built in American factories. One of the first attempts was the Holt Gas-Electric Tank.

The tank was developed by Holt and General Electric and featured an unusual choice of engine. The company fitted a petrol (gasoline) engine connected to an electric generator, which then powered two electric motors connected to the tank track drive wheels. This is why the prototype was called the Holt Gas-Electric Tank.

Engine overheating was an issue and a water cooling system was installed, with the radiator directly above the generator. It is noticeable that in some of the photographs of the tank prototype undergoing tests the two rear armoured doors were fixed in an open position to increase ventilation. This would have been totally impractical on a battlefield, where the crew and the engine would be exposed to small arms fire and shrapnel from exploding artillery shells.

The chassis of the Holt Gas-Electric Tank was based on the Holt 75 agricultural tractor. A new suspension system was designed to take the extra weight and extend the length of the caterpillar track. It had ten road wheels and a return track guide rail. The drive wheel was at the rear and this transferred the power from the engine to the track. The idler wheel was at the front. It could be adjusted forwards and backwards to take up the slack in the track.

The Holt Gas-Electric Tank was armed with a 75mm (2.95in) Vickers mountain gun in the front of the vehicle. The tank tracks would have to be moved so that the vehicle was pointing in the direction of the enemy. The gunner could then make the final adjustments. He would have to constantly co-ordinate with the driver to be able to score a hit on the target.

Two sponsons were fitted to the side and a Browning machine gun was mounted in each. The crew were protected by armour plate that varied in thickness from 6 to 10mm. The front armour was angled like a bow on the front of a ship.

The crew entered the tank through the rear door. If the tank was hit and started to catch fire this one door would be a bottleneck and the lack of other escape hatches could lead to the death of some of the crew. The exact number of tank crew members needed to operate the Holt Gas-Electric Tank is not known. The main gun would have needed a gunner and loader, while the two machine-gunners may have shared a loader. The driver and commander may have had the assistance of a mechanic to look after the complex engine arrangement. The driver sat above the forward-mounted howitzer and looked through small portholes that had a hinged armour cover.

Work on the prototype started in 1917 but it was not completed until 1918 and the trials were disappointing. The tank weighed 25 tons but the engine only produced 90hp. It had a maximum road speed of 6mph (10km/h), which was faster than the British Mark IV but it struggled to climb even slight inclines. It did not have enough power to negotiate the rough, uneven, shell crater-strewn battlefields of north-west Europe and the design was rejected.

The US-designed Holt Gas-Electric Tank was of a very similar appearance to the British 'Little Willie' prototype. Both were armoured boxes built on top of an agricultural tractor tracked system.

# SURVIVING HOLT GAS-ELECTRIC TANKS

The US Holt Gas–Electric prototype tank did not survive.

## Specifications

| Dimensions | Length 16ft 4in (5m)<br>Width 9ft 1in (2.76m)<br>Height 7ft 9in (2.37m)<br>Weight 25 tons (55,000lb) |
|---|---|
| Crew | 6–7 |
| Propulsion | Holt, gasoline, liquid-cooled; 90hp |
| Speed (Road) | 6mph (10km/h) |
| Armament | 75mm (2.95in) Vickers mountain howitzer<br>2 × Browning .30 calibre Model 1917 A1 water-cooled machine guns |
| Armour | 6–10mm |
| Production | 1 prototype |

# US STEAM TANK (TRACK LAYING)

The American-built and designed Steam Tank (Track Laying) was not adopted by the US Army and did not enter service. Only one prototype example was built. Steam-powered agricultural machines known as 'steam tractors' had been used on both sides of the Atlantic since 1885 and it was tried and tested technology.

They normally used large, wide wheels to move around on the farmers' fields but on very wet, muddy waterlogged ground these heavy machines sometimes got stuck. In 1906 David Roberts, chief engineer of Richard Hornsby & Sons, a machinery manufacturer in Lincolnshire, England, patented his design of adding a chain track around smaller wheels to give the steam engine more traction and weight dispersal when negotiating conditions such as this. The company sold the patent to Holt & Co. in America after failing to obtain a British Army contract. (Holt & Co. later became part of Caterpillar Inc. after a merger with C.L. Best.)

In 1917, using a steam engine to power a caterpillar track system was not a new idea. The designers had seen the success the British had with their Mark I tanks in November 1916 and the US Army wanted its own tanks designed and built in the USA.

Gen. John A. Johnson of the US Army's Corps of Engineers started a tank design project. It was developed jointly with the help of Prof. E.F. Miller, Head of the Mechanical Engineering Department at Massachusetts Institute of Technology (MIT). It was built in one of the MIT workshops in Cambridge near Boston and developers consulted with experts from the railways and a company devising steam-driven motor vehicles. It was reported that it cost $60,000 to build and develop.

The prototype was given the name 'America' and was first demonstrated to officials in April 1918. It was given the 'Track Laying' suffix to differentiate it from the steam-powered wheeled armoured tractor prototype under development in the USA. Unfortunately, on its first 'christening' parade on 17 April 1918 in front of Army and Navy officials, it suffered mechanical problems.

The US Tank Commission would not place any orders for this new vehicle without first seeing it undergo trials. However, during the First World War, the Commission was based in Paris, making this difficult. On 22 June 1918 the *New York Herald* ran a report from its man in Paris that the Steam Tank 'America' was being shipped over to France to see how it could handle the rough landscape of the battlefield.

On either side of the tank hull were small sponsons with two holes in each for mounting Browning .30 calibre Model 1917 A1 water-cooled machine guns that could fire 450 to 600 rounds a minute. The tank would be armed with four of these machine guns, to be used to attack machine-gun nests and clear out infantry from enemy trenches.

A flamethrower was to be mounted in the front of the tank hull. This was to be used to attack enemy fortified pillboxes. Capt. Henry Adams, of the US Army Engineer Corps, had developed a flamethrower that could shoot a jet of flame more than 90ft (27m).

It was powered by a 35hp petrol engine fitted inside the tank that could produce 1,600lb pressure per square inch. There was a project to relocate the flamethrower gun nose to a turret on top of the tank but this was never constructed.

The shape of the Steam Tank looks very similar to the British Mark I rhomboid-shaped tanks. Its long length would have helped with crossing the new widened German, anti-tank precaution trenches being built on the Hindenburg Line. The most unusual features of the tank design were the spikes added to the front of the tank. These were attached to the track adjustment mechanism.

The tank weighed 45 tonnes, which was very heavy; a British Mark IV Male tank built in the same year only weighed 28.4 tonnes. It was powered by two 2-cylinder kerosene-burning steam engines, one for each track, which developed a total of 500hp. The steam tank had a maximum road speed of 4mph (6.43km/h). The driver could select from two forward gears and two in reverse.

It needed a tank crew of eight: a commander; driver; flamethrower operator; mechanic and four machine-gunners. They were protected by armour plating, which had a maximum thickness of 13mm.

# SURVIVING US STEAM TANKS

Very little is known about the fate of the US Steam Tank (Track Laying) 'America'. It is believed she was broken up for scrap metal in the 1930s. Only one was built.

## Specifications

| Dimensions | Length 34ft 9in (10.6m)<br>Width 12ft 6in (3.8m)<br>Height 10ft 5in (3.2m) |
| --- | --- |
| Total Weight | 45 tonnes |
| Crew | 8 |
| Crew | 8 |
| Armour | 13mm |
| Main Armament | Flamethrower |
| Secondary Armament | 4 × Browning 0.30in Model 1917 A1 water-cooled machine guns |
| Engine | 2 × 2-cylinder kerosene-burning steam engines; 500hp |
| Suspension | Unsprung |
| Speed | 4mph (6.43km/h) |

The US Steam Tank (Track Laying) was powered by two 2-cylinder, kerosene-burning, 500hp steam engines. It was armed with four Browning .30 calibre Model 1917 A1 water-cooled machine guns.

# US MODEL 1917 6-TON LIGHT TAN

When the United States of America joined the Allies on the battlefields of France and Belgium in the First World War in April 1917, the US Army Expeditionary Force did not possess any tanks. Their officers inspected the British and French types and decided the French Renault FT would meet their needs until more British-style heavy tanks could be manufactured.

They were loaned some Renault FTs and a few British Mark V, V★ and Composite tanks for the final attacks of the First World War. However, the French factories were fully committed to producing tanks to meet the needs of its own army and there was no spare capacity to build additional tanks for the USA.

The Americans quickly conducted negotiations with the French government and obtained the licence to start production of the Renault FT. For security reasons, the early tanks were just called '6-ton special tractors'. Later, they were given the official designation Model 1917 6-Ton Light Tank. This was more commonly abbreviated to just 'M1917'.

The US government placed an order for 4,440 M1917 tanks, but only 950 were produced before the end of the war brought cancellation. Only sixty-four M1917 tanks had been completed by the end of the war and ten were delivered to France but none of them served on the front line.

The letters FT do not stand for 'first tank' or the French terms *faible tonnage* (low tonnage), *faible taille* (small size), *franchisseur de tranchées* (trench crosser), or *force terrestre* (land force). The tank was not named the FT 17 or FT-17 during the First World War. All new Renault projects were given a two-letter product code for internal use, and the next one available was 'FT'. The previous production code was 'FS'.

## DESIGN AND PRODUCTION

This tank should not be judged with modern eyes as tank-on-tank combat was not a consideration in the design.

Light tanks like the M1917 were the solution to the problem of how do you cross no-man's-land under rifle and machine-gun fire and breach the enemy's front line of trenches. Most of the Renault FT tanks used in the war were only armed with machine guns. A few were mounted with cannons to deal with fortified bunkers and machine-gun positions. They worked with machine-gun-armed tanks, which protected them from infantry attack.

The tank was operated by a two-man crew. The driver sat in the front of the tank in the middle and the commander operated the turret and gun. The turret was unpowered, and had no mechanism to move it besides handles. The commander had too much to do; he had to look out for enemy targets and dangers, load the gun, traverse the turret, fire the machine gun and give directions to the driver. He also had to read the map and co-ordinate with other tanks and infantry units. The tanks were not fitted with radios, so the commander had to use flags, hand signals and shout commands at other units.

The tank had a number of good design features that were advanced for the time. For example, the front armour plate that protected the driver was sloped. The armour was thin, but sloping increased the thickness of metal any enemy bullet had to pass through before it penetrated the interior of the tank. The angle of the armour also helped deflect incoming enemy bullets. The tank tracks were comparatively wide for the time and this helped in enabling the tank to cross muddy ground.

## THE AMERICAN VERSION

The American engineers made some alterations to the original French Renault FT design. Some of these features were cosmetic and others were to assist in the problem of supplying non-standard ammunition and equipment to front-line troops.

The most noticeable was the removal of the French Hotchkiss 8mm (.315in) machine gun. It was replaced by an American-made calibre .30 calibre (7.62mm) 1917 Marlin machine gun that accepted the standard US .30 calibre ammunition.

The US designers changed the engine. The French Renault FT was powered by a Renault 4-cylinder, 4.5 litre, thermo-siphon, water-cooled, gasoline petrol engine. The Americans replaced it with a Buda HU modified 4-cylinder, with forced water cooling. This gasoline petrol engine produced 42hp. While the tank wasn't fast by modern standards, the Buda engine did produce a lot of torque, which was more important than speed since that would allow it to cross obstacles and rough terrain more reliably.

This initial engine replacement did not enhance the maximum speed of the tank. It still propelled the vehicle at only 5mph (8km/h) on the road and it only just managed to keep up with advancing friendly troops across country.

It only had an operational range of 30 miles (50km) before it needed to be refuelled. In modern warfare, this would be a problem, but for Allied tanks involved in First World War offensives, the enemy front line was only 100 to 200m away and any breakthrough would normally only cover a maximum of 6 miles (10km).

The Renault FT and the US Army M1917 tank could be individually recognised by the following features. The exhaust on the M1917 was positioned on the left-hand side of the tank instead of on the right. The machine gun and 37mm cannon gun mantlet were replaced with new designs. Solid steel idler wheels replaced the French steel-rimmed, wooden or seven-spoked steel ones on the Renault FT tank.

The American designers added additional vision slits in the armoured bodywork to aid the driver. All US Army M1917 light tanks had polygonal turrets and not the cast-metal circular turrets fitted to nearly 50 per cent of French Renault FT tanks.

For those that like to look closer at the differences between tank types, the frontal armour below the turret on the US M1917 was slightly modified from the original French design. The track tensioning mechanisms, which move the idler wheels forward or backwards, are different. The US Army M1917 tank has an assembly in which a bolt is used to set the tension and two pairs of interlocking, toothed plates that lock together to hold the axle in place, removing strain from the relatively weak bolt.

A self-starter was fitted to the engine and a bulkhead was added to the chassis to separate the crew from the engine compartment. It was still very noisy inside the tank and the commander informed the driver where he wanted him to steer by using his feet on the driver's back: touch the left shoulder to go left, right shoulder to go right and the middle of the driver's back to go straight ahead.

# MANUFACTURER

The US licence-built M1917 light tank was built at three different factories: Van Dorn Iron Works, Maxwell Motor Company and the C.L. Best Company.

# THE M1917 A1 TANK VARIANT

After the First World War, the American engineers wanted to fit a more powerful engine into the M1917 chassis, but it was very restrictive. In 1919, they increased the length of the chassis by around 1ft (30cm) and mounted an American-built Franklin engine that produced 100hp, an improvement on the original US Buda 42hp engine. It only increased the maximum road speed to 9mph (14.5km/h) instead of 5mph (8km/h). It was given the designation M1917 A1.

The octagonal turret was used and a .30 calibre M1919 Browning tank machine gun replaced the .30 calibre M1917 Marlin machine gun. All steel road wheels were fitted to this new tank variant.

Some of the US Army tanks were upgraded to gun tanks by the fitting of M1916 37mm cannons. The shell was a little bit smaller than the British 6-pounder (57mm) high-explosive shell. They could also carry armour-piercing shells for punching holes through concrete bunkers. Behind the armour-piercing head of the shell was a base-detonating fuse system and some black powder that would ignite the primer and charge. It would explode after the shell had hit its target and gone through the concrete or armour.

The tank carried 238 shells; two 100-round ammo racks were fitted in the hull, one each side of where the commander stood, plus a twenty-five-round and thirteen-round ready rack in the turret. This gun tank did not have a machine gun, so it had to rely on other M1917 machine-gun tanks for protection from infantry.

The tanks fitted with the .30 calibre M1919 Browning tank machine guns could carry 4,200 .30 calibre rounds. It is believed 374 upgraded 37mm US Army M1917 gun tanks were built after 1919 and 526 M1917 were fitted with the new the .30 calibre M1919 Browning tank machine guns. They all had the extended chassis and new Franklin engines.

Records show that fifty M1917 signals tanks were built. They had an enlarged non-rotating turret that could carry a radio and space for maps. The French version was called a Renault TSF (*telegraphie sans fil* = wireless radio).

# OPERATIONAL SERVICE

Although ten American-built M1917 tanks were delivered to France in the autumn of 1918, they never saw action before the end of the First World War. It was the tank that would have been used by the US Army in France if the war had progressed into 1919 and beyond.

The US Army was already using some French Army Renault FTs as well as a few British Mark V tanks in France during the First World War. An American Army light tank platoon consisted of five vehicles that were a combination of machine-gun-only and 37mm cannon gun tanks. There was a tank crew height restriction of 5ft 4in (1.62m) or below and a weight limit of 125lb (57kg). If a tanker was taller or larger than this, then he could not fit inside the M1917 tank comfortably and would have had more problems getting out in a hurry.

The M1917, like the French Renault, had a problem with barbed wire wrapping itself around the tracks and drive mechanism, causing the tank to stop. This left the tank crew vulnerable to concentrated artillery fire. Unlike the British heavy tanks, which would lead the infantry in an attack, the M1917 was used to support the infantry from behind.

It needed a barbed-wire-free lane to be cleared during the night or early in the morning of the attack. The infantry would call upon the tanks to suppress machine-gun nests and strongpoints they could not deal with.

Tanks were used to encourage the American people to buy Liberty Bonds to help with the war effort. M1917 tanks in brightly painted green, yellow and tan livery would put on power demonstrations. Some would demolish a house while others would drive through city streets with Victory 'V invest' posters pasted on the sides. Special trains were hired to transport the tanks and other pieces of military equipment across the country as part of the money-raising project.

For financial reasons, the US Tank Corps was demobilised in June 1920 and the tanks were issued to different infantry regiments. The number of working tanks available started to diminish due to accidents, fires and mechanical failures. Some were cannibalised to provide spare parts for others, a few were scrapped, while others were mothballed.

In 1922, the 38th Tank Company, Kentucky National Guard, used some of its Model 1917 tanks to destroy illegal alcohol producing stills during prohibition. These were used in the propaganda war to show the tough stance the US government was taking against bootleggers. The press were invited to take photos of tanks driving over the seized equipment that had been used for making gin and whiskey.

In April 1927, US Marine Corps M1917 tanks were sent to Shanghai, China, under Gen. Smedley D. Butler, to protect the International Settlement and consulates from the Soviet-backed Kuomintang Chinese Nationalist Army and local sympathetic Chinese mobs, which had strong feelings against foreigners. The 3rd Brigade of Marines had a total of 238 officers, 18 warrant officers and

4,170 enlisted men. They worked with the British Army Expeditionary force to protect the settlement.

Nationalist forces continued to extend their control northward, and American property and people were attacked. Gen. Butler with his entire brigade (less the Fourth Regiment), moved up to Tientsin early in June. The American legation guard at Peking (Beijing) then had a total of 17 officers and 499 Marines. Major conflict was avoided, the situation stabilised and the threat from anti-foreigner demonstrations subsided. All units of the 3rd Brigade of Marines in Tientsin including the M1917s were withdrawn in January 1929. There are no reports of the cannon or machine guns of the M1917s being used in anger in China.

In July 1932, six M1917s were deployed in Washington DC during the dispersal of the Bonus Army. George S. Patton Jr states in his diaries that these vehicles were carried in trucks as a deterrent. Photographs of the event show he did not tell the complete story: they were deployed on the streets off the trucks. During the San Francisco general strike of 1934, the governor used M1917 tanks of the 40th Tank Company, California National Guard, on the streets of the city. Some of the tanks used during the strikes had their muffler (exhaust silencer box) removed. This would have made the tanks sound very loud. It is not known if this was done as a tactic to increase fear in the civilian demonstrators or not.

A few of the M1917 tanks were used as war memorials around the USA, although many were scrapped. In 1940, the Canadian Army was offered 250 surplus US M1917 light tanks at scrap value (about $240 each) because, as a neutral country in the early stages of the Second World War, US law stated that it was illegal to sell arms to any combatant countries. The Royal Canadian Armoured Corps gained valuable experience and training on them before embarking to Europe and using more modern equipment. The Canadian Army actually took delivery of 236 surplus M1917s. Fifteen of them apparently went to Camp Borden for training use, while others went to train individual units such as the Fort Garry Horse and possibly another three.

## SURVIVING M1917 TANKS

There are twenty surviving M1917 tanks at various Army bases and museums in America.

# THE TANKS

## Specifications

| | |
|---|---|
| Dimensions | Length Without Tail 13ft 2in (4.02m)<br>Length With Tail 16ft (4.88m)<br>Width 5ft 7in (1.71m)<br>Height 7ft (2.14m) |
| Total Weight, Battle Ready | 6.7 tons |
| Crew | 2 (commander/gunner, driver) |
| Propulsion | Buda HU modified 4-cylinder, 4-cycle, vertical L-band gasoline engine; 42hp at 1,460rpm |
| Speed | 5mph (8.85km/h) |
| Range | 30 miles (48km) |
| Fuel tank | 24 US gallons |
| Armament, Female Tank | .30 calibre M1917 Marlin machine gun or<br>.30 calibre M1919 Browning machine gun (238 rounds) |
| Armament, Male Tank | 37mm M1916 cannon |
| Armour | 6–22mm |
| Total Production | 950 |

US-built M1917 light tank armed with a .30 calibre Marlin machine gun.

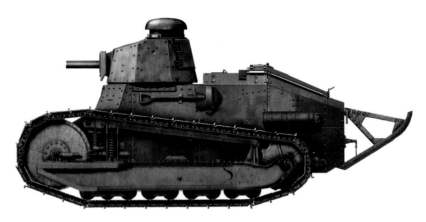

M1917 light tank armed with a .30 calibre M1919 Browning tank machine gun.

M1917 light tank armed with a 37mm M1916 cannon.

M1917 light tank used during the Liberty Bond fundraising event.

M1917 light tank of the 40th Tank Company, California National Guard.

M1917 Wireless Radio Signals Tank.

# US MODEL 1918 FORD 3-TON LIGHT TANK

## THE M1918 TWO-MAN LIGHT TANK

Henry Ford, the car manufacturer, decided to contribute towards the American war effort. His team of engineers developed the Ford 3-ton, two-man light tank M1918. It was very small compared with the French, British and German tanks built during the First World War.

The M1918 was only ever intended to be armed with a single machine gun. The tank crew could not be tall otherwise they would not fit inside. The driver sat on the right at the front and the gunner on the left. The driver had an armoured cupola above his seat so he had good vision of where he was going and possible threats.

The tank was powered by two 45hp Ford Model 'T' 4-cylinder car petrol engines positioned in the back behind the crew. Each engine powered one of the tracks. Like the Renault FT light tank, the M1918 had a pair of metal skids fitted to the rear of the vehicle. These were used to extend the length of the tank to help it negotiate shell craters, ditches and trenches.

The M1918 had a top road speed of 8mph (12.8km/h), which was fast when compared with other tanks. This little tank was very agile, could turn very quickly and had a small turning circle. The large front track wheels were proud of the tank hull and this made negotiating obstructions a lot simpler. It could manage 45-degree inclines with ease.

It had a 17-gallon fuel tank which gave it a maximum operational range of 34 miles (55km).

The original plan was to build 1,500 M1918s. However, only fifteen were built as the war came to a close. The contract was cancelled as the US Tank Corps decided the type no longer met its requirements.

## SURVIVING FORD 3-TON M1918 TANKS

Two have survived. One is part of the US Ordnance collection at Fort Lee, Virginia, and the other is kept at the National Armor and Cavalry Museum restoration workshop at Fort Benning, Georgia.

## Specifications

| | |
|---|---|
| Dimensions | Length Without Tail 10ft 9in (3.27m)<br>Length With Tail 13ft 4in (4.06m)<br>Width 5ft 4in (1.62m)<br>Height 5ft 4in (1.62m) |
| Combat Weight | 3.6 tons |
| Unloaded Weight | 3.1 tons |
| Crew | 2 (driver and gunner) |
| Propulsion | 2 × Ford Model T, 4-cylinder, water-cooled, gasoline/<br>petrol engines; 34hp at 1,700rpm |
| Road Speed | 8mph (13km/h) |
| Range | 35 miles (55km) |
| Trench-Crossing Ability | 10ft (3.04m) |
| Armament | 1 × 0.30 calibre Browning or Marlin machine guns |
| Front Upper Armour | 13mm |
| Front Lower Armour | 10mm |
| Side Front Armour | 13mm |
| Side Rear Armour | 10mm |
| Rear Upper Armour | 10mm |
| Rear Lower Armour | 6mm |
| Top Front Armour | 10mm |
| Top Lower Armour | 6mm |
| Floor Armour | 6mm |
| Total Production | 15 |

The two large tracked front wheels on the M1918 Ford 3-ton two-man tank helped the vehicle negotiate obstacles.

# US SKELETON TANK

In 1917, when the American Expeditionary Force reached the shores of France, not a single tank was available to these units. Plans were made to produce some foreign-designed vehicles, but various difficulties and the American faith in its own capabilities led to the design of several home-grown tanks.

The value of French light tanks such as the Renault FT was recognised; they were easy to produce in quantity and did not require a very powerful engine. However, it was noted that the type's trench-crossing capabilities were inadequate.

The Pioneer Tractor Company from Winona, Minnesota, proposed a rather strange-looking vehicle. Trying to mimic the trench-crossing abilities of the British rhomboid tanks while producing a lightweight vehicle led to one of the most distinctive prototypes of the war.

The tracks encircled a large metal frame, similar in shape to the hull of the British Mark I. The crew was encased in an armoured box at the centre of the vehicle, with a gun turret on top and an engine on each side of the compartment. The driver had a small horizontal vision slit at the front of the tank in the upper middle section of the armoured box. The commander/gunner had a vision slit in the turret.

The tracks were carried on rigidly mounted rollers installed on a tubular frame covered with wood. The pipe construction allowed for the tank to be dismantled and shipped relatively easily and then reassembled on arrival in theatre. Another advantage to this tubular design was that if one of the pipes was damaged it could easily be replaced. By using wood, steel pipes and standard plumbing fixtures the materials and maintenance skills needed to construct, maintain and repair the Skeleton Tank were minimal.

Unlike earlier First and later Second World War tanks, it could wade through deep water. It had more than 3ft clearance, with only its track and frame making contact with the water. The open design meant that what was behind the tank was visible through it, so it did not need a camouflage to merge in with its surroundings.

The crew of two were protected by 0.5in (12.7mm) of armour. The driver sat to the front, with the gunner behind him, manning the turret. The proposed armament was a single .30 calibre machine gun. One Beaver engine and its radiator was mounted inside each side of the armoured compartments, while the transmissions were in a separate compartment at the rear of the vehicle.

The transmission had two forward and one reverse gear, giving a grand maximum speed of 5mph (8km/h). Only one vehicle was built, sporting a dummy gun and turret. It cost $15,000 to construct the one prototype, which is just under $250,000 in today's money. The prototype was ready for trials by October 1918 but when the Armistice was signed in November 1918 most development programmes were cancelled. It was never used in active service.

The tank was driven through the streets of Winona as part of its victory parade celebrations, which were reported in the newspapers. The tank went by different names in those reports: Skeleton Tank and Spider Tank were used. The Skeleton Tank name was the most commonly used but its origins are unclear.

## THE SURVIVING SKELETON TANK

The vehicle was at the US Army Ordinance Proving Grounds in Aberdeen but kept in the open and exposed to the elements. However, it was restored in the early 2000s. All its parts are original except for the wooden frame, which had rotted and needed replacing. It has now been moved to Fort Lee.

The Skeleton is currently out of storage and on display in the Fort Lee military base First World War training gallery, being used for ordnance student training. This vehicle is currently not on public display.

## WHO FIRST CAME UP WITH THE IDEA OF A MILITARY TANK?

This is a disputed subject. The vice president and manager of the US Pioneer Tractor Company, Edwin Wheelock, was contracted to manufacture the prototype Skeleton Tank. He insisted that he completed the blueprints for the Skeleton and brought them over to England months before British Lt Col Ernest Swinton had come up with his idea that an armoured vehicle was necessary to overcome the stalemate of trench warfare by forcing its way through barbed-wire obstacles, climbing over trenches and destroying or crushing machine-gun nests.

Swinton's proposal was submitted in writing to the British War Office on 20 October 1914. He was serving with the British Expeditionary Force in France in 1914 and had seen how bad conditions were on the front line. Swinton had seen American Holt agricultural tracked tractors and recommended that they be armoured and armed with machine guns and an artillery gun.

In August 1914, Wheelock lost a contract to sell Pioneer tractors in Canada because of war being declared in Europe. He started to design a war machine based on the caterpillar tracks used on his tractors but these were lengthened to run along a rhomboid-shaped framework. He tried to sell his idea to the Canadians but again they were not interested.

Meanwhile, in England, the British government Landships Committee granted William Foster & Co. of Lincoln the contract to build the prototype British tank called the 'Number One Lincoln Machine'. This happened in February 1915.

Back in Minnesota, Wheelock hired Frances J. Lowe to try and sell Pioneer tractors and his war machine design to the British. Lowe took the blueprints and some tractors to England. In April 1915, he had a meeting with Col Sir Henry Capel-Lofft Holden, Director of Mechanical Transport at the War Office in London.

Holden dismissed the design as being unworkable because, with the initially proposed weight of 25 tons, the vehicle would be too heavy to cross bridges then found in Belgium and France. Lowe, in a later interview for an American newspaper, said he was then introduced to a Lt Walter Wilson, a Royal Navy officer who was also an engineer. Wilson took the blueprints to study them further and told Lowe that he would contact him if the War Office wanted to place an order. Lowe was never contacted.

Wilson went on to develop the first British tanks with William Tritton of William Foster & Co. The 'Number One Lincoln Machine' prototype was completed on 9 September 1915. It did not look like Wheelock's design and the improved version with longer tracks, nicknamed 'Little Willie', did not resemble Wheelock's design either. Wilson's third prototype, called 'Mother', completed in December 1915, used a lengthened track to run along a rhomboid-shaped framework, which would give the tank better cross-country performance.

It was not until newspaper reports and photographs reached Minnesota showing tanks being used for the first time in battle that Wheelock got a glimpse of what the British Mark I tank looked like. He was shocked at the similarity to his war machine design. He read that a £10,000 financial reward had been offered to the person who came up with the idea of using a tank in battle. He sent Lowe back to England to claim that reward and find out why his company had not been given the construction contract.

Lowe was not given any information. He could not even find out what had happened to the company's blueprints that he had submitted because, owing to the war, nearly all information was classified as secret. Wheelock made a formal claim for the £10,000 prize money but after two different hearings a British Prize Court awarded the money to Lt Col Ernest Swinton.

Wheelock's claim was not backed up by validated documentation. He never filed a patent or kept a copy of his blueprints. Lowe said he handed the only copy to Wilson and was never given it back.

Realistically the British government, when at war, would not have entered negotiations with a private company of a neutral state to develop and build a new weapon. That company would not legally be able to sell that weapon without breaching its country's neutrality. There was also a risk, in 1914, of the USA entering an alliance with the German Empire and therefore any new weapon could be used by the enemy. Communications and logistics problems also made the idea of a contract being awarded to an American company impractical in 1914.

## Specifications

| Dimensions | Length 25ft 0in (7.62m)<br>Width 8ft 5in (2.56m)<br>Height 9ft 6in (2.89m) |
| --- | --- |
| Total Weight | 8 tons |
| Crew | 2 |
| Max Speed | 5mph (8km/h) |
| Armour | 59in (1.50m) Frontal |
| Powerplant | Two Beaver 4-cylinder, water-cooled gas engines; 50hp |
| Armament | One Browning .30 calibre Model 1917 A1 water-cooled machine gun |
| Production | 1 prototype |

The crew of the US Pioneer Tractor Skeleton Tank was encased in an armoured box at the centre of the vehicle, with a gun turret on top and an engine on each side of the compartment. The driver had a small horizontal vision slit at the front of the tank in the upper middle section of the armoured box. The commander/gunner had a vision slit in the turret.

# KILLEN-STRAIT ARMOURED TRACTOR

One of the first contenders to be a battlefield barbed-wire-cutting tank was the Killen-Strait Armoured Tractor. The Killen-Walsh Manufacturing Company made farm tractors. It changed its name to Killen-Strait in 1914, to build the agricultural tricycle Strait's Tractor, designed by William Strait. The company's factory was in Appleton, Wisconsin, in the USA.

The tricycle configuration had one caterpillar track at the front and two at the back. The front track was used to steer the vehicle; the two at the rear provided the propulsion. A small directional metal vane was fitted above the front caterpillar track to show the driver which way the front track was pointing as visibility from the driver's seat was poor. The tracks were held together with chains and made of hardwood, and the working surfaces were faced in steel sheets. The links were joined together with case-hardened steel pins 1in (2.54cm) in diameter and 13in (33.02cm) long. These pins had a weight-bearing surface over their entire length.

The wheels served to keep the track in line, but were not used to transmit any power. The power was positively applied to the track by driving sprockets with detachable case-hardened rims. Three links of the chain engaged the sprocket at one time, thus minimising the wear. The chain could be tightened when necessary by moving the front set of idler wheels forward. The links had depressions in them to engage with the drive sprocket teeth.

The steep angle of the tracks at the rear allowed it to reverse over difficult obstacles that were impassable for other tracked tractors. It has been argued that these upward-tilting tracks on the Killen-Strait Tractor inspired the rhomboid-shape tracks on the front of the future British Mark I, but others disagree.

The company's catalogue promoted the following selling point: 'One great objection advanced against traction engines has been the way in which they packed the soil. The weight of the Strait Tractor is distributed over 3,000 square inches of bearing surface making the machine exert less pressure per square inch on the ground than a man would … The strait will run easily and lightly over freshly ploughed ground without packing at all.'

The first version was powered by a 4-cylinder, 6 × 7in bore and stroke Doman engine that produced 40hp. It was known as the 30-50 model. The later version was called the Model 3 15-30 Tractor but had a less powerful engine. It was powered by a 4-cylinder 4½in × 5¾in bore and stroke Waukesha engine that produced 30hp. It was advertised as being able to pull two or three 14in ploughs.

The Killen-Strait Tractor used a 1914 car-type transmission gearbox with cut steel, case-hardened gears running in a bath of oil. The connection to the engine was via a sliding cone clutch faced with Raybestos. The spur gears had 4in faces and a heavy pitch; they had ample strength to take the strain put on them. There were two speeds forward and one reverse gear.

On 30 June 1915, Killen-Strait shipped one of its tractors over to London so it could demonstrate its cross-country qualities to members of the British government and Army High Command. Winston Churchill, the 1st Lord of the Admiralty, and the Minister of Munitions, the future First World War Prime Minister David Lloyd George, were in attendance. Other observers were the Duke of Westminster, Sir Frederick Black (Director of Munitions Supply), Maj. Gen. Sir Ivor Philipps, Maj. Gen. Scott-Moncrieff, Col Holden, Brig. Gen. Louis Jackson (Head of Trench Warfare at the Ministry of Munitions). Jackson later went on to support Swinton and Tulloch demonstrate the American Holt tractor that was used on the 'Little Willie' tank prototype. The demonstration took place at the Talbot Recreation Ground adjoining the Royal Naval Air Service (RNAS) Armoured Car Division HQ at the Clement Talbot Works, in Wormwood Scrubbs, London.

Churchill was on the lookout for a caterpillar track-fitted vehicle that could cross enemy trenches and destroy all wire entanglements. The Ministry of Munitions was looking for a vehicle that could cut the no-man's-land battlefield barbed wire.

On the same day, the British War Office issued its specification for a 'machine-gun destroyer' to the Admiralty's Landships Committee, based at 83 Pall Mall and chaired by Churchill. The phrase 'machine-gun destroyer' can be interpreted in two ways: one is that it is a vehicle that kills machine-gun nests and the other is it is a vehicle like a fast agile Navy destroyer-class ship armed with machine guns. Early tanks, following the adopted Navy terminology, were known as Landships.

Lt Oliver Thorneycroft fitted two scissor-like Royal Navy torpedo net cutters at the end of two protruding metal poles to the front of the Killen-Strait tractor. The machine was driven into a cat's cradle of tensioned barbed wire that for demonstration purposes had been prudently strung up at precisely the cutter's height. It did not work so well on randomly spaced barbed wire at different heights.

The trials were not successful for the Killen-Strait Manufacturing Company. Although its tractor had good mobility and could negotiate many obstacles put in its way, it was not powerful enough to rip through barbed wire and drag it out of the way to create a path for infantry. When the wire cutter was fitted to the front of the vehicle it took too long to cut the wire and sometimes it failed to do so.

Lt Symes fitted a turretless Delano-Belleville armoured car hull on to the tractor chassis, and a standard armoured car turret could have been fitted at a later date. It was envisioned that this new vehicle would join the ranks of the RNAS Armoured Car Section but the turret made the vehicle very top-heavy and gave it a very high profile. This would have made it an easy target for German gunners. However, the main reason the Tractor did not enter production as a Landship tank was that it could not cross wide trenches.

The RNAS Armoured Car Section was formed for fleet reconnaissance, patrolling coasts for enemy ships and submarines, and attacking enemy coastal territory. To cover the great distances along the coast it used armoured cars but it found the poor conditions of French and Belgian roads limited its activities. The unit saw in the Killen-Straits armoured tracked tractor a vehicle it could use to get to locations where there were no roads, or where they were in very bad conditions. As the unit grew it was renamed the Royal Naval Air Service Armoured Car Division (RNACD) and spilled into twenty squadrons. In the summer of 1915, the RNACD was disbanded as trench warfare developed.

The Killen-Strait Tractor during the experiments at Wormwood Scrubbs in June 1915. (Imperial War Museum Q14618)

# THE FATE OF THE KILLEN-STRAIT TRACTOR

The armoured Killen–Strait Tractor ended its days as a tow tractor at the RNAS Barrow Airship Station. It arrived there in September 1915. Its exact final fate is not known but it has not survived.

The armoured Killen-Strait Tractor was not used in combat because it had problems crossing trenches. It was used as a tow tractor at the RNAS Barrow Airship Station.

# RUSSIAN TSAR TANK

Russia never managed to develop its own tank during the First World War. The Imperial Russian Army was presented with a number of plans and suggestions but the Central Technical Committee of the Army's Military Technical Administration only helped finance two projects.

One of these was the Nepotir tank (Bat tank). The reason for this strange name is that when the working model was picked up by its rear wheels it resembled a sleeping bat. It was later called the Lebedenko tank after the designer and given the nickname of the Tsar Tank (Czar Tank). It was a unique design with huge proportions. The Russian Army needed a vehicle that could cross rough ground, shattered woodland, lines of barbed wire, shell craters and trenches to silence enemy machine guns.

Only one prototype was built. Two giant spoked wheels more than 29ft 6in (9m) tall were attached to the front of a central armoured compartment. At the rear was a metal tail that transferred some of the weight down to the ground via three smaller roller wheels. It was a tricycle configuration (although technically it had five wheels) that was steered via the three rear wheels.

In 1915 the designer gave a presentation in front of a high-ranking audience that included the Russian Empire Tsar Nicholas II, using a working model that was powered by a clockwork spring motor taken from a gramophone. Thick books were laid in front of the model and it managed to successfully negotiate all obstacles put in its path.

The crowd were impressed and funding was promised. The Tsar invested 250,000 rubles into the tank's development: this sum was the equivalent to around $3 million in 2017. Owing to this commitment it became known as the Tsar (or Tsar's) Tank.

The engineer Nikolai Lebedenko worked with his nephews, Boris Stechin and Alexander Mikulin, and a fellow engineer, Nikolai Zhukovskiy, to finalise the plans and build the mechanical demonstration model. Lebedenko normally helped design artillery weapons and the plans of the Nepotir battle machine looked very similar to the layout of some artillery gun carriages.

Most sources state that each giant wheel was powered by a captured 250hp German Maybach Sunbeam Zeppelin airship engine, but this has not been confirmed and a different engine may have been used. On a flat surface it is believed that the tank had a top speed of 10.56mph (17km/h). This was a lot faster than the slow British Mark I tank, which had a maximum speed of 3.7mph (5.95km/h). However, the cross-country speed was a lot slower.

It is not known what weapons were to be fitted to the Tsar Tank but belt-fed Maxim 7.62mm machine guns were in use with the Russian Army at this time. The tank may have been planned to be armed only with machine guns.

Some historians have argued guns such as a 6-pounder cannon capable of firing high-explosive shells, solid rounds and grapeshot would have been fitted in some of the sponsons. However, this information is not documented.

Above the central crew compartment there was a turret with space for one or more weapon mountings. Some historians have argued that this was a non-rotating superstructure, not a turret, with mountings for forward- and rear-facing machine guns.

The 'turret' gave the tank a maximum height of 39ft 4in (12m), which is taller than the roof of most two-storey houses. The two side sponsons could have been fitted with a cannon or a machine gun. The bottom 'turret' had room for mounting one or more machine guns. The large front wheels meant that there were blind spots; the wheels limited the forward arc of fire from the top and bottom turrets.

By the end of July 1915 the prototype was ready for its first test. It was transported in separate components to the proving grounds near Moscow and then assembled. In August, during a presentation before high-ranking officials, it initially performed well. However, near the end of the demonstration the rear wheels became stuck. The engines were not powerful enough to drive the two big main wheels to extract the rear roller wheels from a ditch.

There were plans to fit more powerful engines but at a meeting a decision was made that there was no future for the Tsar Tank. The main concern was not its ability to cross rough terrain but its vulnerability to artillery bombardment. The tall tank was an easy target to spot, even from great distances. As soon as it appeared on the battlefield every enemy gun would open fire and it could not be concealed by a smokescreen. The construction of the wheel made it susceptible to high-explosive and solid armour-piercing shells.

# THE FATE OF THE TSAR TANK

The Tsar Tank was never recovered from the ditch. It remained there, overgrown, until it was cut up for scrap in 1923.

The second tank project that received finance was totally different from the Tsar Tank. It was small and had an armoured shell over a wide single track. It was called the Vezdekhod ('Go Anywhere') tank. In March 1915 the test chassis was completed but it was not fitted with its armoured shell. The vehicle was steered by two wheels at the front each side of the track, on the exterior of the single central track. They offered resistance to the soft ground and acted like rudders. The senior officers of the Imperial Russian Army were not impressed with its abilities and declined to fund further development or authorise its production. It was never tested with the outer armour body fitted.

## Specifications

| Dimensions | Length 58ft (17.8m)<br>Width 30ft (9m)<br>Height 39ft (12m) |
|---|---|
| Total Weight | 60 tons |
| Crew | 10 |
| Propulsion | 2 × 240hp Maybach |
| Speed (road) | 11mph (17km/h) |
| Armament | Not known |
| Production | 1 prototype |

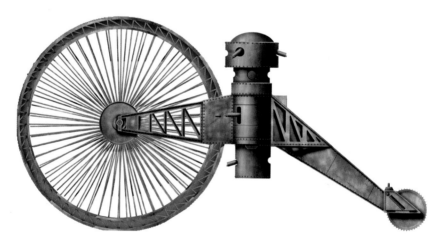

The Russian Army needed a vehicle that could cross rough ground, shattered woodland, lines of barbed wire, shell craters and trenches to silence enemy machine guns. Only one Nepotir prototype Tsar Tank was built.

# THE BATTLES

# THE FIRST TANK BATTLE

On Friday, 15 September 1916, for the first time in history, tanks were used on a battlefield. The British faced 100,000 German soldiers over a 7-mile defensive trench system that was protected by layer upon layer of barbed-wire fences and machine-gun posts.

They would go into battle just north of the river Somme along a fighting front between the villages of Flers and Courcelette, 99 miles (160km) north of Paris.

This new attack was part of the four-month Battle of the Somme that started on 1 July 1916. Not very much ground had been captured but the fighting had caused 300,000 Allied casualties. The senior British commander, Sir Douglas Haig, was desperate to stop the losses. He was under a lot of political pressure to reduce the casualties and make a breakthrough.

Many history books have portrayed Haig as an over-confident traditionalist stuck in the past, who was not willing to try new tactics and had a disregard for the suffering of the fighting men under his command. Haig and members of his staff had witnessed demonstrations of the tank's abilities: how it could cross trenches, clear paths through layers of barbed-wire defences and lay down machine-gun fire and high-explosive shells on enemy positions while keeping the tank crew protected behind an armoured shell. He was confident in the potential of this new weapon and was eager to let it loose on the battlefield.

Rather than waiting for the numbers of British Mark I tanks available in France to be of a sufficient number to overwhelm German forces, he demanded the few that had arrived be deployed immediately in the next major attack.

The British Empire forces had 200,000 infantry, more than 700 artillery pieces and 49 of the brand new Mark I tanks available for this new offensive, scheduled for 15 September 1916. Twenty-five tanks were issued to 'C' and 'D' Company of the Heavy Section, Machine Gun Corps. A few had broken down in training and needed repairing. 'A' and 'B' Company had not yet arrived in France.

The tanks were not sent into battle in one large group. They were instructed to drive in front of the infantry in small groups of two or three tanks and breach the German defences to allow the following troops to assault the enemy trench network. They were tasked with attacking and destroying machine gun posts.

# DEVILS WOOD

Before the main attack could be launched, the Germans in Delville Wood to the east of the attack route, known to the British as Devils Wood, had to be dealt with first to prevent a flanking attack.

Four 'D' Company Tanks were assigned Delville Wood as their objective. On 15 September 1916 at 5.15 a.m., under the cover of darkness, they advanced. One of the tanks, D4 No. 516 commanded by 2Lt C.E. Storey, entered the wood but became badly ditched and could not move.

The terrain had been shelled and was full of muddy craters and fractured tree stumps among the lines of barbed wire. There was no green woodland left because of the constant shelling. The second Female tank, D5 No. 540, called 'Dolphin' (some sources say it was 'Delphine') commanded by 2Lt A.H. Blowers, became stuck on the rough, slippery ground but was pulled out of trouble by the third Male tank, D3 No. 728, commanded by 2Lt H.G. Head.

They headed north, in the direction of Flers village from the northern edge of Delville Wood. They were now behind the advancing infantry because of the unditching problem. As they reached the first objective, Switch Line trench, they found that the infantry had already captured it without the tanks' help, after it had been pounded by an artillery barrage.

The two tanks moved on to the second objective, called Gap trench, near the southern edge of Flers village. The tanks suddenly spotted two German 77mm field guns that were very capable of knocking them out of action. They fired at them not knowing they had already been captured by British soldiers.

The tanks were now crossing the flat open land to the east of Flers. They reached the Rue de Gueudecourt (known as Bulls Road). They had leapt ahead of the infantry so they turned back as they were coming under heavy enemy fire.

2Lt Blowers' tank, 'Dolphin', was asked to help deal with a German strongpoint at the edge of Flers village. As it got close the vehicle was hit by an artillery shell. Two of the tank crew were killed and three others injured, including 2Lt Blowers. The tank was knocked out and caught fire.

2Lt Head's tank nearly made it back to the start line on the northern edge of Delville wood but was abandoned. It is not known if it suffered a mechanical breakdown, ditched or simply ran out of fuel.

The last of the four tanks, Male tank D1 No. 765 called 'Daredevil', was commanded by Capt. Howard W. Mortimore. He recorded seeing lots of flashes coming from the remains of the wood. These were the muzzle flashes of German machine guns and rifles and their bullets bounced off the tank's armour. His tank crew fired back with their machine guns and the 6-pounder guns.

'Daredevil' managed to reach the enemy Hop trench and Ale Alley trench on the east side of Delville Wood and cleared them of defending German troops. He told his family after the war that he remembered peering through his viewfinder as he approached the enemy trenches and saw the German troops take one look at the tank and run.

He then moved off along Beer trench but his tank was hit by a high-explosive shell that broke the track. The crew managed to get out but some were injured, although not seriously. Capt. Mortimore was gassed twice and eventually sent home. He survived the war and served as an officer in the Home Guard in the Second World War.

## THE MAIN ATTACK

Out of the forty-nine Mark I tanks that were assigned to the battle only thirty-two were ready to advance into no-man's-land that morning. Nine broke down shortly after they moved off, while a further nine had difficulties keeping up with the advancing troops due to mechanical problems. Five were abandoned after getting stuck in shell craters or trenches.

The final nine managed to reach the enemy lines. The going was slow even though it was dry, and artillery shell craters made progress difficult. The tanks intimidated the German troops who had never seen such a mechanical monster before. They appeared to be invulnerable to machine gun and rifle fire and the German infantry soldier had no means of stopping them.

At the end of the day the villages of Courcelette and Flers had been captured. Some tanks had reached and passed the third and final objective of the day. The infantry, with the help of the tanks, had managed to advance 2,500yd (2km) over a 3-mile front.

The tank attacks, even though they occurred on the same day, are best looked at as a series of individual advances, each with their own narrative, rather than one concerted co-ordinated event.

Many of the abandoned tanks and those that had suffered mechanical problems were recovered and repaired.

The first battle where tanks were used can be best described as a limited success. Those nine tanks that engaged the enemy in their own trenches had shown what they could do: cross a hostile battlefield covered in barbed-wire fences and other obstacles while under fire, breach defensive lines of trenches, destroy machine-gun posts and create a path for supporting infantry to follow.

Deficiencies in the tank's design and abilities also became apparent. When machine gun bullets hit the armour plating, the metal on the inside splintered and sent sharp fragments flying around the inside of the tank that injured the crew.

There were weak spots in the armour that machine gun bullets could exploit and force their way through, killing the men inside. When glass prisms used in vision slits were hit by a bullet they could shatter and blind the user.

Although in training it looked like the Mark I tank could drive over most obstacles, on the battlefield it had problems dealing with deep shell holes and shattered tree stumps.

When a tank was hit by high-explosive artillery shells it would be knocked out of action. Sharp shrapnel would penetrate the armour and kill or maim crew members. If the fuel tanks leaked or were hit, some tanks just exploded or caught fire, killing everyone inside. This happened to the crew of tank D14, commanded by 2Lt G. F. Court, on 16 September as they tried to stop a German counter-attack near the village of Flers with two other tanks.

Sir Douglas Haig was impressed that the tanks had managed to breach the German front line. Four days later he ordered an additional 1,000 tanks. His comment was: 'Wherever the tanks advanced, we took our objectives and where they did not advance, we failed to take our objectives. Go back (to Britain) and make as many more tanks as you can.'

# BOULEAUX WOOD

Six tanks from the 3 and 4 Section of 'C' Company, Heavy Section Machine Gun Corps, were given orders to move with the infantry from a start line that ran between the villages of Ginchy and Combles towards the villages of Lesbœufs and Morval.

Mark I Female Tank C16 No. 510, commanded by 2Lt E.L. Purdy, was given orders to attack and subdue the German trenches that ran between Leuze Wood and the village of Combles, then move up the south-east side of Bouleaux Wood towards Morval. It was fitted with the anti-grenade wooden mesh roof for added protection.

2Lt Purdy's tank reached the trenches and drove up and down them firing its weapons. Suddenly the tank was hit on the right track by a high-explosive shell, which immobilised it. The German troops tried to throw grenades on to the tank but the crew used their 0.303in calibre Vickers water-cooled machine guns to drive them off. The infantry eventually captured enough of the German Loop trench system to enable the tank's crew to escape. They set fire to their tank before abandoning it.

Two tanks were assigned to advance on the north-western side of Leuze and Bouleaux Wood: Male Tank C13 No. 716 commanded by Lt Sir J. Dashwood and Mark I Female tank C14 No. 509 commanded by 2Lt F.J. Arnold. Lt Sir Dashwood's tank track came off as he advanced so 2Lt Arnold's tank moved on alone. The tank crossed the front-line trenches and moved along behind them firing its machine guns, waiting for the infantry to catch up and secure the trench.

It reached Middle Copse and nearly to the end of Bouleaux Wood but turned back to deal with the German machine guns and rifles that had started to fire upon the flank of the advancing British infantry. The Germans were using the concealment advantage and relative safety of the woods. 2Lt Arnold's tank C14 opened fire. Disaster struck as near the German 'Beef Trench', the tank fell into a shell crater from which it could not get out.

# THE QUADRILATERAL

Lt Basil Henriques was the commander of the British Mark I Female tank C22, No. 533, 4 Section, 'C' Company, Heavy Section Machine Gun Corps, on 15 September 1916. His tank with two others had orders to advance towards a

German defensive trench system called the Quadrilateral with infantry following behind. It was halfway between the villages of Guillemont and Morval.

An artillery barrage would be raining fire down on enemy troops to the left and right of the advance. A gap was made so that the British troops and tanks could attack through it.

The other two tanks suffered mechanical breakdowns so Lt Hendriques' tank was on its own. By mistake one of the tank crew fired on some of his own troops. Their commanding officer had some strong words with the crew and pointed them in the correct direction of attack.

The tank reached its objective, the Quadrilateral, and opened fire at the German troops. German artillery fired at the tank and the advancing British infantry. One high-explosive blast smashed the tank commander's thick glass vision prism. Lt Hendriques suffered multiple cuts to his face because he was looking through it at the time of the explosion. He recovered in hospital but he used one of the pieces of glass pulled from his face as a 'stone' that he commissioned to be mounted in a gold ring and then gave it to his wife. That ring is on display at The Tank Museum, Bovington.

At 1 p.m. two tanks renewed the attack on the Quadrilateral trench system. One of these was one of the two that had broken down, Mark I Female tank C20 No. 523 commanded by 2Lt G. MacPherson. They came under fire from guns firing armour-piercing bullets. 2Lt MacPherson was killed and the attack was cancelled.

# GINCHY

Ten tanks in three groups from 'C' Company, Heavy Section Machine Gun Corps, started their attack from the village of Ginchy with orders to head towards the villages of Lesbœufs and Morval. They were to attack along three prearranged gaps in the artillery barrage that would bombard the enemy trenches.

Three tanks moved off at 5.40 a.m. towards the German front line called Straight trench. One of the Mark I Male tanks, No. 714, broke its rear steering tail as it moved over the rough ground and turned back to get it fixed. The other two tanks continued on. The German machine-gunners opened fire from directly ahead in Straight trench and then machine-gun fire came in from the right flank from German infantry in the Quadrilateral trench, causing casualties among the British infantry.

One of the tanks, a Mark I Male, No. 746 commanded by 2Lt J.P. Clark, managed to breach the German rows of barbed wire and cross the front-line trench. He turned left, heading northwards, firing from behind the enemy Straight trench with his two 6-pounder guns and 0.303in (7.62mm) Hotchkiss air-cooled machine guns. He managed to put six enemy machine guns out of action, which enabled the British troops to capture that section of the trench. As it moved into the back of the next trench system known as 'The Triangle' the commander had to make the decision to turn back. They were low on fuel.

Mark I Female tank No. 508 called 'Casa', commanded by 2Lt L.V. Smith, followed 2Lt Clark's tank over Straight trench, providing additional firepower. Smith followed Clarke north up the rear of Straight trench, then veered off to the right heading towards Lesbœufs over the flat open countryside, firing at any enemy troops they encountered. After about half a mile the tank developed engine problems so it had to turn around and hobble back to the start line in Ginchy.

The next group of three tanks were to have followed the left side of the Givenchy to Lesbœufs road called Sentier de Lesbœufs. The infantry had to fight their way towards the trenches known as the High Road and Switch Line without tank support. Two of the tanks suffered mechanical breakdowns at the start line just outside Ginchy. The third tank ditched as it moved off and was stuck. Although the trenches were bombarded by British artillery, the attacking infantry suffered high casualty rates from enemy machine-gun fire.

The third group of tanks started from the west side of Ginchy but one broke down and did not cross the start line. The other tanks moved off at 5.30 a.m., heading north of the town to punch a hole in the German trench system known as Pint trench that ran along the Ginchy to Flers road called Grande Rue.

Some German machine gun crews managed to hide as the tanks went past their position. When the following troops reached the trench they were cut down by machine-gun fire. Mark I Male No. 714, commanded by Lt L.J. Bates, then managed to silence many of the machine guns. The other Mark I Male, No. 760 commanded by Lt H.B. Elliot, also attacked the machine gun positions before moving off in a northwards direction with Lt Bates' tank, heading towards the their first objective, the Switch Line trench.

Both tanks breached that trench, firing at the defenders and helped secure prisoners with the help of the British infantry. They then moved off towards the second objective called Gap trench, south-east of Flers village. Lt Bates' tank ditched in a crater near the trench and could not get out. Lt Elliot's tank also reached the Gap trench but was very short of fuel and had to turn back. His tank had to be abandoned near the north end of Pint trench when the fuel ran out.

The tenth tank of this group was No. 505 commanded by 2Lt H.R.C. Cole. He was instructed to head towards a German trench called New trench on the south-east corner of Delville Woods (Devil Woods). He found that the enemy had withdrawn from the woods after the earlier assault. The tank's track was damaged and it had to turn back.

# LONGUEVAL

The next group of ten tanks from 'D' Company, Heavy Section Machine Gun Corps, moved off from a start line north of the village of Longueval on the north-west side of Delville Wood. They were tasked with helping the British and New Zealand infantry capture the village of Flers and then move on to the village of Gueudecourt.

Mark I Male tank D6 No. 747 was commanded by 2Lt R.C. Legge. It moved off a little bit late so instead of being in front of the infantry attacking Switch trench after the artillery barrage lifted, it was coming up from the rear. By the time the tank reached this first objective it found that the trench had been captured by the foot sloggers.

2Lt Legge moved off towards the eastern edge of the village of Flers to give much-needed support to the attacking troops. They managed to silence some machine-gun nests that were firing at the advancing infantry. At 10.15 a.m. the tank continued heading northwards along the east side of the village until it reached Rue de Gueudecourt (known as Bulls Road). 2Lt Legge spotted some German field guns and instructed his gunners to open fire on them.

He then continued on towards the village of Gueudecourt, the final objective of the day. Two trenches protected the village: Grid trench and Grid Support trench. In between the two was a gun battery near the road called Pilgrims Way, which opened fire on the slow-moving tank. Three crew and 2Lt R.C. Legge were killed. One member of the crew was captured but three made it back to British lines.

'Dracula' was the macabre name given to Mark I Female tank D16 No. 538 commanded by Lt A.E. Arnold. Mark I Female tank D15 No. 537 was commanded by 2Lt J.L. Bagshaw and Mark I Male tank D18 No. 743 was commanded by 2Lt L.C. Bond. These three moved off northwards along the Tea Lane trench chasing the artillery barrage with the infantry following behind. 2Lt Bagshaw's tank was hit by a German shell. Two members of the crew were killed and the others were wounded by rifle and machine-gun fire as they abandoned it.

'Dracula' breached the barbed-wire fences and trench of the first objective, Switch trench. It drove along the length of the trench firing at the enemy soldiers trying to shelter inside and destroyed any machine-gun nest it found. The following infantry were then able to capture the trench.

Both tanks then moved on to the next job: assaulting the Flers trench that was just south of Flers village. This was the second objective. They were joined by Mark I Male tank D17 No. 759, called 'Dinnaken', commanded by Lt S.H. Hastie. The three tanks attacked together ripping up, cutting and crushing the defensive lines of barbed wire and leaving a big enough gap for the following infantry to get through unhindered. As the tanks crossed Flers trench they stopped to enable their machine guns to fire down into the trenches, killing anyone inside. The infantry were then free to capture and hold the rest of the trench.

Lt Arnold's 'Dracula' and 2Lt Bond's tank drove north along the west side of Flers village while Lt Hastie's tank 'Dinnaken' went straight up the main road into the centre of the village. They fired on any German troops they came across and put out of action a number of machine guns. This enabled the village to be captured. By noon Flers was under the control of New Zealand soldiers. Lt Hastie's tank 'Dinnaken' returned towards the start line but his tank broke down north of Delville Woods.

The Germans counter-attacked at 2.30 p.m. to try and regain control of the village but the two remaining tanks helped the infantry stop the assault. They moved out north of the village towards three small trench systems called Grove Alley, Box and Cox, firing their weapons at the enemy troops before returning to the village and later to the start line.

Two of the ten tanks ditched before they reached the start line and could not get out. Two other tanks ditched after crossing the start line and a fifth got stuck after trying to get help one of the others. None of these five tanks made contact with the enemy.

# FAT TRENCH AND GROVE ALLEY

Four tanks of 2 Section, 'D' Company, Heavy Section Machine Gun Corps, were to support the New Zealand infantry as they moved either side of the Rue du Calvaire road north of Longueval village and capture a stretch of the Switch Line trench (the location of which is now marked by the New Zealand Army war memorial). The tanks arrived late and followed the infantry attack as the artillery barrage lifted, rather than leading the attack.

The infantry captured and occupied Switch Line trench and then the tanks moved northwards along Fish Alley trench to the second objective Fat trench with the New Zealanders following. The tanks used their weapons to shoot at any German soldiers they spotted. These two trenches were soon captured as well, but tank D10 No. 535 commanded by 2Lt H. Darby was knocked out as it moved along the northern spur of Fat trench.

To the right was the northern end of the Flers trench. It was heavily protected by rows of barbed wire. At 10.30 a.m. Mark I Female tank D11 No. 547 commanded by 2Lt H.G. Pearsall attacked the centre of the trench and his crew machine-gunned both sides as they crossed it. The New Zealand troops were able to walk over the crushed barbed wire to attack and occupy the enemy trench.

2Lt Pearsall continued north-west and then headed north-east along Grove Alley trench, firing at the German defenders with the assistance of two other tanks from a different section (No. 743 and No. 538). He spotted two field guns and attacked them. The trench could not be held so he covered the withdrawal of the troops back to the Bulls Road third objective just north of the village of Flers.

Mark I Male tank D8 No. 720 commanded by 2Lt H.G.F. Brown had followed 2Lt Pearsall's tank as he moved north-west against Grove Alley trench, but instead of turning north-east along it, 2Lt Brown continued over it, firing at Germans in the rear connecting trenches.

Mark I Male tank D12 No. 719 commanded by Capt. G. Nixon crossed the second objective trench where Fat trench met Flers trench to the west of the village. At 9.15 a.m. he moved towards a machine-gun nest that was firing from inside a farmhouse in the north part of the village. It was pinning down the attacking infantry. A high-explosive shell damaged the track and it slid into a ditch while trying to retreat for repairs. The tank was knocked out and caught fire after it was hit by more artillery rounds.

# MARTINPUICH

The eight tanks of 4 Section, 'D' Company, Heavy Section Machine Gun Corps, were tasked with capturing the village Martinpuich. Their start line ran between the south-western edge of High Wood, north-east of the village of Longueval, to a position about half a mile north-east of the village of Bazentin.

Only five tanks managed to move off past the start line. Tank D21 No. 512 got stuck when it ditched on the way to its starting position. Mark I Male tank C23, called 'Clan Ruthven', ditched in a British trench 50yd beyond the start line and could not get out. It was later hit by shell fire. Tank D23 No. 528 broke a track en route to the start line and it could not be fixed in time.

Mark I Male tank D22 No. 745, commanded by Lt F.A. Robinson, moved off from its start position at the crossroads south of High Wood into what remained of shelled woodland. The crew found the going problematic because of natural obstacles such as shattered tree stumps and the man-made ones including shell craters and enemy barricades, so they left the wood.

The D22 tank crew mistakenly identified some British soldiers of the 6th Battalion (City of London) Rifles, who were manning the Worcester trench, as enemy infantry and opened fire, killing several men before realising their horrific error. The tank then ditched and only after fourteen hours of hard work was it finally freed from the depression and returned back to British lines.

Just after 6 a.m. Mark I Female tank D13 No. 548, called 'Delilah' and commanded by 2Lt Sampson, also entered High Wood. It came under fire from rifle and machine guns. The tank was rushed by German infantry, who had been hiding in trenches and behind barricades. Some climbed up on to the tank. One of the enemy soldiers managed to force his rifle into the tank's 'pistol port' loophole and fired at the crew, injuring one. The crew fired back and drove them away.

As 'Delilah' reached a second trench within the wood it broke down. Now that it was a stationary target artillery shells started to fall around the tank. Two high-explosive rounds hit 'Delilah' so the crew were forced to abandon it and make their own way back to British lines. The British infantry found it very hard to remove the German infantry from their prepared defensive positions inside High Wood.

Without the support of the tanks they suffered many casualties. The Germans only surrendered when they realised that British troops had worked around the outside of the wood and were now firing at them from their side and rear.

At 6.03 a.m. two tanks, Mark I Female D25 No. 511, commanded by 2Lt E.C.K. Colle, and Mark I Male D24 No. 751, commanded by Lt W. Stones, moved northwards towards the western end of Hook and Switch trench, half a mile south of the village of Martinpuich. The artillery barrage had lifted. The British troops were following just behind the tanks rather than waiting 100m behind them. This limited the ability of the tanks' machine gun crews to fire at the German soldiers they were passing because of fears of hitting their own men.

The first objective was taken and both of these German trenches were now under British control. The tanks and infantry moved forward again heading for the village of Martinpuich. Lt Stones' tank was hit by two artillery shells, which damaged its track and forced the crew to abandon it about 5yd north of Switch trench.

2Lt Colle's tank had better luck. It reached the village and engaged three enemy machine gun positions, putting them out of action. This enabled the following infantry to move into the streets and clear out any remaining defenders. By the end of the day Martinpuich was in British hands. The tank had developed problems with its steering mechanism so it made its way back to British lines to be repaired.

Mark I Male tank D20 No. 744, commanded by 2Lt H.C.F. Drader, headed towards the western end of Martinpuich. It had to attack Bottom trench and Tangle trench first; both had been bombarded by artillery. By the time 2Lt Drader's tank reached each Bottom trench he found that the German troops had retreated or were waiting to surrender.

The tank advanced along a sunken road that had embankments either side. The Germans had built protective dugouts into the limestone soil. The tank crew fired into each one as they passed. When they reached Tangle trench they fired at the German defenders and those fleeing. The village was finally captured at 3 p.m.

# COURCELETTE

The six tanks of 1 Section, 'C' Company, Heavy Section Machine Gun Corps, were tasked with capturing the village of Courcelette on the far left of the attack front. They were supporting the Canadian Division.

Two of the six tanks, Mark I Female tank C2 No. 522, called 'Cognac' and commanded by Lt F.W. Bluemel, and Mark I Male tank C1 No. 709, called 'Champagne' and commanded by Lt A.G.C. Wheeler, did not have a very good day. Their start point was about half a mile north of the village of Pozières.

Both tanks moved off but ditched. The 'Cognac' tank managed to get back on the move but ditched again. This time they were stuck fast and under fire from the enemy, so the tank had to be abandoned. The 'Champagne' crew tried to get their tank moving again but failed and they were also under fire. Their driver was killed trying to unditch the tank and was also abandoned.

Mark I Female tank C6 No. 504, called 'Cordon Rouge' and commanded by 2Lt J. Allan, had moved off from the same start point but had better luck. It headed for a sugar factory, situated south of Courcelette, as ordered and engaged with the enemy troops concealed in the trenches after the artillery barrage had lifted. The tank's gunners managed to silence a number of German machine guns. This enabled the Canadian infantry to continue their attack. 'Cordon Rouge' reached the sugar factory and kept firing on the defenders.

Three tanks were ordered to move off from a start point by the Pozières windmill (now a war memorial) situated on the Route de Bapaume D929 road. Two of them failed to move past the start point: Mark I Male tank C3 No. 701 'Chartreuse' ditched and could not get out and Mark I Female tank C4 No. 503 'Chablis' damaged a track and could not move forward.

The remaining Mark I Male tank C5 No. 721 'Crème de Menthe', commanded by Capt. A.M. Inlis, joined Cordon Rouge at the sugar factory and opened fire with its 6-pounder gun and machine guns. The Germans who had been defending the factory surrendered. The Canadian Infantry went ahead in the afternoon and captured the village of Courcellette.

# CONCLUSION

Many tanks suffered from ditching and mechanical problems and the condition of the terrain the tanks had to cross limited their use. The heat and poisonous fumes given off by the engine made working conditions inside the tank horrendous. The limited fuel storage capacity meant that a few tanks had to withdraw early to refuel rather than stay with the attacking troops.

Despite these problems, where tanks did assist infantry assault trenches and silence machine gun positions in woods, farmhouses and villages, the infantry succeeded in capturing the objective with reduced casualty rates. The tank showed it could punch holes through rows of barbed wire and breach enemy trenches. Sir Douglas Haig was now convinced that the tank had proven it was an effective weapon on the battlefield. He gave instructions for hundreds more to be built immediately.

# THE NAME

The Heavy Section Machine Gun Corps (HSMGC) was redesignated as the Heavy Branch Machine Gun Corps (HBMGC) in November 1916. The Tank Corps was formed from the Heavy Branch MGC on 27 July 1917. It was given the name Royal Tank Corps (RTC) on 18 October 1923. On 4 April 1939, the Royal Tank Corps was renamed the Royal Tank Regiment.

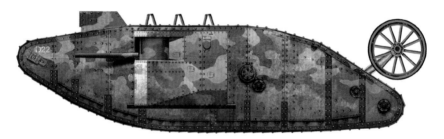

This Mark I Male tank, No. 745, saw action on 15 September 1916 as part of 'D' Company, 4 Section. Unfortunately the crew mistook some British soldiers as the enemy, firing on and killing some of them. The rear tail could be locked in the up position when necessary. The three 'A' shaped bits of metal on the roof were covers for the three engine exhaust pipes in the roof.

Mark I Female tanks took part in the Battle of Flers-Courcelette on 15 September 1916. They were armed with four 0.303in (7.62mm) Vickers water-cooled machine guns in side sponsons and a 0.303in (7.62mm) Hotchkiss air-cooled machine gun on the front cabin. A two-wheeled steering tail was attached to the rear. Tank No. 511 was commanded by 2Lt E.C.K. Cole on that day as part of 'D' Company, 4 Section, Heavy Section Machine Gun Corps (HSMGC). It was given the unit number D25. It engaged the enemy and returned to Allied lines at the end of the day.

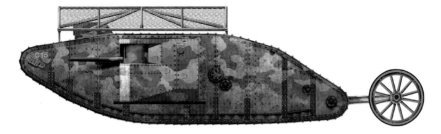

A wooden and wire mesh frame was added to the roof of the Mark I to deflect hand grenades thrown by German infantry. On 15 September 1916 2Lt J.P. Clark commanded this Mark I Male No. 746 in 'C' Company, 3 Section, HSMGC. It was later given the unit number C15. It crossed German trenches and attacked enemy positions, returning to Allied lines at the end of the day.

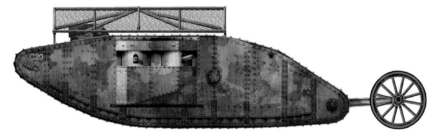

Mark I Female No. 523 C20 under the command of Lt MacPherson, 'C' Company, 4 Section, HSMGC, was due to be part of the attack on 15 September 1916. However, like many other tanks, it broke down. It was repaired by the afternoon and tried to catch up with the advancing units. However, it had to be abandoned on the battlefield on 16 November 1916 after it ditched and could not get out.

# THE BATTLE OF CAMBRAI

'The first time tanks were massed together for an attack was on 20 November 1917 during the Battle of Cambrai.' This often used statement is not quite true. It was the first successful use of massed tanks and combined arms tactics in a large-scale operation. Large numbers of tanks had been used before in 1917 but without the proper co-ordinated support of the Air Force, artillery and infantry. Prior to 1917 tanks had been sent into battle in small groups.

Although the tank action at Cambrai was successful it did not result in a complete victory and most of the successes gained during the attack were reversed after a few weeks following the battle. It could not really be called a tank battle as only one side, the British, used armour.

The French city of Cambrai is 109 miles (176km) slightly north-east of Paris near the border with Belgium. Between the city and the British front line to the south-west was the German Army's defensive Hindenburg Line (Siegfriedstellung). In November 1917 it was heavily defended with more than 250,000 troops, machine-gun posts, trenches, artillery and row upon row of barbed wire.

The object of the attack was to breach the line, break through into the open countryside behind it and occupy the Bourlon Wood Ridge.

## POLITICS

It was odd that the British started the Battle of Cambrai in the first place, having just ended a long and exhausting battle at Passchendaele that resulted in more than 250,000 casualties. The whole Army needed a rest, not another offensive. However, Douglas Haig, the British commander-in-chief, was under pressure to produce results. The Prime Minister, David Lloyd-George, had publically expressed his and the Cabinet's frustration at apparently futile attacks at the Somme and Passchendaele. Haig badly needed a victory to save his own career and the British nation also needed one after three years of stalemate and high casualty figures with little result.

THE BATTLES

# THE PLAN

British Lt Col John Frederick Charles 'Boney' Fuller, a Tank Corps staff officer, put forward a tank raid plan in the Cambrai area. He had observed how tanks had failed at Passchendaele because they had been used on unsuitable ground. The terrain around Cambrai had not yet been turned into a lunar landscape from continuous artillery bombardment. It would be ideal tank country so long as there was no pre-attack large-scale artillery bombardment. He proposed a surprise attack with initially only 200 tanks.

Artillery commander Brig. Gen. Hugh H. Tudor of 9th (Scottish) Division, IV Corps, was instrumental in changing artillery practices. Using new technology and mathematics, the artillery could deliver precise, effective and accurate bombardments without giving the enemy time to seek shelter. Tudor also submitted a proposal that these new techniques should be used as part of a surprise attack.

During the first three years of the war, prior to any attack, a week of artillery bombardment was required to try to flatten the barbed wire strung up in no-man's-land, with the element of surprise lost. Reinforcements and reserves could be rushed to the location of a suspected attack. However, the tactics used in the Battle of Cambrai changed that.

Elements of the plans were merged and submitted to Haig and he authorised its launch for November 1917.

# THE TWO ARMIES

Three German 'Second Army' Corps were posted to the Cambrai section of the front line in late 1917. Troops from XIII Corps, known as Gruppe Caudry, were occupying the trenches when the British attacked. The other two corps were being rested or held in reserve away from the front.

They consisted of four infantry divisions: in the north was the 20th Landwehr Division; in the middle was the 54th Infantry and 9th Reserve Division; in the south of the line was the 183rd Infantry Division. Each division was comprised of three regiments. They were under the command of Gen. Georg von der Marwitz, a tough and innovative commander.

In 1917 a British Army battalion was made up of four companies. Each company was divided into four platoons and each platoon was subdivided into four sections of twelve men each.

A brigade contained four battalions, a division was made up of three brigades, and a corps contained two divisions. Each corps in theory had around 20–24,000 front-line soldiers, support staff and officers, but not all units were up to full strength. The British attack at Cambrai would be launched by III and IV Corps, Third Army, with the Tank Corps and Cavalry Corps. V Corps would be in reserve.

# THE ATTACK PLAN – CODENAME OPERATION GY

The British Imperial forces fielded a total of 476 tanks for the first assault, some of them supply tanks. By the end of the first day 179 tanks were not fit for battle the following day. Some had been knocked out by enemy artillery fire; others had broken down or got stuck on unsuitable, muddy, ground covered in deep shell craters.

The Mark IVs' impressive gains in captured territory were not properly exploited by the supporting infantry and cavalry as had been planned. A tank is the correct tool for taking enemy positions, but it cannot hold them for very long.

The Tank Corps consisted of three armoured brigades. The 108 vehicles of the 1st Tank Brigade were used to support the 51st and 62nd Infantry Division of IV Corps. The 216 tanks of 2nd and 3rd Tank Brigades were given the role of providing support to the 6th, 12th and 20th Infantry Division of III Corps.

An armoured section of dedicated wire-crushing tanks was made up of three tanks, often one Male Mark IV gun tank supported by two machine gun-only Female Mark IVs. They would advance in a V shape in front of an infantry company, crushing down or ripping up the 100yd-deep belts of German barbed wire using a trailing grappling hook. Some of the wire was more than 6ft tall in places and ranged between 50 and 100yd deep.

The tanks' machine guns would put down suppressive fire on the enemy trenches and the Male tank's 6-pounder gun would try to knock out machine-gun nests with high-explosive shells. As the tanks crossed the trenches they would deliver enfilading fire along their length.

They would be followed by a second wave of eighteen fighting tanks per brigade front and the rest of the tanks and infantry would push through in a third wave.

Once the Hindenburg Line breakthrough had been achieved, III Corps, operating in the southern part of the 6-mile front between St-Quentin Canal and Bonavis, would aim to capture the canal crossings at Masnières and Marcoing. This would enable the following cavalry to ride towards the village of Walincourt-Selvigny and provide flank protection. At the same time IV Corps would be in the north and attacking the defended high ground of Bourlon Ridge after having first captured the village of Flesquières.

The capture of the town of Cambrai was never the primary objective of the British attack as they did not want to get bogged down in street fighting. If the attack had advanced as far as Cambrai the troops were instructed to encircle the town and cut off all roads into it. They never reached that far.

# PREPARATION

All tank, artillery gun and troop movements had to be undertaken at night so as to avoid detection. The tanks were transported up to the front from training grounds by train. They then made their way to their start positions under their own power. Camouflage nets were then used to hide them from enemy reconnaissance planes. The tanks were kept 1,000yd away from the front line and machine-gun fire was used to hide the noise of tank engines from the Germans.

The Royal Flying Corps (RFC) fitted some of its aircraft with 20lb bombs that could be released by pulling a cable. The crews practised bombing pinpoint targets during early November as using aircraft in a ground-attack role to support troops on the ground was still experimental in 1917. The pilots had been given a diverse list of targets ranging from supply routes and enemy airfields to front-line trenches.

On the morning of 20 November 1917, battalion officers and some of their men marked the route the tanks were to follow with white tape. The tanks would be moving to the start line, a few hundred yards from the British front-line trenches, in the dark. They would need the white tape to prevent them getting lost.

# FASCINES

An RFC reconnaissance aircraft spotted new German anti-tank obstacles; some trenches had been widened to around 16ft to make them difficult to cross. The British found the solution to this new problem by looking back in history. In Medieval times, knights in armour had solved the problem of how to cross moats and other large ditches by tying bundles of long, thin branches together and rolling them into the ditch. When the ditch was full of these bundles they could walk over them.

These 15ft-diameter bundles of wood were called a 'fascine'. The British Army adapted the Mark IV to carry larger versions of these fascines on top. Long roof rails were fitted along the vehicle's length and the wood was cut to the same size and bound with chains. The bundles measured about 10ft (3m) long and 4ft 6in (1.4m) wide.

The fascines were secured to the tank's roof with straps that could be released from the relative safety of its interior. As the lead tank reached the edge of the German trench the straps would be released and the bundle of wood would roll forward into the ditch. That tank would then move right and machine gun the enemy troops in the trench on its left, to make way for the next tank to deliver its load. The next tank would move forward and drop its fascine in the same place and move left to machine gun down the length of the trench on its right. This continued until the widened anti-tank trench was full of enough wood fascines to allow the rest of the tanks to breach the gap and attack the Germans' rear communication trenches and supply lines.

# THE NEW ARTILLERY TACTICS

The success of the British attack on 20 November cannot just be put down to the use of tanks in large numbers. It was the new tactical way of combining airpower, artillery, infantry and armour by using infantry infiltration tactics, predicted artillery fire, sound ranging, battlefield intelligence and infantry-tank co-ordination. This new tactic was called 'combined-arms warfare'.

The initial attack was a success because the enemy were taken by surprise. This was achieved through night-time transportation of supplies, men, tanks and guns to the front line to avoid detection and not following the traditional tactic of using artillery to 'soften up' enemy trenches days before the actual attack went forward.

Predicted artillery fire is a method of shelling enemy positions based on detailed calculations and maps, often called 'map shooting'. It enables shells to be fired on German trenches without first alerting the soldiers with ranging shots, which enabled them to seek shelter in deep dugouts before the main bombardment fell on their position. This new method of indirect fire could also deliver smoke shells to the correct location to cover the advance of the tanks and infantry.

The artillery needed good maps. By 1917 the British Army's Field Survey companies, with the help of old maps and aerial photographs, were able to produce accurate maps of the front line and beyond, deep into enemy territory. British artillery gun batteries could now use these new maps to plot their position and that of the intended target. They could work out the range, bearing and elevation needed to bombard the area without having to use ranging shots first.

In the past, too many tanks had been abandoned having fallen into or got stuck in deep shell craters. Major attacks in 1914 and 1915 had been preceded by a large blanket artillery barrage, which made the terrain very difficult for tanks to negotiate.

To avoid this, a new type of shell with a No. 106 shell fuse was introduced. It was designed to deliver high-explosive shrapnel-filled shells to the target but without leaving a deep crater. As soon as the spindle sticking out of the nose of the shell hit anything solid it moved backwards and caused the fuse to detonate instantaneously. This above-surface exploding shell fuse was also used to cut barbed wire and burst smoke shells.

At the start of an attack, like that at the Battle of Cambrai, British heavy artillery guns tried to put German artillery batteries out of action by using counter-battery suppression fire. Their positions would have been worked out on a map using a sound ranger. This involved a soldier listening to a pair of microphones a few kilometres apart. When the enemy guns fired he would use a stopwatch to record the time between the sound arriving at the different microphones. Other soldiers would be tasked with detecting gun flashes and using a theodolite or compass to work out the bearing. Using this information artillery officers could then calculate the co-ordinates of the hostile battery.

All three main types of British artillery were used during the Battle of Cambrai: more than 1,000 guns were available for fire missions. The Royal Garrison Artillery (RGA) manned the long-range, heavy-calibre guns that could fire high-explosive shells a distance of just over 7 miles (13,000yd, 11.88km). The front-line field guns were operated by the Royal Field Artillery (RFA) and the Royal Horse Artillery (RHA), who used light- and medium-calibre guns with ranges of just under 3 or 4 miles respectively (5,000 to 7,000yd, 4.57 to 6.4km).

# 20 NOVEMBER 1917 – DAY ONE

At 6.20 a.m. on 20 November 1917 the British offensive at Cambrai began with a surprise artillery mass barrage directed on the German trenches as the infantry and tanks moved forward. Smoke was fired first, followed by high-explosive surface-detonating shrapnel shells that cut barbed wire and killed German soldiers without making deep impact craters. The artillery lifted their barrage forward to stay in front of the advancing tanks and troops.

Even before the tanks reached the enemy trenches, conditions inside these vehicles were already very unpleasant. The crews had to work in the choking fumes coming from the engine and guns. The exhaust pipes going up to the roof were now red hot and causing sweat to run down the men's faces and backs. The noise from the engine and the rattling machine-gun fire was so loud that they could not hear the person next to them, even if they shouted. The driver had to use a metal bar to bang on the engine cover to signal to the secondary gearsmen to change gear.

Lt D.E. Hickey recalled what happened to his tank as he crossed no-man's-land: 'Inside the tanks the crews wrestled with the new technology under fire. Just at this critical moment the autovac that supplied petrol to the engine failed. The engine spluttered and stopped. We were now a stationary target. In the sudden silence we could hear the thud, thud, of falling shells and metal and earth hitting the sides of the tank. The atmosphere inside the tank was foul. With tense faces the crew watched as the second driver coolly and methodically put the autovac right, ignoring the proffered advice from the rest of the tank crew to give it a good hard knock.'

With the help of the tanks the 51st and 62nd Divisions of IV Corps advanced towards the village of Havrincourt. The Hindenburg Line trenches in front of the village were captured in a two-hour battle that lasted from 7 a.m. to 9 a.m. Some German soldiers abandoned their weapons as they ran to the rear. Retreating infantry gave an account to a German artillery field gun officer of swarms of tanks, so many that it was absolutely impossible to stop them.

German snipers and machine gun teams occupied the damaged buildings of Havrincourt. They inflicted a lot of casualties on the infantry of the

62nd Division. The village was finally taken at 10.30 a.m. with the use of the Mark IV tanks to get close to the enemy positions and put down suppressive fire.

To the far north of the attack ran the Canal du Nord, and none of the canal bridges were strong enough to take the weight of the British tanks. The German trenches that lined the east bank were taken by the 10th Royal Inniskilling Fusiliers without tank support by 9.15 a.m. This secured the left flank of the attack from enemy counter-attacks.

To the south, on III Corps' attack front, the advance was going well. The tanks had cleared the barbed wire to allow the infantry to follow them into the Hindenburg Line trench system in front of the village of Ribécourt. The new 'map shooting' artillery bombardment had worked well and the German troops had not had time to shelter in their deep bunkers. Many men were killed or reduced to quivering wrecks because of the intensity of the bombardment. There were many reports of troops surrendering upon seeing and hearing the advancing tanks of the first and second waves.

The village of Ribécourt was captured and the men and machines of III Corps advanced towards the villages of Masnières and Marcoing to take the St-Quentin Canal crossings. By 11 a.m. the 29th Division reported that tanks plus their men had reached the canal and were fighting their way into the two villages.

A dramatic indication that real progress had been made was the sight of British field artillery limbered up and going forward, first at a trot and then at a gallop. Battery after battery were to take up new positions on the captured front line.

It was now nearly five hours since the start of the attack and the German commanders started to send reinforcements and organise a defence; the initial shock was wearing off. Enemy troops used the buildings to their advantage and British infantry were pinned down by enemy fire. Heavier weapons had been brought forward and anti-tank rifles were used to penetrate the tank's armour, while machine-gunners loaded their weapons with armour-piercing bullets. Tanks had to fire their weapons at nearly point-blank range as they navigated the village streets.

The Germans had wired the canal bridge at Marcoing for demolition and if it blew up this would cause serious problems for the next planned advance. Eight Mark IV tanks of 'A' Battalion reached the bridge and managed to prevent this happening. Tanks from 'B' Battalion arrived at the bridge at 11.30 a.m. but there was not enough infantry support to force an attack over to the other side. All the tanks could do was hold the west side of the canal while firing at the enemy on the east bank.

A tank called the 'Flying Fox II' of 'F' Battalion tried to cross the Masnières canal iron girder bridge. Unfortunately, the bridge had been partially damaged when the Germans tried unsuccessfully to blow it up with a demolition charge. It could not take the weight and came crashing down with the tank stuck in the middle, although the crew managed to scramble out.

The Germans were in houses on the other side of the canal so the other tanks of 'F' Battalion, trapped on the west bank, patrolled up and down the canal for the next two hours firing at targets as they became visible. The crew were happy in the knowledge that they had reached their objective 5 miles behind enemy lines; this was a feat that had not happened before. As one side of the tank was shielded from the enemy the members of the tank crew that were not firing their guns were able to get out and breathe fresh air.

Infantry units including the Newfoundland Regiment and the 2nd Hampshire Regiment had managed to get across the canal, secure the east bank and head towards the Siegfried II Line trenches. On the western side of the canal the trenches at Noyelles and Nine Woods, part of the Siegfried II Line, had already been captured.

With the houses on the east bank of the canal now empty of enemy soldiers the tank crews were stood down and replacements took over the running of the tanks. Supply tanks arrived and unloaded fuel and ammunition.

At the end of the first day troubling news came back to Tank Corps HQ that a large number of tanks had been lost or were no longer fit for action. German artillery had knocked out sixty-five. Some of the tanks had to be abandoned because they got stuck fast in a deep muddy crater or trench: forty-three tanks were recorded as being unavailable through 'ditching'.

Around seventy-one tanks suffered a variety of mechanical failures ranging from broken tracks to blown engines. Tanks that could not be moved then became fixed targets for enemy artillery. The tank crews had to abandon their vehicle for the relative safety of a nearby trench or shell hole under enemy fire. Many did not make it.

## THE GERMAN FIELD GUN PROBLEM

As the British tanks and infantry passed into open country, in the distance, at the top of the hill, they could see the outskirts of Cambrai.

The British had achieved a lot of their military objectives on the first day of the attack but not all of them; some of the villages in front of Cambrai remained in German hands. The tanks and assault troops of the first wave bypassed these pockets of resistance, expecting them to be 'mopped up' by the following waves of infantry.

One of these villages was Flesquières (pronounced *fles-key-yeah*) and lurking nearby was one of the few German artillery batteries that had received training on how to knock out tanks. The tank battle was not over.

A new, direct fire, anti-tank field gun was used for the first time on the front line. It was called the 7.7cm Feldkanone 16 Field Gun and was manufactured by Krupp. It had originally been designed as an artillery howitzer but it had been modified for direct fire against tanks and could fire a 6kg (13lb) armour piercing shell over a distance of a mile. A battery of these German guns, commanded by Lt Jakubasch of 4th Battery, 213th Field Artillery Regiment, was hiding behind bushes near the village of Flesquières waiting for the British tanks to come into its sights.

'H' Battalion, Tank Corps, Mark IV tanks moved up the slope. As they went over a ridge and started to gain speed, one of the tanks, called 'Hong Kong', was hit and knocked out. Tanks 'Huntsmen' and 'Harvester' were also hit and had to be abandoned. 2Lt Gordon Hassel commanded the Mark IV tank called 'Harrier'. He recorded hearing a huge explosion and seeing one of his tank's tracks go flying through the air. A second shell took off the roof and the third penetrated the rear of the tank.

German artillery battery commander Lt Richter remembered the shock of seeing a British tank emerge from the village: 'I gave the order, "275m fire. Damn too far, fire. A little to the right, fire." A hit, oh Lord a column of fire was bursting out of the monster. Two of our men ran to the tank and when they returned they described the half-burned bodies of the crew.'

A German gunner recalled: 'Nine British tanks rolled towards us. The captain orders, "steady men, wait for it." When the enemy was less than 100m away the command rang out, "rapid fire". The first tank rears upwards. Those following halt. One direct hit after another.' The guns destroyed around thirty-two tanks near Flesquières.

More were crippled by stormtroopers in the narrow streets of Fontaine-Notre-Dame. British Lt Col J.F.C. Fuller, who had contributed to the planning of the Battle of Cambrai, recalled: 'There was horrible slaughter in the streets of Fontaine-Notre-Dame. I had spent three weeks before the battle thinking out its possibilities. I never tackled the subject of village fighting. I could have kicked myself again and again for this lack of foresight. It never occurred to me that our Infantry Commanders would order our tanks into such places.'

The German Army did not have enough of these direct fire anti-tank guns to stop all the advancing British tanks and they could be put out of action by British high-explosive tank shells and machine guns. The dilemma for the British tank commander was, did he order the tank to stop so the gunners could take an accurate shot at the field gun and become an easy target at the same time or move forward hoping that by changing direction regularly the enemy gun would miss. The British Mark IV 6-pounder gun could not be fired accurately on the move.

With the help of the infantry the village of Flesquières was taken during the night after the Germans had moved back to more defendable positions to the north at Fontaine and Cantaing.

## CHURCH BELLS

On 21 November 1917 church bells rang out across Britain to celebrate the victory. It had only cost 4,000 casualties compared with the 159,000 during the advance at the Battle of Arras. But bells had also rung out in Germany for the first victory against the French at Verdun. Again, the celebrations were a little hasty.

## DAY TWO

The British Army started to use infantry infiltration tactics rather than just attacking in one large wave. Multiple waves of men would be used, each with a different task to complete. The first wave of infantry had the job of penetrating as far as possible and leaving enemy strongpoints to be dealt with by follow-up waves of soldiers who were more heavily armed.

The German infantry also used this method of attack. It called the infantry sent in first *Stoßtruppen* (stormtroopers or shock troops). The Germans would use infiltration tactics to great effect during the Battle of Cambrai counter-attack.

By the morning of 21 November 1917, British and Commonwealth soldiers were exhausted from the effects of combat and sleep deprivation. It had been a damp and cold night and only 55 per cent of the tank force were available, divided up between III and IV Corps. There were problems getting supplies up to the forward troops because of German Artillery fire. By 10.30 a.m. the villages of Fontaine and Cantaing had fallen to the British. The mounted cavalry of the 2nd Dragoon guards took part in the action to clear the enemy out of Cantaing. Tanks assisted the Scottish 4th Seaforth Highlanders and 7th Argyll and Sutherland Highlanders to capture Fontaine. At 4 p.m. the village of Noyelles was captured. To the east, the British 87th and 88th Brigades crossed the canal and started the advance from Marcoing and Masnières between 2 and 2.30 p.m.

## DAY THREE

There was intense fighting on 22 November 1917 all along the Battle of Cambrai front, especially between the villages of Fontaine and Bourlon. This German resistance stalled the British advance. German forces launched a local counter-attack at the village of Fontaine and recaptured it at 2.30 p.m. The Scottish Highlanders were attacked by a strong force of infantry from the German 46th Regiment. They were outnumbered and suffered 319 casualties before withdrawing from the village. The build-up in German strength was an indication that reinforcements were starting to arrive.

## DAY FOUR

On 23 November 1917 the British tried to recapture Fontaine and take Bourlon, Bourlon Wood and the village of Moeuvres using combined arms tactics that had worked so well on the first day of the attack. Both sides received additional reinforcements during the night. A total of eighty-eight tanks were available for the continued offensive push across the whole 6-mile front.

By 11.30 a.m. nineteen tanks of 'B' and 'C' Battalion had managed to reach the streets of Fontaine but were stopped or repelled by accurate anti-tank fire. The Germans used a new tank-stopping weapon for the first time. They had the bright idea of using a 7.7cm anti-aircraft gun, mounted on the back of a lorry, to fire on British tanks with armour-piercing shells. Two lorry chassis were used, the Daimler K-Flak (Kraftwagenflak) mit Krump 7.7cm L/27 M1914 BAK and the Ehrhardt E-V/4 K-Flak (Kraftwagenflak) mit Rheinmetall 7.7cm L/27 M1913 BAK. The guns were known as Ballonabwehrkanone (BAK = anti-balloon cannons). The Germans feared that the British would use airships like the Zeppelin to bomb their troops and cities. Their fear was unfounded as the British did not successfully develop such a fleet during the war. Only six tanks survived the assault.

The Daimler K-Flak (Kraftwagenflak) mit Krump 7.7cm L/27 M1914 BAK anti-aircraft gun platform was designed to attack British airships and aircraft. It was used to fire on advancing British tanks.

The attempt to capture Bourlon village and Bourlon Wood failed as tanks could not be used in the dense woodland. Welsh and Scottish Highlander troops fought their way through the wood and managed to get to the far northern edge but a fierce German counter-attack pushed them back to the middle of the wood, where both sides dug in.

The attack on the village of Bourlon was uphill in open ground. An attack by the British 36th Division on the west of the village had failed; this meant that troops involved in the main attack on the village were being shot at from the front and left side. A few tanks and soldiers from the 13th Green Howards and 12th South Wales managed to reach the outskirts of Bourlon but they were pushed back.

Irish infantry attacked the village of Moeuvres to the west of the Canal du Nord and Bourlon. Again the countryside was open farmland with very little cover. They managed to capture the village but were then forced to retreat when the Germans launched a strong counter-attack. There were many casualties on both sides.

# DAY FIVE

On 24 November 1917 the British tried yet again to take the village of Bourlon. Only twelve tanks of 'I' Battalion supported the renewed attack up the gentle incline over fields and along the main road. The 1st and 2nd Cavalry Battalions, 40th Division, were now fighting alongside 121st Brigade. Eight of the twelve tanks were knocked out as they entered the streets of Bourlon. They were stopped by a variety of weapons ranging from grenades to field guns. The outskirts of the village were captured but the centre remained in German hands. Later, enemy troops managed to surround and cut off the 14th Highland Light infantry (HLI) in the village.

To the east of the village hard fighting continued in Bourlon Wood for most of the day. At 4.15 p.m. the last Germans soldiers were forced out of the northern tree-lined edge. The British were finally in command of the wooded ridge that had been one of the Day One objectives.

# DAY SIX

On 25 November 1917 German troops continued to arrive to reinforce the defences along the 6-mile front. Haig had hoped that the wide open farmland would have been ideal for the British cavalry to exploit and push forward. However, the lack of cover and good visibility were ideal conditions for enemy snipers and machine gun teams to cause havoc and stop the advance of horse-mounted soldiers. Also, the number of tanks available to support attacks continued to dwindle.

The 13th East Surreys tried to rescue the cut-off 14th Highland Light infantry (HLI) in Bourlon but were forced back and the eighty surviving Highlanders had to surrender. The Germans now had total control of the village of Bourlon.

# DAY SEVEN

No more advances were made in Bourlon during 26 November but German strength continued to grow along the whole front. It was obvious that they were preparing to mount a massive counter-attack. That night the weather worsened and it started to snow. The Germans continued to send waves of infantry to try to regain Bourlon Wood but these were cut down by the steadfast defence of the 19th Royal Welsh Fusiliers. Both sides' artillery continually bombarded each other's forward positions.

# DAY EIGHT

On the morning of 27 November the British launched two attacks. The first one tried to recapture the village of Fontaine but resulted in heavy casualties. The understrength Guards Division was sent in supported by only twelve tanks, hence there simply were not enough manpower and tanks to take this reinforced German strongpoint. Their artillery had taken the opportunity of zeroing their guns on to the battlefield in front of the village and the approaching tanks and British infantry were subjected to a heavy barrage of accurate high-explosive shells and machine-gun fire. The assault was launched in near blizzard conditions.

The 350 British artillery guns laid down a creeping barrage to cover the advance of the few tanks and infantry but it was not enough. The British tanks of 'F' Battalion, Tank Corps, managed to reach the streets of Fontaine but they were attacked by infantry units armed with bombs and grenades. The Guards Division could not keep up with the tanks and many were killed as they headed towards the village. Some did reach the village and were engaged in house-to-house, hand-to-hand combat. The attack was over by 10 a.m. and those few that survived retreated back to the start lines.

A new attack was sent into Bourlon, this time from two different directions. The tanks managed to reach the streets but were attacked by field guns, troops armed with demolition charges and bundles of grenades. Fourteen tanks were knocked out. Hard fighting occurred in the streets and houses at close quarters. More troops were rushed to the front to hold the line and a German counter-attack was halted by the 186th Brigade. Haig ordered the offensive to cease and sent three new infantry divisions to strengthen the front line and deal with the oncoming mass assault.

# THE BATTLES

## DAY NINE & TEN

28 and 29 November 1917 were spent preparing for the German counter-attack. German artillery were sending over shells to register their guns by bracketing shots to make sure the main barrage landed in the right place. The British troops in Bourlon Wood were shelled with phosgene and mustard gas.

## DAY ELEVEN

The Germans sent two army groups to attack the British positions, which were now outnumbered. This major counter-offensive started at 6 a.m., 30 November 1917, with their *Stoßtruppen* leading the way firing light machine guns and flamethrowers. They bypassed areas of resistance, which were dealt with by troops in the second wave.

Units put up a strong defence and the British lost 6,000 prisoners. Snow started to fall again as fighting continued throughout the afternoon.

The furthest distance the Germans advanced was 3 miles from their start line and they captured the village of Gouzeaucourt. It was later recaptured when the 1st Brigade, Guards Division, were rushed to the area.

## DAY TWELVE

The British 3rd Army launched an attack at 6.50 a.m. on 1 December 1917 against the advancing Germans. The Guards Division and the Ambala Brigade, 5th Cavalry Division, launched an attack at 7.15 a.m. at Gauche Wood and the village of Gonnelieu with thirty-nine tanks in support. Twenty of these tanks headed towards the village, where they clashed with several German battalions that had been sent to continue their advance. Fighting was brutal; Gauche Wood was captured but the British were pushed back to the edge of the village.

At 9.35 a.m. the third assault began against the village of Villers-Guislan by the 2nd Lancers and the 5th (Mhow) Cavalry Brigade. The sight of a full, traditional, large cavalry charge initially alarmed the Germans, who fled. Small arms fire and the bullets from machine guns further back from the charge caused heavy casualties among the men and horses and the village was not captured. In the afternoon, fighting continued at many points along the front. Aircraft from both sides bombed and machine-gunned enemy troops and artillery guns.

## DAY THIRTEEN

On 2 December 1917 the village of La Vacquerie was attacked by German forces but this was repelled by the defending British troops. Attacks against positions south of Moeuvres and the village of Marcoing were also repelled.

## DAY FOURTEEN TO DAY EIGHTEEN

On 3 December 1917 commander-in-chief Douglas Haig sent out orders that between 4 and 7 December the British 3rd Army would start a phased retreat to the more defendable Flesquières Ridge line and dig in. Regular and Pioneer troops had been busy preparing strong defensive trench systems behind the front line since 1 December. Both sides stopped any further local attacks; the Battle of Cambrai was over. It was a miserable and disappointing draw after such a promising start.

## CONCLUSION

Although they were pushed back and lost a lot of ground after their initial successes, the Battle of Cambrai was crucial for the British. They had gained valuable experience with their tanks and cracked their artillery problems. Vital lessons were learnt about teamwork on the battlefield and the tactics of 'combined arms'.

Failing to deal with the German counter-attack and hold captured ground has been blamed on a number of factors such as poor leadership at General Headquarters or the fact that the cavalry failed to turn up as arranged. It is just as likely that the failure to exploit the gains were purely because nobody had expected the tanks to advance as far as they did.

The big tactical and logistical challenge for both sides was to master what happened after a breakthrough. The Germans had failed to consolidate their initial breakthrough at Verdun and the British failed to do the same at Cambrai.

The Battle of Cambrai had shown what could be achieved by the latest Mark IV tank on good ground. The generals now understood just what a tank could really do if deployed in the right locations with infantry and artillery support. Their place in the British Army was never in question again.

Mark II training tanks were not intended to go into battle so they were not constructed with hardened armour plating. Amazingly, they were used once in action at the Battle of Arras in April 1917, as not enough Mark IVs had been delivered to the front line. They were replaced by Mark IV tanks.

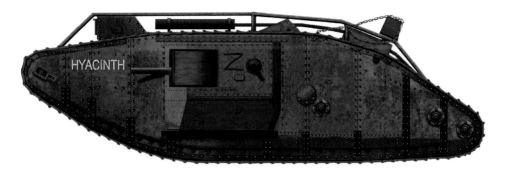

The Mark IV Male 'Hyacinth' H45 of 'H' Battalion, 24th Company, 10 Section, was ditched in a German trench while supporting the 1st Battalion, Leicestershire Regiment, a mile west of Ribécourt. It was commanded by 2Lt F.H. Jackson. It reached the starting point and the first objective as it attacked the Hindenburg Line trench system. Notice the red letter Z hand-painted over the vision slit in an effort to conceal its locations from snipers and machine-gunners. There were no red and white identification stripes at the front yet as German tanks or *Beutepanzern* had not been encountered on the battlefield.

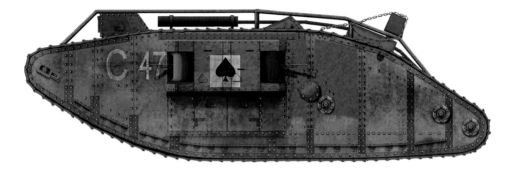

British Mk IV Female No. 4651 'Conqueror II' C47 of 'C' Battalion, 9th Company, went into battle on 20 November 1917. It was commanded by 2Lt W. Moore. The tank attacked the enemy and successfully returned to Allied lines. On 23 November 2Lt W. Moore led his tank crew into battle again. While attacking German positions it was knocked out by a penetrating armour-piercing shell that set it on fire. It was photographed burnt out in Fontaine-Notre-Dame. On the right-hand side the crew had painted a caricature of a frightened-looking German soldier. In April 1918 it was photographed again in No. 21 German tank repair workshops.

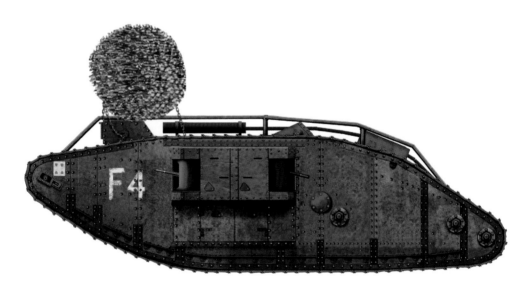

To help the Mark IV cross wide trenches it was fitted with a large round bundle of wood called a 'fascine' on top of the roof. When it came to a trench the commander and driver released the securing cables and let the fascine fall into the trench before driving over it. Mark IV tanks were mainly painted brown.

# FRENCH TANK BATTLES

Artillery colonel Jean-Baptiste Estienne was given the task of organising the French tank units. The French Army did not create a new branch like the British Tank Corps. Tanks were under the control of the artillery, the Artillerie Spéciale (AS). Schneider assault tanks were organised into a *groupe*. Four tank batteries made up a group, while a tank battery comprised of four tanks. On paper an AS *groupe* had a strength of sixteen tanks but this number varied due to vehicles suffering mechanical breakdowns. Seventeen Schneider-equipped groups were formed and allocated the numbers AS 1 to AS 17.

Col Estienne established his headquarters at Champlieu, near a tank camp. He established a tank training centre at Cercottes near Orléans. The tank crews were recruited from the Army and Navy, but the biggest proportion came from the cavalry. By April 1917 Estienne had formed thirteen AC *groupes* of Schneider tanks and two of Saint-Chamond tanks. Around 200 tanks were now available, four times the number the British had used on the Somme.

During the Battle of the Somme British commander Sir Douglas Haig was desperate to stop the high casualty rate and was under a lot of political pressure. Rather than wait until enough British and French tanks were available to be deployed in one large group, then used to make a knockout breakthrough, he sent a small group of forty-nine British Mark I tanks into battle for the first time on 15 September 1916.

Estienne was annoyed as the element of surprise had been lost and the Germans now started to implement anti-tank counter-measures. Trenches were widened and field guns were established behind the front line to deal with tanks that breached them. German defenders were instructed to let the tanks go past them but then try to stop or delay the following Allied soldiers. This would mean that the advancing tanks would not have infantry support. Unmolested by Allied infantry machine gun or rifle fire the German gun crews could then target the slow-moving tanks.

French High Command had to come up with new tactics. Infantry were trained to assist the tanks in crossing obstacles. There was better co-ordination between the artillery, air force, ground forces and tanks. Tank supply vehicles were introduced to resupply tanks that had managed to force a breakthrough in the enemy lines.

# NIVELLE OFFENSIVE

On 2 April 1917 French artillery started a fourteen-day bombardment of German positions in the Champagne area of France. At 6 a.m., 16 April 1917, French commander-in-chief Gen. Robert Nivelle launched a massive attack. This new offensive is known as the Second Battle of the Aisne and the Third Battle of Champagne. It was also called the Nivelle (Spring) Offensive.

The object of the attack was to capture the ridges, known as the Chemin des Dames, that overlooked the battlefield and gave the Germans good views of the French positions. The Germans learned about the attack and had pulled back most of their front-line troops. When the artillery barrage ended, these troops rushed back to meet the attacking forces.

On day one, 128 Schneider tanks went into action for the first time but these contributed very little to the outcome of the battle. The pulverised earth, after fourteen days of artillery shelling, was left like a moonscape, full of craters and muddy ditches; the tank crews found it very difficult to cross this type of terrain. The first lessons of tank warfare were being learnt.

Unlike the British Gen. Haig, French Gen. Estienne believed that tanks would only be successful if they were used en masse. He ordered that they were not to be used in small numbers before his planned assault.

Estienne had to change his initial plans as the British had used tanks during the Battle of the Somme in September 1916. To deal with the widening of German trenches as an anti-tank defence French tactics changed. The first thing they did was widen the front-line trenches so they could not be breached by advancing tanks.

In addition, combat pioneer units were attached to the armoured assault groups to help them construct breaches on the far trench walls so that the tanks could climb out.

Eight groups of tanks were put into the main assault supporting the 32nd Corps attack. Some 208 Schneider tanks had been delivered by the time of the planned attack, 100 of which were the Schneider CA *surblindé* (up-armoured) versions. The additional armour was needed to protect the crews from the German 37mm light field guns that had started to be moved to the front-line trenches as a defence against tank attacks.

Fifty Schneider assault tanks in AS 3, AS 7 and AS 8 were assigned to the 5th Corps assault, to the west of the village of Miette. They were called Groupement Chaubés.

Eighty-two tanks in AS 2, AS 4, AS 5, AS 6 and AS 9 were used in the assault on the German front line between the villages of Berry-au-Bac and Juvincourt. They were called Groupement Boussut.

At first the tanks were going to be used at the front of the assault to punch through the enemy's front lines, but news of the Germans' new anti-tank defences prompted a change in tactics and instead the Schneider tanks were to be used as artillery support vehicles. They would take over the role of the field guns once they had moved beyond the range of the divisional artillery and beyond.

At 6 a.m. on a misty, overcast morning the attack moved forward as artillery continued to bombard the German trenches. The advancing tanks were spotted by a German reconnaissance aircraft and this sighting was quickly communicated back to the German artillery batteries. Most of the French tank losses were caused by artillery shells.

Groupement Chaubés lost just over half its tank force due to enemy artillery fire. Twenty-six tanks were knocked out and fifty-one tank crew members were killed or wounded.

In Groupement Boussut, thirteen Schneider assault tanks broke down or became 'ditched' – stuck in the mud or in a deep shell crater from which they could not extricate themselves. The crews had to abandon them and try to get back to their own lines. Thirty-one were disabled or knocked out by artillery fire. More than half of the initial tank force was out of action and 129 tank crew members were killed or wounded, including the Groupement Boussut commander, Commandant Louis Bossut.

One of the Schneider AS groups managed to push 3.10 miles (5km) behind the German front line, showing what armoured vehicles were capable of, but they had to return to their front lines due to lack of infantry support.

The performance of French tanks, used on the battlefield for the first time, was not what had been expected. Too many had been lost to artillery attack. An investigation found that part of the problem was the placement of the fuel tanks near the front of the vehicle. They often ruptured, spilling their contents inside the crew compartment. When the fuel ignited the tank either exploded or burst into flames. They were repositioned to the rear of the tank on all new models under construction and existing tanks were retrofitted with new fuel tanks either side of the rear hatch.

To reduce crew casualties, a new large hatch was fitted to the side of the tank to help crew members get out faster. However, the additional armour on the *surblindé* versions of the Schneider CA was not enough to stop German armour-piercing shells.

## LAFFAUX MILL

During the minor attack near Laffaux Mill on 5 May 1917 the French Army sent its new Saint-Chamond tank into action for the first time. The attack was part of the Second Battle of the Aisne, which resulted in a German victory.

Eight groups of tanks were put into the main assault supporting the 32nd Corps attack. Two groups of Schneider tanks and one Saint-Chamond group took part in the battle.

The French Army attacked south-east of Vauxaillon, capturing Moisy Farm and Laffaux Mill. The German counter-attacks were repulsed. By the end of the day the French Sixth Army had reached the outskirts of Allemant and taken around 4,000 prisoners.

The tanks had problems negotiating the rough ground, although the Schneider tanks performed better than the Saint-Chamonds. Some tanks did not make the start line as they suffered mechanical breakdowns. Three Schneiders and three Saint-Chamond tanks were knocked out and lost. German battle reports noted that the tanks silenced a number of its machine gun positions and assisted the French infantry in their advance.

## GENERAL PÉTAIN

The year 1917 saw several mutinies in the French infantry at the front, who perceived a disregard for their lives and living conditions after suffering defeats. They held the line and would fire at attacking Germans but refused to participate in any more offensives until their concerns were addressed. In response to this unrest, Nivelle was replaced as commander-in-chief by Gen. Philippe Pétain.

Rather than ordering hundreds of firing squads, Pétain looked at different ways of addressing this problem. He saw the potential of the tank as a morale-raising tool. Infantry that had gone into battle with tanks wanted them to be part of the next attack.

Unlike Col Estienne, Pétain realised that the tank was not a wonder weapon; it had limitations but they could be overcome. He introduced infantry and tank co-operation training exercises, and the role of artillery was re-examined.

The Malmaison attack was to be led by fifty-six Saint-Chamond tanks and thirty-six Schneiders. In the early morning of 23 October 1917 they headed off from the start line through the early morning mist. These conditions helped the French attack as the German artillery spotters could not see their targets.

The Schneider CA *surblindé* tanks had better armour protection and the German armour-piercing SmK rounds could not penetrate it. The small local offensive against Malmaison was a success and this encouraged Pétain to order an increase in the Artillerie Spéciale French tank corps.

More supply vehicles were ordered and some new Saint-Chamond tanks were converted into *chars caissons*, used to recover broken-down or knocked-out tanks for repair. They were identical to the gun tanks except the gun was removed and blanked off with armour plate.

An experiment in battlefield communication was tested successfully in this attack. Two Saint-Chamonds and two Schneiders were converted into wireless radio tanks (*char télégraphie sans fils TSF*). This enabled the tank groups to be in communication with divisional headquarters and infantry units. Later, Renault FT tanks were also converted into Renault TSF vehicles.

## BEE SWARM THEORY

Col Estienne put forward the 'bee swarm theory' on future tank deployments because the big Saint-Chamond and Schneider tanks had shown that they were vulnerable to artillery bombardment. They were too thinly armoured to survive a direct hit. Rather than relying on one or two big armoured tanks attacking a trench system, the survival odds would be improved if a swarm of smaller, cheaper to build tanks were used instead. He argued that five smaller, faster tanks armed with machine guns or a cannon were better than one big tank. The German defences would be overcome by the sheer weight of numbers. The smaller, more agile tanks would be harder to target and knock out.

Gen. Pétain agreed with this new tactic. On 20 June 1917 he increased the order for Renault FT *char légers* (light tanks) from 1,500 to 3,500. He viewed the increased availability of tanks to support the infantry as an important ingredient in restoring the fighting spirit of the French Army.

The new, large order was for 1,150 machine gun Renault FT tanks, 1,950 armed with the 37mm gun, 700 support tanks armed with the 75mm short-barrelled howitzer, and 200 wireless radio TSF tanks. In October 1918 the order was further increased to 7,820 tanks.

Gen. Pétain did not want to test this new 'bee swarm' theory until enough tanks were available. The new light tank battalions were organised in a different way from their bigger cousins. At full strength each tank company had seventy-five Renault FTs; a battalion would have three companies. On paper each company was supposed to have four radio tanks, forty-one machine gun tanks and thirty 37mm gun tanks. The Battalion Headquarters unit would have a company workshop and transport detachment. The recovery section would be issued with three tanks: two 37mm gun tanks and one machine gun tank. For protection it would have three sections of five tanks: three 37mm gun tanks and two machine gun tanks. The reserve section consisted of five replacement tanks. A radio TSF tank was used for communication. This was a total of 249 tanks in the HQ unit.

Before a battle, mechanical breakdowns would alter these figures. After combat a battalion may have to cope with half its tank numbers lost through ditching, mechanical failure or enemy action. In May 1918 battalions were brought together to form a larger military body called a Régiment d'Artillerie Spéciale (RAS). They were formed from three tank battalions. On paper one RAS had 747 tanks on its strength.

In May 1918 Gen. Pétain had planned to launch a mass attack of French infantry and Renault FT tanks but the German spring offensive disrupted this plan. They pushed so far into the Allied lines that the French tank base at Champlieu had to be evacuated to a new location.

On 31 May 1918, 200 Renault FT tanks were used in an attack for the first time. They came from 501e RAS and were supporting Moroccan infantry near Ploisy-Chazelles. In open countryside they were able to assault the enemy positions and silence their machine guns. Their armour protection allowed them to machine gun the troops in the trenches, and this allowed the following infantry to occupy these positions.

An unforeseen advantage of using smaller tanks was their ability to negotiate narrow tracks in woodland that would be impassable for the bigger British Mark IVs and the French Saint-Chamonds and Schneiders. Where there were tanks, advances were made because they encouraged the attached infantry units.

There were not enough Renault FTs available to properly try the 'bee swarm' tactic. After the first week of battle tank availability, numbers had been severely reduced through mechanical breakdowns, ditching and losses by enemy artillery fire. The crews were exhausted but, unlike the British system, there were not enough personnel to rotate tank crews on a daily basis. Tanks were often used in small numbers to fight off counter-attacks. Although the Renault FT did suffer with mechanical problems, it was more reliable than the other Allied tanks.

# MATZ VALLEY

On 11 June 1918, ninety-six Saint-Chamond tanks and fifty-one Schneider tanks were used in a new attack in the Matz valley. In the intense fighting thirty-seven Saint-Chamonds and thirty-five Schneiders were put out of action. Despite the losses, the tanks helped the infantry stop the German advance.

# SOISSONS

On 18 July 1918, 255 Renault FT tanks were used to spearhead some of the attacks near Soissons. Some 123 Schneider tanks and 100 Saint-Chamond tanks were also deployed. This was the biggest collection of French armour used in one offensive. The faster Renaults provided the impetus for the attacks, although sometimes they had to wait for the following infantry to catch up. Tanks are good at destroying machine-gun posts and neutralising enemy resistance in trench networks but they cannot hold ground.

# LIAISON

Co-ordination between infantry and tanks was still problematic as the RAS battalions did not want to release tanks for training exercises. After a day's use they would need a full mechanical inspection and service, and some would break down and be out of action for a week while parts were found and fitted. This would reduce the number of tanks available for active service on the battlefield.

Co-operation with the artillery was often poor. French battle plans called for the artillery to fire smokescreens in advance of an attack. This would make the tanks and infantry harder to see and target. A good smokescreen would save lives and was instrumental in making sure that enough men and machines made it safely across no-man's-land to assault the enemy trenches.

Effective smokescreens were not always delivered. Enemy artillery shells were responsible for knocking out 356 Renault FT tanks during the war out of a total figure of 440 losses. This number could have been reduced if the German artillery observer had not seen them.

Renault tanks were successful when they worked together to deal with threats. They were faster than their larger cousins, so could rush German field guns. As they were more agile, the German gunners found it difficult to score a hit before they were overrun. In the last few months of the war the Germans tried to counter this tactic by grouping more field guns together in one location, but by that time more Allied tanks were arriving in greater numbers.

Pioneer troops were assigned to assist Renault FT tanks breach the high walls of enemy trenches. Unlike the longer British tanks that could successfully cross both walls of most trenches, the smaller French tanks found this a problem. These engineers or specially trained infantry would use brute force and spades to make a ramp into the far side of a German trench after it had been made safe by the tanks' machine guns.

In reality these sappers (diggers) had difficulty keeping up with the tanks and this delayed the attack. New methods were being looked at to solve this problem but no solution was found before the war ended.

# THREATS

In 1918 the Germans started to lay anti-tank landmines on routes they believed enemy tanks would use. There were many different types as most were built on the battlefield from explosives or artillery shells. If the crew of a Renault FT had the misfortune to drive over one of the bigger improvised explosive devices they normally did not survive. However, the use of minefields was not very widespread across the battlefields of France and Belgium and it is believed that only thirteen Renault FTs were destroyed by mines.

The armour on the Renault FT tanks held up quite well to German anti-tank rifle rounds. The angled front hull armour made penetration difficult. The cast-metal Renault FT Girod turrets were not as strong as the flat armour plate used on the polygonal turrets but their shape helped in deflecting some of the rounds. German machine-gunners and infantry with anti-tank rifles were instructed to fire at weak spots such as the driver and commander's vision slits. Although their bullets might not penetrate the armour they would cause the metal inside the tank to fracture into tiny sharp pieces that would cut exposed flesh and cause blindness.

## THE HUNDRED DAYS OFFENSIVE

With the German spring offensive of 1918 halted, the Allies started to fight back with lots of small attacks all along the front line. It became known as the 'Hundred Days offensive' and ran from 8 August to 11 November 1918. More than 2,000 Renault FT tanks had now been delivered so finally 'bee swarm' tactics could be put into action to overwhelm the enemy.

More men had to be trained to operate the tanks and additional RAS tank battalions formed. They were used in ten, planned, small attacks following the July Soissons offensive but the next large-scale battle took place on the morning of 28 August 1918, when the plan was to attack the area around Crécy-au-Mont/ Crouy. More than 580 Renault FT tanks from seven tank battalions of the 502e, 503e and 505e RAS took part. After five days of vicious fighting, the French managed to push the German defenders backwards in retreat over large areas of occupied land.

The final Allied attacks of September and October were marred by wet weather and were fought over muddy, slippery, waterlogged countryside. The Renault FT Régiment d'Artillerie Spéciale battalions were used for attacks in Champagne and Flanders that started on 26 September 1918. Some German infantry units continued to fight hard up until the Armistice of 11 November 1918.

The fighting of late summer 1918 was very different from previous years. The use of tanks had meant that the infantry had now broken through the lines of defensive trenches and were fighting over flat farmland – ideal tank country. There were very few artillery shell craters to cause problems.

However, it was not as easy as it sounds as the Germans adapted to the new type of fighting and still offered strong resistance in places. They used ridges, villages and woods as strongpoints. German artillery and field guns could see their targets from a long way off and open fire. It was through the Allied use of large numbers of men, tanks, aircraft and co-ordinated artillery fire directed at specific targets that the Germans were finally overwhelmed and defeated.

# TANK *v.* TANK BATTLES

There is no record of a French tank meeting a German Sturmpanzerwagen A7V heavy tank or a captured British Mark IV *Beutepanzer* in battle during the First World War.

A Schneider CA Char Ravitailleur (supply tank). In mid-1918 all early production models that had survived were sent to training duties and, later, most of the late production Schneider CA tanks were converted to supply tanks. Their superstructure was altered, they gained extra armour, lost their heavy Blockhaus gun (which was replaced by a new hatch), and also had their machine guns removed.

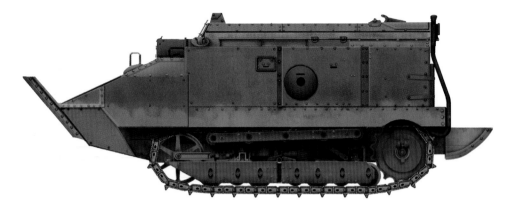

One of the first Schneider CA tanks engaged on the front in April 1917, at Berry-Au-Bac, part of the Nivelle offensives. The olive livery was not a standard one, but it was the standard factory paint. When the first units arrived they were put in combat in such haste that most of them appeared in this livery.

A late 1917-built Schneider CA tank in February 1918, in a training unit near the front, freshly camouflaged with an unusual pattern of sand, dark brown, khaki green and pale blue over a dark blue-grey basis. Later these took part in the July 1918 offensives launched by Ferdinand Foch, where 350 French tanks were committed.

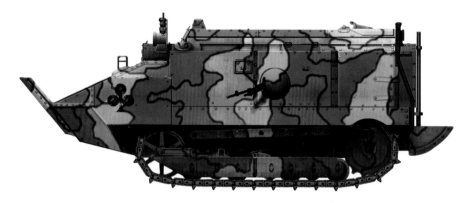

The last Schneider CA tanks committed in action were the ones participating in the French August counter-offensive under Gen Gouraud's command, after the failure of the Ludendorff summer offensive. The livery is the one used in early 1918, with bright colours separated by black lines, creating a paving effect to disrupt the outline of the tank. However, these colours made the tanks even more visible on a uniform grey-brownish battlefield. The French usage of playing card symbols to identify units by their letter stuck until the Second World War.

One of the very first French Saint-Chamond tanks engaged in operations, Lauffaux plateau, May 1917. Notice the flat roof, angled vision kiosks and the M1915 heavy field gun. The unspotted, unblended three-tone livery was usual in 1917, often featuring stripes as well.

One of the late production French *char* Saint-Chamond, engaged in counter-battery support in June 1918.

Renault FT light tank with the octagonal variant of the 'Omnibus turret' developed by Berliet, which was probably the cheapest to produce.

Renault FT tank armed with a 37mm gun. They were fitted with metal 'skids' at the rear to help them cross trenches and ditches.

'Le Tigre' in autumn 1917. 'The Tiger' was the nickname of the popular French president, Georges Clémenceau.

'Char canon', armed with a 37mm gun, in 1918. The bordering black stripes were often omitted by then.

Renault FT, Berliet model with the Girod turret, 506è Régiment d'Artillerie Spéciale (RAS), 1918.

Renault TSF radio tank, in olive green livery, in early 1918. TSF stands for *télégraphie sans fil* (wireless). There was no armament and it had a three-man crew.

# THE FIRST TANK *v.* TANK BATTLES

On 24 April 1918, three British Mark IV tanks of the 1 Section, 'A' Company, 1st Battalion, 3rd Tank Brigade, were involved in the first tank-on-tank battle against German-built Sturmpanzerwagen A7V heavy tanks near the town of Villers-Bretonneux south of the river Somme.

The Mark IV Male tank, A1 No. 4086, armed with two 6-pounder, quick-firing guns positioned in side sponsons and also machine guns, was under the commanded of 2Lt Frank Mitchell. The two Mark IV Female tanks, armed only with machine guns, were commanded by Lt Edward Hawthorne and Lt J. Webber.

The crews had endured an earlier gas attack. The Germans had been shelling the area with mustard gas and high-explosive shells since 3.45 a.m. in an attempt to dislodge the British and Australian troops that held the town. Traces of the poisonous gas still lingered inside the tanks and mixed with the exhaust fumes and heat coming from the engine. The crews' eyes were sore from the chemical attack, most had headaches from carbon monoxide poisoning and some were physically sick, yet they still battled on.

As the tanks approached the forward Allied trenches that ran between the town of Villers-Bretonneux and the village of Cachy they received information from a British soldier that German tanks had been spotted in the area. These trenches had been dug along the south-east side of the road known as the Cachy Switch, now called the D168.

Frank Mitchell, in command of the Male Mark IV tank, spotted the German A7V tank No. 561 called 'Nixe' about 500m away to the south-east, in front of a ridge. German troops were coming over the ridge crest behind it. There were two white Roman 'V' numerals painted on the front of the tank either side of the black and white cross. This indicated it was the fifth vehicle of the 2nd Sturm-Panzerkraftwagen Abteilung (tank battalion). The letters A7V are an abbreviation for Abteilung 7 Verkehrswesen, the military department tasked with development of the German Sturmpanzerwagen A7V tank.

After safely crossing the trenches and line of barbed wire Sgt J.R. McKenzie manning the right-hand 6-pounder gun of the British Mark IV Male fired the first shot while the tank was moving. It missed, landing behind the German tank. He fired a second shot but this one landed to the right of the enemy tank.

The British lead tank then came under heavy machine-gun fire, which caused bits of sharp metal fragments to tear away at high speed from the armour plate inside the tank and cut any exposed flesh. The driver continued straight ahead into the hail of bullets.

The British tank's outline merged with the dark trees of the Bois d'Aquennes woods that were behind the three tanks. In the mist, it was difficult for the lead Sturmpanzerwagen A7V tank commander to locate them, and this is why he did not return fire immediately. German Lt Wilhelm Blitz commanded the A7V No. 561 'Nixe' tank. Unusually, he wore civilian dress as there was no official tank crew uniform.

When he did spot them he ordered his driver to reverse in order to get to a better firing location. He ordered his gunner to fire at Mitchell's tank with his 57mm howitzer at a range of under 1km (0.6 mile). Believing he had knocked out that threat, he turned his attention to the two supporting Mark IV Female tanks.

His gunner was a good shot; he managed to score direct hits on both tanks. The German tank shells made large holes in the armour plate, leaving the British crews vulnerable to machine gun and small arms fire. They were not armed with a weapon that could knock out the A7V so both commanders decided to withdraw.

However, Mitchell's Mark IV had not been hit and he instructed his driver to use a dip in the landscape to better target the lead A7V 'Nixe' with the left-hand 6-pounder gun. The first shot landed 30m in front of the enemy tank and the second shot also missed.

The German tank commander did not realise that the Mark IV Male tank had not been knocked out and he closed the gap between the two vehicles as he advanced towards the road and the woods. However, the German infantry had no such illusions; they saw the British tank was still operational and moving forward. They maintained machine-gun fire on the tank and one of the tank Lewis Gun crew was seriously injured in both legs.

Mitchell ordered his driver to keep moving towards the enemy. Despite taking careful aim, the port gunner missed again and the shell landed in front of the A7V tank. Trying to score a direct hit while the tank was moving over rough ground was very difficult.

The British tank was turned and halted to enable McKenzie on the starboard gun to have another shot while the vehicle was stationary, but still the aim was off target. Finally, a British 6-pounder shell hit the A7V on its right front armoured plate near the 57mm gun. The German gunner was killed, two other crewmen mortally injured and three others injured. The explosion set off boxes of ammunition and hand grenades carried inside the tank. The crew abandoned the A7V fearing more hits from the Mark IV and they were fired upon by its machine guns.

Mitchell then spotted in the far distance two more A7V tanks, 'Siegfried' No. 525 and 'Schnuck' No. 504, driving towards the British trenches in front of the village of Cachy. He gave chase and fired at them at long range but the shells missed. He now turned his attention to the advancing German infantry in front of him that was threatening the British trenches. Mitchell ordered his machine-gunners to open fire and his 6-pounder gunners to use high-explosive shells to try and stop the attack.

German artillery then tried to knock out Mitchell's tank. This forced him to zigzag back towards the relative safety of the woods behind the Cachy Switch road. A German ground attack aircraft also tried to bomb the fleeing tank but its payload exploded in front of it without causing any damage.

Mitchell's tank then came under fire from accurate mortar shells. One damaged the tracks, causing the vehicle to turn in a circle before coming to a halt. The tank was now facing back towards the enemy so Mitchell ordered all the remaining 6-pounder high-explosive shells to be fired at the attacking German troops before the crew abandoned the disabled vehicle for the relative safety of a dugout.

On 24 April 1918 three British Mark IVs of the 1 Section, 'A' Company, 1st Battalion, 3rd Tank Brigade, were involved in the first tank-on-tank battle against German-built Sturmpanzerwagen A7V heavy tanks near the town of Villers-Bretonneux, south of the River Somme. This Mark V Male and A7V replica can be seen at The Tank Museum in Bovington.

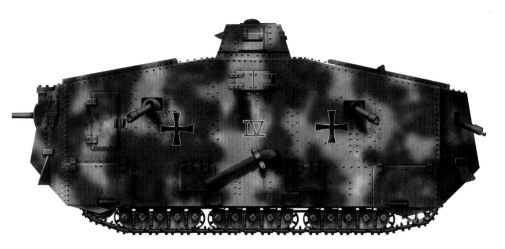

The German Sturmpanzerwagen A7V's quick-firing 57mm Maxim-Nordfeldt QF cannon could fire high-explosive and canister shot shells at soft-skinned vehicles, artillery field guns and troops. For armoured targets such as the Mark IV and Whippet tanks it could fire armour-piercing Panzerkampf shells. It was also armed with six machine guns.

Once the German crew of Sturmpanzerwagen A7V 'Nixe' felt they were safe they returned to their tank. The engines still worked so they drove back with their injured and dead comrades. However, after only a mile the engine ran out of oil and stopped working, so they had to make the rest of the journey on foot. Their tank was recovered later that evening.

2Lt Frank Mitchell was awarded the Military Cross. He survived the First World War and worked as a bank clerk after the war. German Lt Wilhelm Biltz also survived the war, winning the Iron Cross 1st Class. He returned to his position as a lecturer at the Clausthal University of Technology and later accepted the position of professor and Director of the Inorganic–Chemical Institute at the University of Hanover. He died in Heidelberg on 13 November 1943.

## WHIPPET'S FIRST TANK *v.* TANK BATTLE

Slightly later on the same morning, an RAF plane on a reconnaissance patrol spotted German troops moving towards the village of Cachy. He dropped a warning message to the British troops held in reserve behind the Cachy Switch trenches by the Bois l'Abbé woods north of the village of Cachy.

Two Sturmpanzerwagen A7V tanks of the 2nd Sturm-Panzerkraftwagen Abteilung (tank battalion) – 'Siegfried' II No. 525 commanded by Lt Friedrich-Wilhelm Bitter and 'Schnuck' No. 504 commanded by Lt Albert Müller – were driving towards the British trenches in front of the village of Cachy in support of the advancing infantry.

At around 12.20 p.m., seven British medium Mark A Whippets of 'X' Company, 3rd Battalion, 3rd Tank Brigade, armed only with 0.303 calibre Hotchkiss machine guns, moved towards the advancing German infantry, which they managed to halt and in some areas turn back.

The German infantry commander contacted Lt Bitter and directed him towards the Whippets; Lt Müller's tank was too far south at that stage.

Caught out in the open flat farmland with a German heavily armed tank aiming its 57mm gun at them, the Whippet tank commanders soon realised the perilous situation they were in. They had no weapon that could knock out the enemy tank, so tried to escape. The German A7V tank's quick-firing 57mm cannon could fire high-explosive and canister shot shells at soft-skinned vehicles, artillery field guns and troops. For armoured targets such as the Whippet tank it could fire armour-piercing Panzerkampf shells.

Lt Bitter's gunner's first shot missed 2Lt Harry Dale's Whippet No. A256 but his second shot at a range of 200m set it on fire. The German gunner then fired at 2Lt D.M. Robert's Whippet No. A255 at a longer range of around 700m. Again his first shot missed but he hit with his second shell, knocking it out of action.

However, the A7V's gun firing pin's striker springs then broke under stress and it no longer had a 57mm gun with which to fire at the enemy tanks. Unlike British Mark IV Male tanks that were armed with two cannon, one on each side in a sponson, German tanks only had one main gun.

Lt Bitter engaged a third British Medium A Whippet with machine guns. No. A244 was commanded by 2Lt George Richie. It was damaged and could not move, then further machine-gun fire hit either the fuel tanks or ammunition and set it on fire.

The four remaining Whippets started to withdraw from the battlefield towards the protection of the woods. As they went, they continually fired their machine guns at the German infantry. Lt Albert Müller's tank No. 504 'Schnuck' emerged through the mist near the village of Cachy and fired at the enemy tanks. 2Lt Thomas Oldham's Whippet No. A236 'Crawick' was knocked out and caught fire. The other three tanks, 'Crustacean' No. A286, 'Centaur III' No. A277 and 'Crossmichael' No. A233, made it back safely to British lines at 3.30 p.m.

One of the first medium Mark 'A' Whippets, No. A321. It saw action in March 1918.

A late production medium Mark 'A' Whippet, No. A259 'Caesar II', now in The Tank Museum in Bovington.

This Whippet is No. A347 'Firefly'. It is on display at the Royal Army and Military History Museum, in Brussels, Belgium. (Musée Royal de l'Armée et d'Histoire Militaire Bruxelles en Belgique).

The Whippets had done the job to which they were assigned; they had stopped the German infantry capturing the village of Cachy. The Germans were forced to dig trenches 500m–1km to the east of the British trenches and the village.

While the town of Villers-Bretonneux did fall to the Germans for an evening, the following morning was ANZAC Day and the Australian Infantry not only took the town but 1,000 prisoners with it. The German advance had been broken; the city of Amiens would never fall to the Germans.

# *BEUTEPANZERN*

The German Army only operated twenty A7V heavy tanks and it deployed more captured British tanks on the battlefield than German-built ones. They were known as *beute*-tanks or *Beutepanzern* – trophy tanks. As most of the captured tanks were British Mark IV heavy tanks they were also referred to as *schwerer-Kampfwagen* (*beute*).

By the beginning of summer 1918 the Germans had recovered a large number of abandoned Allied tanks. After the successes of the spring offensive in 1918 and the recapturing of most of the November 1917 Cambrai battlefield, more than 300 damaged tanks were now situated behind German lines.

The Bayerischer Armee-Kraftwagen-Park (BAKP 20, the Bavarian Army-Motor-Park) special recovery units went out on to the old battlefields with the objective of salvaging as many Allied tanks and parts as was possible and bringing them to their tank repair workshops in Monceau-sur-Sambre, Marchienne-au-Pont and Roux, all near Charleroi. It was here that the tanks were refurbished and prepared to fight for their new masters. This unit, commanded by Oberst Meyer, had been operational at this location since 12 November 1917 after it transferred from the Eastern Front following the Russian Revolution and the subsequent ceasefire. It was at full capacity by February 1917 and more than 100 captured tanks are known to have been repaired.

Apart from changes made to the weaponry of the captured tanks, very little was altered apart from a large escape hatch being fitted to the driver's cabin. This feature later appeared on the British-operated Mark V tank. (No British Mark V tanks were ever used as *Beutepanzern* during the war.)

The Germans had access to a supply of Belgian 5.7cm quick-firing Maxim Nordenfelt Model 1888 guns and ammunition. Supplies of British 6-pounder ammunition were very hard to obtain so the guns on the Male tanks were replaced. The 1888 could fire two types of rounds: a 2.7kg shell with a range of 2.7km and a grapeshot shell used by the Navy that could project 196 lead balls against infantry up to a range of 300m. The German Army called these guns 'Belg 5.7cm K'.

Grapeshot was recorded being fired at British infantry from a Belgian 5.7cm-armed Mark IV Male *Beutepanzer* belonging to Abteilung 16 as it joined a German counter-attack near Séranvillers on 8 October 1918. It avoided the British tanks and withdrew once it had used up all its ammunition. Its Lewis guns were damaged and five of the tank crew wounded.

It had been accompanied by two other machine gun-only Female tanks but they were both knocked out by 6-pounder shells and set on fire during a tank battle with two British Mark IV Males, L45 and L49, from 'C' Company, 12th Tank Battalion, Tank Corps.

On some vehicles Mauser 13mm *Tankgewehr* (anti-tank rifles) replaced machine guns. Produced after May 1918, the Mauser was a single shot bolt-action rifle that fired armour-piercing, hardened steel-cored, 13mm semi-rimmed cartridges. Each round had an initial velocity of 785m/s (2,580 ft/s) and could penetrate 22mm armour plate at 100m.

Each *Beutepanzer* appears to have had its own different camouflage pattern. There does not seem to be any standardisation, although some of them were painted very similarly to the German-built A7V tanks. This may have been because these tanks were also serviced at this location. Some of the workshops were based in Belgian railway facilities. It has been suggested that the paints used by Belgian railway engineers were commandeered by the Germans and used to paint the A7V tanks as well as the captured Allied tanks.

The colours used for the Belgian railway rolling stock were cream/ivory, red/brown and dark green. The Germans would have had access to their Army-standard *feldgrau* grey paint. A large German Army black cross, called a 'Bundeswehr Schwarzes Kreuz', which was a type of Christian cross with arms that narrowed in the centre and had a white border, was painted on the captured tanks to identify the fact they were under new management. The design of the German identification black cross changed in the second half of 1918 to the 'Balkenkreuz' (beam or bar cross). Some of the later repaired *Beutepanzern* had this newer cross design painted on their sides instead.

The British tanks in 1918 were now painted with large white-red-white strips on their sides and roofs so they could be distinguished from German-operated Mark IVs.

When a *Beutepanzer* suffered a mechanical breakdown or ditched on the battlefield they were very rarely recovered; after the weapons were removed the tank was abandoned and blown up. A newly repaired one from the Charleroi workshops was sent to the front to fill the gap in the *Abteilung* (battalion) allotted vehicle strength. As time went on and losses increased, BAKP 20 could not keep up with the demand for newly repaired captured tanks.

A small number of other captured Allied tanks were used by the Germans. Between ten and fifteen medium Mark A Whippets were captured but only two were repaired to operational condition and painted with Bundeswehr Schwarzes Kreuz crosses. One of them was sent to Abteilung 13 for the

German tank crews to use. Whippets that were beyond repair were still sent to the *Abteilungs* so they could inspect them and be familiar with the enemy's tanks. There are no records of a Whippet *Beutepanzer* being used in action during the war.

Most of the captured French tanks were used for evaluation and not operationally. There is a First World War photograph of a Renault FT, known as the *leichten Kampfwagen* FT-17 Renault 'Hargneuse III', parked next to a *Beutepanzer* Mark IV but there is no evidence to suggest it was used in action. There are lots of photographs of Renault FTs with black Balkenkreuz crosses on

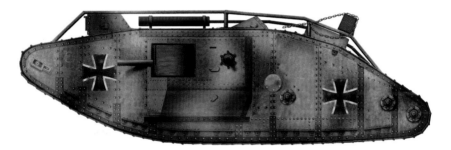

Captured British Mark IV Male *Beutepanzer*. The British 6-pounder gun was replaced with a Belgian 7.5cm Model 1905 gun that had a range of 8km. The tank was redesignated Panzer 107 'Ännchen'. It was abandoned by its German crew near Fort de la Pompeile on 1 June 1918.

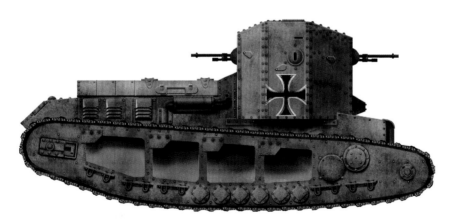

Captured *Beutepanzer* medium Mark A Whippet. Large German Army Bundeswehr Schwarzes Kreuz black crosses were painted on the captured tanks to identify the fact that they were under new management.

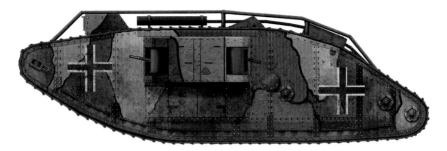

Captured Mark IV Female. The design of the German identification black cross changed in the second half of 1918 to the 'Balkenkreuz' (beam or bar cross). Some of the later repaired *Beutepanzern* had this newer cross design painted on their sides instead.

them but nearly all these were taken during the Second World War when they were used for internal security work in occupied countries.

There are a number of photographs of a working Saint-Chamond French tank under German control. It was called 'Petit Jean Pas Kamerad' ('No Mercy Little Jean') and it is believed to have been used just for evaluation. The same weapons used on the Mark IV *Beutepanzern*, the Belgian 5.7cm QF gun and the 13mm *Tankgewehr* (anti-tank rifle), were intended to be fitted to the tank but it is not known if they were mounted and tested as there are no documents or photographic evidence to prove this at present.

There is a photograph of a late production French-built Schneider CA.1 *Beutepanzer* that had been used in action against the US 1st Infantry Division and was then knocked out by artillery shells near Froissy on 20 July 1918. There are no documents or other evidence that shows the use of any more Schneider CA *Beutepanzern* by the German Army.

Mark IV *Beutepanzern* were involved in the last recorded battle of the First World War where German-controlled tanks were used on a battlefield. This occurred on 1 November 1918 near Sebourg. Five tanks were due to move off from the start line at the beginning of the counter-attack, but only three managed to advance with the infantry. Two were quickly knocked out by artillery shells. The third tank lagged so far behind the attacking soldiers that it never saw action.

# MARK IV *v.* MARK IV TANK BATTLES

On 8 October 1918, ten captured British Mark IV *Beutepanzern* were used by the Germans to counter-attack a British infantry advance, south of Cambrai. This is an important date as it was the third and last time that tanks fought tanks in the First World War. It was also the first time British Mark IV tanks fought captured Mark IV tanks.

According to battalion records dated 19 August 1918, 'A' Company, 12th Battalion, fielded seven tanks and three supply tanks: L6 Female No. 4510 'Lily' commanded by 2Lt J.S. Wright; L7 Female No. 8034 'Looter' commanded by 2Lt A.R. Martell; L8 Female 'Lukoie III' commanded by 2Lt N. Carmichael; L9 Male 'Lightning III' commanded by Lt F.R. Warsap; L11 Female tank No. 8021 'Liaison' commanded by 2Lt Graty; L12 Male No. 8103 'Lochiel' commanded by 2Lt C.B. de la Mare; and L16 Male 'Lion II' commanded by Capt. Roe. 'A' Company saw action on 8 October 1918.

The British were given orders to capture the enemy defensive positions running along the Cambrai–Esnes road up to the village of Niergnies as part of an encirclement of the city of Cambrai. The first objective was to take and hold an enemy trench system west of the village of Niergnies. The second was to capture the village, and the third was to take control of the road and the land as far east as the railway line.

The attack started at 4.30 a.m. in the dark. The tanks crossed the front line at 5 a.m. and by 6 a.m. the first objective, the trench system, had been secured with the assistance of Male L12 (and possibly L6).

The attack on the village of Niergnies was not so easy. At 6.40 a.m. severe enemy opposition was encountered near the cemetery and La Belle Etoile at the southern end of the village, but with the support of Male tanks L9 and L16 the village was in British hands by 8 a.m.

Female L7 was hit by artillery and knocked out near Ranger Wood: three crew members were killed. Its commander, 2Lt Martell, joined tank L6. Female L11 was immobile after its track broke and Female L8 was hit by a British smokescreen shell that damaged its track near the railway level crossing on the Rumilly to Cambrai road. The crew were captured but 2Lt N. Carmichael convinced his captors to surrender to him instead. They were given over to the custody of the infantry when they caught up with the tank.

The Germans sent four captured British Mark IV *Beutepanzern* of Abteilung 15 (15th Battalion) as part of the counter-attack in support of the infantry. At

8.30 a.m. they moved forward under the protective cover of a smokescreen laid down by German artillery shells. When the British tank commander saw the familiar rhomboid-shaped tanks emerge from the smokescreen he naturally believed that they were Allied tanks. He got a shock when they opened fire at close range.

Male L16 was the first to fire its 6-pounder gun at the leading German *Beutepanzer* No. 218, commanded by 2Lt Heuser. The shell hit the track but failed to immobilise the tank. The gun crew of the enemy tank then scored two direct hits, knocking out the British Mark IV L16. The crew bailed out but the tank commander Capt. Roe and two crewmen were wounded.

The captain joined the crew of tank L9. It had been hit and was partially on fire but still drivable. Both 6-pounder gun crews were injured. The tank headed towards the German tank No. 218 firing its Lewis machine guns but it was hit again and caught fire. The crew bailed out and the tank was blown up to prevent it being captured.

*Beutepanzer* No. 218 now turned its attention to British Mark IV Male L12. It was hit twice by 6-pounder shells and knocked out. Seven crew members were injured.

The Mark IV Female L6 came under fire from anti-tank rifles, which damaged three of the Lewis guns. At the same time it suffered a radiator defect and had to return to the lines for repair.

The L6 commander, 2Lt Martell, left his tank when it drove past a captured German field gun under the control of a British artillery officer. After he explained what had happened the gun was moved into position and fired at *Beutepanzer* No. 219 commanded by 2Lt Paul. The shell hit the fuel tank and put it out of action. *Beutepanzer* No. 218 was also hit but withdrew. British tank L54 attacked two *Beutepanzern* to the south of Niergnies and drove them off.

'B' Company, 12th Battalion tanks also took part in the battle around Cambrai on 8 October 1918. They encountered two enemy Mark IV *Beutepanzern* near the village of Esnes. The company was commanded by Maj. H.J. Inglis, who had seven tanks under his command. His orders were to support the New Zealand troops attacking the village of Lesdain and then move on to hold the Cambrai to Esnes road, the D960. Four tanks were to drive along the line of the Torrent d'Esnes valley while three others supported the troops crossing the farmland to the south.

'B' Company was operating further south on the attack front away from the tanks of 'A' Company and 'C' Company. The tanks moved off at 4.30 a.m., crossing the front line at 5 a.m. Three tanks were involved in the street battle inside the village of Lesdain while one headed towards the village of Esnes across open flat farmland.

By 8 a.m. the New Zealanders had reached their second objective and taken control of their section of the road that ran south of the village of Le Grand Pont, past the western edge of Briseux Wood and down to Hurtabise Farm.

The infantry further to the south had reached their section of the road at 10.30 a.m. They had needed the help of two of the three tanks assigned to them to deal with enemy machine-gun posts along the Beaurevoir line, Bel Aise Farm, Hurtebise Farm and Pelu Wood. One of the British tanks was hit and knocked out by an artillery shell at the start of the attack very early on in the morning, and four of the crew died. Later in the morning the second tank ran out of petrol and had to return to get refuelled. The third overheated and was also forced to go back.

The New Zealanders recommenced their attack at 9.30 a.m. and the village of Esnes was soon taken. German infantry then counter-attacked from the north-east of the village supported by two captured Mark IV tanks. The troops held their ground and the enemy tanks were driven off with the help of two 'C' Company tanks.

'C' Company, 12th Battalion tanks were commanded by Maj. D.H. Richardson MC. He had eight under his command and was ordered to support the troops attacking the central area around the village of Séranvillers-Forenville. 'A' Company tanks were to the north and 'B' Company's were to the south.

The tanks moved off at 4.30 a.m. in the dark but only seven crossed the front line at 5 a.m. as one had broken down. The villages of Séranvillers-Forenville, La Targette and Forneville Farm were attacked. 2Lt Ransley commanded one of the tanks supporting the British infantry during these attacks. His gun crew managed to silence a number of German machine guns in the villages and in a nearby wood before being hit four times by artillery shells and catching fire.

At 8.30 a.m. German infantry counter-attacked. They had the support of two captured Mark IV Female tanks that were armed only with machine guns. They belonged to the same tank battalion, Abteilung 15, that had attacked the tanks of 'A' Company further to the north.

These two *Beutepanzern* (trophy tanks) were given the numbers 134 and 138. A British Mark IV Female tank, L54, was commanded by 2Lt J.B. Walters. He spotted the danger and headed towards the enemy. During the firefight the German tanks' machine guns were damaged so they both withdrew. One of these German tanks was commanded by 2Lt Semmler. He reported later that his tank had been knocked out by high-explosive mortar shells; they had been fired by the 99th Light Trench Mortar Battery.

Two British Mark IV Male tanks, L45 commanded by 2Lt Clark and L49 commanded by 2Lt Sherratt, were positioned to the east of Séranvillers. They had reached the tree-lined Cambrai to Esnes road when they spotted two advancing German Mark IV Female *Beutepanzern* belonging to Abteilung 16. These enemy tanks, along with infantry, were moving from the north-east towards the village of Esnes, machine-gunning British soldiers in their path.

The two British tanks moved forward until they were about 300m away. They opened fire with their 6-pounder guns and hit their targets, setting them on fire. A third German Mark IV Female *Beutepanzer* commanded by 2Lt Hoffmann was not spotted by British tanks. It attacked British troops north of Séranvillers-Forenville but came under heavy machine-gun fire. Five of its eight-man crew were wounded and all its Lewis guns were put out of action, forcing it to withdraw.

On the same day, further to the south, around twenty Mark V tanks of the 301st Battalion, US Tank Corps, and sixteen Whippets, were in action supporting British and American troops in an attack north-east of the village of Joncourt, towards the village of Prémont. This was the second time American tank crews had seen action, although they did not encounter any enemy tanks.

Visibility was very good and smoke shells were fired at German positions to hinder them locating targets. By 11 a.m., with the help of the American tank crews, the enemy machine-gun nests in and around the village of Brancourt-le-Grand were put out of action. They reached their final objective by 2.15 p.m.

During the advance, tanks were targeted by German artillery and also bombed by enemy aircraft. Four were knocked out after receiving direct hits. Eleven tanks managed to reach their objectives. Eight of the Mark IVs suffered mechanical failure and, of these, three never got past the start point at Joncourt.

# THE BATTLE OF AMIENS

During the Battle of Amiens in the summer of 1918 a few British medium Mark A Whippets showed what devastation could be caused when tanks break through enemy lines and attack the rear. This was open, not trench, warfare.

After the breakthrough, battles took place over flat farmland with little cover. It was ideal tank country but it also meant that German field gun batteries could easily find their slow-moving targets. Only the use of the 'Combined Arms' tactics would work: artillery, cavalry, tanks, and ground attack aircraft of the RAF working together with the infantry to overcome the enemy defences.

The battle began on 8 August 1918 and is also known as the Third Battle of Picardy. It was the opening phase of the major Allied offensive that led to the end of the First World War, later known as the Hundred Days offensive.

Allied forces achieved a breakthrough in the German front-line defences and pushed forward 7 miles (11km) into enemy territory. This was the greatest Allied advance achieved so far in the war. In the Battle of Cambrai on 20 November 1917, Allied troops had only been able to advance 5 miles (8km). German Gen. Erich Ludendorff described the first day of the battle as 'the black day of the German Army'.

## BACKGROUND TO THE BATTLE

On 3 March 1918 the new Bolshevik government of Soviet Russia and the Central Powers (Germany, Austria–Hungary, Bulgaria and the Ottoman Empire) signed the peace treaty of Brest-Litovsk that ended Russia's participation in the First World War.

This released thousands of men, machines and weapons from the Eastern Front to the Western Front, and forty-two German divisions were sent west. For a temporary period the Germans had an advantage in manpower and materials over the Allies. They knew this would not last, as more boats full of American Army soldiers and equipment were landing in Europe each month. The German High Command knew it had to win the war soon.

They poured their new-found strength into breaking the Allies' front line and launched five main spring offensive attacks: 21 March–5 April, Operation Michael; 9–11 April, Operation Georgette; 27 May, Operation Blücher-York; 9 June, Operation Gneisenau; and 15–17 July, Operation Marne-Rheims.

These were mainly aimed at the positions of the British Expeditionary Force (BEF), which the Germans believed had been weakened from the 1917 battles of Arras, Messines, Passchendaele and Cambrai. A large bulge in the Allied lines appeared and German troops managed to advance 40 miles (65km).

All these attacks made advances but none resulted in the decisive breakthrough the German High Command was looking for. British reserve forces managed to halt the attack before the cities of Amiens and Arras. By the end of July German supplies were running short, lines of communication were stretched, troops were exhausted and their numbers were depleted.

Gen. Henry Rawlinson submitted a plan for a new major attack to British High Command. It was inspired by the success of the 4th Australian Division troops, supported by sixty tanks, attacking the enemy defences in front of the village of Hamel. This advance had resulted in 1,500 German soldiers being taken prisoner from their forward lines of defence.

Marshal Ferdinand Foch agreed that the attack be jointly mounted with the French First Army under the Command of French Gén. Debeney with the whole operation under the command of British Field Marshal Douglas Haig.

# THE PLAN

The Allied High Command wanted to regain lost ground suffered in the German spring offensive and straighten the front line. It wanted to drive the Germans away from the strategic Paris to the Avricourt railway line.

The British held the north section of the planned attack front. The Australian and Canadian infantry were in the middle and the French in the south. At the Battle of Cambrai the British had developed the ability to initiate a surprise armour-supported attack using advanced artillery 'map shooting' tactics. They did not have to bombard the enemy positions for thirty-six hours before the attack to 'soften them up' and alert them of a forthcoming offensive.

British artillery, using good maps and mathematics, could use indirect artillery fire to land smoke and high-explosive, surface contact-exploding HE shells on the enemy trenches at the same time as the tanks moved off from the start line. Prolonged bombardments and ranging shots were no longer required.

The British use of 'sound ranging', gun flash spotting and aerial photography meant that the German artillery batteries would also be targeted as soon as the battle started. Some 503 of the 530 German guns had been located before the attack started.

The French Army and artillery units were not as technologically advanced and they also lacked tank numbers. It was agreed that the French Army would launch its attack forty-five minutes after the British so as not to spoil the surprise.

A total of 580 tanks were going to be used in this attack, more than the total used in the mass tank attack at the Battle of Cambrai in 1917. Some of these were supply tanks. The British III Corps, 10th Tank Battalion, had thirty-six Mark V tanks.

The British Cavalry Corps, 3rd Tank Brigade, was comprised of two tank battalions. The 3rd and 6th Tank Battalions were allocated thirty-six Medium Mark A Whippets each. The 9th Tank Battalion was held in reserve to deal with counter-attacks. It had thirty-six Mark V tanks.

The Canadian Corps, 4th Tank Brigade, comprised four tank battalions. The 1st Tank Battalion fielded thirty-six of the new elongated Mark V* tanks. The 4th, 5th and 14th Tank Battalions each had thirty-six Mark V tanks. Unarmed supply tanks were used to bring ammunition forward under battlefield conditions.

The Australian Corps, 5th Tank Brigade, comprised four tank battalions. The 2nd, 8th and 13th Tank Battalion each had thirty-six Mark V tanks. The 15th Tank Battalion crewed thirty-six elongated Mark V* tanks.

The new elongated troop-carrying Mark V* tanks were used for this battle. Conditions were so bad inside the vehicle that the machine gun squad carried at the back was often too ill to fight due to the heat and the noxious fumes from the engines and guns.

The French Army lacked large numbers of heavy tanks with which to make a breach in the German defences. They used the lighter 6-ton Renault FT armed with either a Hotchkiss machine gun or a 37mm cannon to support the infantry advance after a heavy artillery bombardment.

The newly formed Royal Air Force was tasked with providing battlefield reconnaissance, fighter and bomber cover. It would also send out patrols to deny the enemy the use of observation balloons and aircraft.

In an effort to keep the attack secret, a detachment of two infantry battalions, a clearing station and a wireless unit were sent to the Ypres front as a bluff. The Allies mounted a number of small counter-offensives away from the Amiens area to make the Germans believe that the next major offensive was going to happen elsewhere.

The German Army had issued instructions on how troops were to deal with enemy tanks. This advice was based on knowledge gained at battles including

Cambrai in November 1917 where 77mm field guns had successfully knocked out many British tanks that were not supported by covering infantry.

Those same conditions were to be recreated if possible. The tanks were to be let through the German lines but the following infantry were to be engaged and held up. Field guns, trench mortars, clusters of bagged grenades, anti-tank rifles and machine guns were then to be let loose on each unsupported tank in the rear.

## THE BATTLE – DAY ONE

The Allies were blessed to have dense fog covering most of the battlefield early on the morning of 8 August 1918. The River Somme cut the attack front in half. The British began their attack north of the river with the Australians (plus the American troops of the 33rd Division) and Canadians to the south. The artillery opened fire at 4.20 a.m. as the tanks and troops left their start lines.

## THE BRITISH

One of the first objectives for the British was to reach the far side of Malard Wood and capture the riverside village of Sailly-Laurette. Unfortunately, the mist caused a few problems: although it hid the advancing troops and tanks from the Germans, it prevented the Mark V tanks from following the infantry closely and giving accurate covering fire.

British infantry fought their way into Sailly-Laurette on the banks of the Somme and had secured the village by 7 a.m. They then advanced towards the village of Chipilly. The eastern side of Marlard Wood was reached at 8 a.m.

British troops fighting to the south of the village of Morlancourt over the open featureless flat farmland in the far north of the battlefield ran into stiff opposition. The German troops at the front of the attack decided to counter-attack immediately rather than wait in their defensive trenches. Many soldiers on both sides were killed in close-quarter fighting in the mist. It was only after British reserve units were sent in that the attack moved forward. Those sent to capture Morlancourt had some initial success.

By 8.20 a.m. the mist had started to clear and this gave the German machine gun crews and riflemen easy targets on which to concentrate their fire over the open farmland. A lot of fighting happened around Gressaire Wood, to the south-east of Morlancourt, and grew along the northern valley side of the Somme. It was a second British attack objective.

In the afternoon the second attack was cut down by machine-gun fire from German defensive positions in the land above the village of Chipilly and in Gressaire Wood to the north-east.

More German reinforcements were rushed to the area and they launched a successful counter-attack, driving the forward line of British units back past the Chipilly–Morlancourt road. The British were continually under air and artillery attack and suffered many casualties.

# AUSTRALIAN TROOPS

The Australians quickly punched through the early morning mist and the German defences, taking control of the high ground south of the River Somme known as the Gailly Ridge and the village of Lamotte-Warfusée. The mist had started to clear, allowing the Australian tanks to keep up with the infantry without fear of inflicting friendly fire casualties on them. A German artillery battery positioned in the Vallée Jean Quart, north of Lamotte-Warfusée, was taken by surprise and overrun.

The Australian troops started to come under fire from the south. Germans positioned in the village of Marcelcave had seen the attack to the north of them and opened fire. Although this village had been assigned to the Canadians to attack, the Australians crossed into their sector and captured the village to stop the threat to their flank.

Australian tanks and infantry had some problems during their advance on the village of Cerisy on the south bank of the Somme. As the advanced troops walked over the crest of the valley ridge they were spotted by waiting German machine gun crews, who opened fire.

The following tanks of the Australian 8th Tank Battalion crossed the ridge and advanced downhill to attack the German machine guns. One tank suffered a mechanical breakdown and was immediately attacked, as the infantry had been forced to retreat behind the ridge line because of the murderous machine gun fire.

With the tanks now on their own, the Germans fired armour-piercing bullets at vulnerable points in their armour, such as vision ports, to make the crew take cover. They then managed to get close enough to the tanks to hurl modified hand grenades with extra explosive 'heads' at the tracks and roofs.

Two Australian tanks were set on fire and their crews captured by this method. A stalemate was avoided by the Australians managing to outflank the defenders to the north and also attacking them from the side while they were concentrating on the tanks coming over the valley ridge line to the west. At 9.20 a.m. the German commanding officer gave the order for his troops to retreat.

This episode was a good indication that the German 1918 tactic on how to deal with enemy tanks could work so long as the tanks were separated from their supporting infantry.

To the south of Cerisy, other Australian units captured thirteen German artillery batteries in the valleys south of Morecourt. One tank rolled over trying to get down the steep slopes of the Somme valley. The other tanks stopped and looked for a different route.

At 8.20 a.m. most of the mist had cleared and the Australian second attack wave was launched, supported by eighty-four tanks and twelve armoured cars. Artillery batteries moved forward and Whippet tanks of the 1st Cavalry Brigade advanced on the right flank.

In the absence of the traditional creeping artillery barrage, the tanks took on the role of finding and destroying German strongpoints with 6-pounder high-explosive shells and machine-gun fire. The RAF was used to create a smokescreen, using phosphorous bombs to help hide the advancing units.

South of the Roman road a number of tanks were knocked out by German artillery field guns, which had been pulled out of their gun emplacements and fired directly at the trundling tanks. To counter this new threat, the Australian infantry and a few tanks worked their way around the sides of these gun positions and captured them. The advance continued quickly over flat farmland towards the village of Bayonvillers, which was soon captured. The cavalry pushed on south-eastwards towards Harbonnières, attacking retreating German troops and their transport and supply vehicles.

The advancing infantry had temporarily lost their tank support but they were suddenly helped by the arrival of armoured cars using the Roman road, moving on towards the village of Foucaucourt. They fired their machine guns at German left flank positions as they passed. A message had been received by the field artillery, who also opened fire, thus allowing the infantry to advance along both sides of the Roman road and break up the defending Germans, who retreated under this combined attack.

The RAF had spotted a large German 28cm (11in) SL L/40 railway artillery gun north of the village of Harbonnières and attacked the train, putting it out of action. Cavalry of the 5th Dragoon Guards converged on the location and captured the gun. Australian infantry and tanks soon caught up with them as they pushed forward to the villages of Vauvillers, Framerville-Rainecourt and Rainecourt. This gun fired a 700kg shell to a range of 18.64 miles (30km) and posed a major threat to the important Amiens rail junction. After the war it was taken as a trophy to Australia, where it can be seen today at the Australian War Memorial in Canberra.

Armoured cars drove deep into the rear areas of the German defences, machine-gunning any targets they saw in Framerville, Proyart and Chuignolles. One squadron had to turn around after they came under fire from field guns just outside Foucaucourt when their advance was halted by a traffic jam of retreating German transport vehicles.

Cavalry and Whippet tanks around the village of Guillaucourt pushed the defending Germans back. German reserve units started to arrive and using machine guns and trench mortars they knocked out a number of tanks east of the village of Harbonnières, forcing the infantry and surviving tanks back into the village. The terrain was flat and without cover, so they could easily observe the fall of their mortar shells and make the necessary adjustments to hit their intended target.

The Germans took up a defensive position in and between the villages of Vauvillers, Framerville-Rainecourt, Proyart and Méricourt-sur-Somme.

## CANADIAN TROOPS

The terrain the Canadians fought over was more undulating and wooded than the flat, open, northern farmland the British and Australians were marching across. This was because the small river La Luce meandered west to east along their line of attack.

Initially the mist and boggy soft ground near the river caused problems for the Canadian tank commanders, who were co-ordinating their attacks with the supporting infantry. There was heavy fighting around the woodland near the village of Hangard but the armoured breakthrough occurred further east at the village of Démuin at around 7.30 a.m.

The Canadian 4th Tank Division tanks engaged with all the Germans in their path, causing many to retreat. Some of the defenders followed orders and let the tanks go by as they took cover. After the tanks had gone they attacked the following infantry, who now did not have tank support.

By 11.30 a.m. the Canadians had captured the village of Cayeux-en-Santerre. To the north, 14th Battalion tanks were used in an outflanking manoeuvre. They attacked the artillery gun batteries west of Wiencourt-l'Equipée from the south while the infantry successfully fought the Germans who occupied the small hill east of the nearby village of Guillaucourt.

With the help of the cavalry and sixteen 3rd Tank Battalion Whippets, the village of Beaucourt-en-Santerre was captured by the Canadian infantry and around 300 prisoners were taken. They came under heavy machine-gun fire as they pushed further east towards Beaucourt Woods.

Slightly to the south, concealed German field guns opened fire at ten advancing 'A' Company tanks as they approached the village of Le Quesnel. Nine were knocked out by enemy fire. The countryside was flat and the gun teams had good vision of the approaching slow-moving tanks, for whom there was no cover.

Cayeaux Woods to the north-east were rushed by other Canadian troops. A German artillery battery, a number of enemy troops, and machine guns were seized. At 1 p.m. the move forward recommenced. By 4.30 p.m., exhausted by hard fighting, the Canadians halted their attack on the high ground ridge line and the road that runs between the villages of Caix and Le Quesnel.

# FRENCH TROOPS

The French Army units began their attack at 5.05 a.m., forty-five minutes after the rest so as not to spoil the element of surprise. The German defensive trench system in the Moreuil Wood along the River L'Avre valley was soon breached following the 45-minute artillery bombardment. By 7 a.m. French troops were on the eastern edge of the wood.

A further artillery barrage, 300m in front of the new French line, commenced while the troops paused. At 7.43 a.m. the attack restarted as soon as the shelling stopped. The town of Moreuil was enveloped and later captured. At a 600m-wide section of the river, German machine-gun fire from the Bois de Genonville woods and Genonville Farm inflicted a lot of casualties on the attacking troops. French troops had captured the Bois de Genonville and the Bois de Touffu woods by 9.30 a.m.

Further south along the river valley, smoke shells were fired at the defenders' position on the opposite banks of the L'Avre River to screen advancing units. This tactic was more successful. Two crossing points and the immediate high ground were soon captured.

The French infantry and tanks advanced east over the flat open farmland and attacked the German-held village of Villers-aux-Erables. There was little cover. The mist had cleared and the enemy opened fire from the village and the Bois du Dé woods 400m to the south and the village of Mézières-en-Santerre to the east. At around 10.30 a.m. they moved north to try and outflank both villages.

French African colonial troops had problems removing the Germans from around the area of Genonville Farm Hill, which overlooked the river L'Arve valley. It was only when the Germans' line of escape eastwards, back to the village Le Plessier-Rozainvillers, was in danger of being cut by other French troops that the order was given to withdraw. At 11.40 p.m. the Genonville hill and farm were captured. The African troops then attacked the enemy positions in the Bois de Genonville woods, finally securing it and Hill 95 at 3 p.m.

Other French troops captured the village of La Neuville-Sire-Bernard and advanced towards the village of Le Plessier-Rozainvillers. The village of Mézières-en-Santerre and the Bois du Dé woods were finally captured by the French in the afternoon.

At 6.30 p.m. the French attacked the village of Fresnoy-en-Chaussée and pushed the defensive German line based along the Mézières-en-Santerre to Hangest-en-Santerre road backwards. An artillery barrage was fired at the village and also at enemy troops in Petit Bois woods to the south-west of the village. Tanks and infantry struck at the north-west and southern edges of the village and the defensive positions. After fierce house-to-house fighting, by 10.30 p.m. the French 31st Corps had secured Fresnoy-en-Chaussée and pushed the Germans 300–500m to the east. The French had fought their way 5 miles (8 km) into German-held territory.

# DAY TWO

On 9 August 1918 the front line had now outrun the range of some of the supporting artillery batteries. The number of tanks available for battle had been seriously reduced due to breakdowns, ditching in deep shell holes and trenches, plus enemy artillery. Congested roads hindered the reinforcement units' ability to push through and continue the advance.

## THE BRITISH – DAY TWO

British III Corps troops were ordered to launch assaults towards Etinehem but first they would have to capture Gressaire Wood on the steep north-western side of the Somme valley and the Chipilly Spur. The American 131st Regiment took part in the assault on Gressaire Wood but both assaults on these locations were held up for many hours by accurate German machine-gun fire. It was only with the help of the Australians attacking from the rear of the village and the use of a smokescreen that the enemy resistance in the Chipilly Spur was finally overcome at 8 p.m. The enemy withdrew from Gressaire Wood as it got dark and the American troops dug in for the night.

Morlancourt was not in British hands. Unfortunately a tank moved forward fifteen minutes before the attack was due to start and was knocked out by a German field gun. This alerted all the German defenders and the British had to rush the open countryside under heavy machine gun and mortar fire. They eventually managed to get around the eastern side of the village and capture the village.

## AUSTRALIAN TROOPS – DAY TWO

The Australian troops were ordered to launch assaults towards Lihons. They started their attack from Harbonnières towards the village of Vauvillers. A single German field gun, positioned in the village, opened fire on the advancing tanks and troops and knocked out a few of the tanks. The Australians retaliated by firing trench mortars at its position and put it out of action. RAF ground attack aircraft helped the infantry and tanks assault the defenders.

The Germans still commanded the steep, wooded ridge of Chipilly Spur, enabling them to fire on the advancing Australians. A small party of Australian infantry swam across the river and captured the village of Chipilly, neutralising that threat.

Australian infantry moved out of the village of Bayonvillers and headed east across the farmers' fields in the direction of Herleville with a view to joining in the attack on Lihons from the north-west. They got as far as capturing the village of Framerville-Rainecourt before they met stiff resistance from German reinforcements.

At 1.45 p.m. seven tanks moved off to support the infantry attack that had started in Vauvillers and headed south-east towards the village of Lihons. Thanks to good visibility, German artillery guns near Lihons quickly targeted the slow-moving tanks and knocked out five of them. The infantry used the old 1917 trench systems to advance under cover towards enemy positions.

Just outside the village was an old trench system, behind and either side of Crépey Wood. German reinforcement units were arriving on the battlefield in strength and they occupied this position. The Australians attacked with thirteen Mark V★ tanks and two infantry brigades.

## CANADIAN TROOPS – DAY TWO

The Canadian troops were ordered to launch assaults towards the Roye–Hattencourt–Hallu road. At 4.30 a.m. the Canadians started their advance by attacking the village of Le Quesnel, which was taken after an hour of fierce resistance. The Germans fought hard while retreating through the woods and trench systems to the east of the village.

The German reinforcements had marched through the night on orders to set up defensive locations between Arvillers and Saulchoy-sur-Davenescourt, situated on the slightly higher ground running between the two villages and between the villages of Folies and Bouchoir, so utilising the existing trench system that linked the two villages.

Fourteen Mark V tanks and seven Whippets were used to attack the villages of Vrély and Warvillers from 1 p.m. The ground was flat farmland with very little cover and casualties were high. The Germans fired at the attackers from dug-in locations in the woodland called Hatchet Wood between the two villages. After heavy fighting, the wood and the two villages were in Canadian hands by 4.30 p.m.

Slightly south, seven Whippets were used to support the Canadian troops attacking the villages of Beaufort-en-Santerre and Rouvroy-en-Santerre, again over flat farmland. The village of Beaufort-en-Santerre fell first and its defenders retreated eastwards to bolster the numbers of defenders at Rouvroy-en-Santerre. That village was only captured at 9.20 p.m.

At 9.15 a.m. seven tanks were ordered to support an infantry attack on the village of Folies to the south-west of Rouvroy-en-Santerre. That village was captured at 4.15 p.m. The attack on the village of Bouchoir to the south met stiffer resistance but it was in Canadian hands by 5 p.m.

The Canadian forces that had fought along the La Luce valley to the north of La Quesnel on the previous day then attacked the village of Rosières-en-Santerre. They had the support of five Mark V tanks, ground attack aircraft and trench mortars. After the forward defences were dealt with, the Canadians moved into the village streets at around 1.30 p.m. It took a long time to clear each road and house of enemy soldiers but by 4.30 p.m. the Canadians had finally captured the village.

While the street-to-street fighting was going on in Rosières-en-Santerre, other Canadian troops were crossing the open farmland to the south of the village heading towards the village of Méharicourt. They were supported by fourteen tanks of 14th Tank Battalion, who actively hunted German machine-gun posts. At 5.30 p.m. the Canadians had passed the village and started to dig defensive trenches.

## FRENCH TROOPS – DAY TWO

More troops crossed the river L'Avre, this time at La Neuville-Sire-Bernard, and advanced east. The village of Hangest-en-Santere was in French hands by 10.20 a.m. but a further advance towards the next village, Arvillers, was held up by a strong German counter-attack. This was stopped and defeated and French troops finally moved forward and captured Arvillers at 5.45 p.m.

Troops that crossed the river L'Avre at Braches forked right and headed towards the town of Davenescourt around the Bois St Hubert wood. French troops, slightly south down the river valley, had problems crossing the marshy lowland near Hargicourt and Pierrepont-sur-Avre. However, as it got dark they had reached the outskirts of the Davenescourt.

The French opened a new attack front late in the afternoon, around the town of Montdidier and the village of Assainvillers in the south, with orders to advance towards the town of Roye. Assainvillers was reported captured by 6.05 p.m. The advance moved forward but had to stop as it got dark.

The French often call the Battle of Amiens the Battle of Montdidier.

# DAY THREE

On 10 August 1918 only thirty-eight heavy tanks were fit for duty.

## THE BRITISH – DAY THREE

The British consolidated their positions as more German reinforcements arrived.

## AUSTRALIAN TROOPS – DAY THREE

The Australians' orders for 10 August were to recommence their attack eastwards towards the village of Lihons. Unfortunately no tanks were available for this initial assault and the 7.45 a.m. artillery barrage landed behind the front row of enemy defences. As the Australians advanced at 8 a.m. they were met with machine gun and rifle fire, and the attack floundered.

The Germans launched a counter-attack that the Australians managed to fight off. They held the ground they had captured, dug in and stayed there overnight, having failed to capture Lihons.

At 7 p.m. other Australian units crossed the River Somme and marched north through the village of Chipilly and Gressaire Wood to be ready for a night assault, then south, into the Etinehem spur through Tailles Wood and east towards the town of Bray-sur-Somme. The attack started at 10 p.m.

The Corbie to Bray-sur-Somme road was chosen as the line of attack in assisting night time navigation. The infantry, marching in three columns, were led by three tanks of the 8th Tank Battalion. They were spotted by a German bomber, which dropped its load of bombs. This was followed by a hail of machine-gun fire from the defending German infantry just outside the village of Bray-sur-Somme. They were using armour-piercing bullets and these started to cause casualties inside the tanks.

The advance was halted as the troops took cover. German artillery sent high-explosive and gas shells over the top of the column and caused casualties at the rear. At 3.30 a.m. the order was to withdraw.

The Australian night attack down the Etinehem spur was much more successful. It was led by two tanks of the 2nd Tank Battalion, which were able to deal with enemy machine gun positions and generally cause fear in the defenders. The Germans withdrew south across the River Somme so as not to be cut off. At 11.59 p.m. the Australian troops dug in for the night east of the village of Etinehem.

At 5.30 p.m. the Germans started a counter-attack at Crépey Wood but this was repulsed.

## CANADIAN TROOPS – DAY THREE

Canadian Corps orders for 10 August were to continue the attack eastwards towards the railway line that linked Chaulnes with Roye. At 4.20 a.m. Canadians attacked the small village of Le-Quesnoy-en-Santerre with the help of four tanks from the 5th Tank Battalion. All the tanks were knocked out but the village was taken.

As the Canadians moved on towards the village of Parvillers-le-Quesnoy they were reinforced by more troops and twenty tanks of the 4th and 5th Tank Battalions. This landscape was riddled with old defensive trench systems. The defending Germans used them with skill to hide while spraying the attacking force with deadly machine-gun fire.

The Canadians were stopped about 500m west of the village near Square Wood. Four of the tanks had been knocked out by field guns. The Germans counter-attacked at 1.30 p.m. but were repulsed. The Canadians dug in. Four more tanks arrived at 2 p.m. to help defend their current position.

Troops to the north, attacking the village of Fouquescourt, found themselves in a similar position. The German defenders were making use of the old trench system just west of the village and this made attacking difficult and slow. This attack also stalled 500m to the west of the village on the old British front-line trenches. The advance was halted at 3 p.m. With the arrival of more troops the Canadians infiltrated the old trench system and eventually pushed their way into Fouquescourt by 6 p.m. They then continued the advance towards the Chaulnes–Roye railway line.

Further north the Canadians had better luck and by 1.30 p.m. had captured the villages of Maucourt and Chilly. They pushed on towards the next village, Hallu, but this is where they encountered the same old trench system. After a short fight the village was captured by 2 p.m.

The Canadian attack on the village of Lihons to the extreme north of their battlefront was halted just outside by heavy machine-gun fire.

Seven Whippets of the 6th Tank Battalion were knocked out during an attack over farmland between the villages of Rouvroy-en-Santerre and

Parvillers-Le-Quesnoy. The cavalry were ordered to take the village of Nesle and the high ground above the town of Roye. They managed to take the village of Andechy but could not reach either of their objectives because of heavy machine-gun fire. The Canadians dug in for the night just west of the village of Damery.

## FRENCH TROOPS – DAY THREE

New French troops were available for deployment on 10 August 1918. At 4.20 a.m. the French launched an attack south-east of Montdidier. At 4.30 a.m., further north-east, other French troops recommenced their attacks towards the town of Roye.

By 10 a.m. the town of Montdidier had been captured. These troops pushed further east and captured the village of Faverolles and Etelfay. They continued east, crossing flat farmland until they encountered heavy resistance just west of the village of Grivillers.

Other troops moved north to attack the village of Tilloloy but encountered German infantry using the old 1916 defensive trench systems and the attack was halted.

The French joined up with the Canadian cavalry, which had captured Andechy and moved on towards Villers-lès-Roye, the last village before the town of Roye. At 3 p.m. this attack was halted by heavy machine-gun fire from 'Z' Wood.

The villages of Saulchoy-sur-Davenescourt, Warsy, Guerbigny and Marquivillers were captured but these troops halted for the night just before the villages of L'Echelle-saint-Aurin and Armancourt.

## DAY FOUR

This day, 11 August 1918, was mainly about holding the new battlefield line. The German spring offensive bulge had been straightened. Local attacks still went on but there were no more major advances.

## THE BRITISH – DAY FOUR

The British held their positions north of the River Somme along a line that ran north-west, just in front of the town Bray-sur-Somme.

## AUSTRALIAN TROOPS – DAY FOUR

At 4 a.m. the Australian Corps attacked north and south of Lihons. Only six tanks were available to support the operation but the artillery provided a heavy creeping barrage. The thick morning mist had returned and this hindered the German defenders when looking for targets.

This battle was being fought over the old 1916 trenches. To the north of Lihons the Germans counter-attacked at 8.45 a.m. as the mist lifted. They were attacked by machine guns, which halted their advance along the Lihons to Framerville road. At 9.30 a.m., to the south of the village, another counter-attack was instigated but this was halted by heavy artillery bombardment along the Lihons to Chilly road. The Germans tried again at 1 p.m. and later at 4.30 p.m. but each time their attack was repulsed.

Further attacks were made along the Roman road just north of Framerville-Rainecourt. No tanks were available. The troops were under constant machine gun and sniper fire in the open countryside. They dug in and consolidated their position after the mist lifted.

At 8.30 p.m., under the cover of an artillery barrage, Australians moved north to seal off the Méricourt-sur-Somme spur of land on the southern side of the River Somme. The Germans had already started to withdraw from this exposed position but 300 prisoners were taken before everyone could be evacuated.

The Australians north of the river in the Etinehem Spur found in the morning that their positions were exposed and they suffered casualties from enemy gunfire. Reinforcements could be seen moving into the town of Bray-sur-Somme and the Australians spent the day at this location preparing for a German counter-attack that never materialised.

## CANADIAN TROOPS – DAY FOUR

At 4.20 a.m. the Canadian and French troops were ordered to recommence their attacks, but because of the problems of getting the surviving tanks into position, the Canadian advance did not happen until 9.30 a.m. The French started their attack at 4.20 a.m.

Attacks were started in order to capture the villages of Damery and Parvillers-le-Quesnoy, north-west of the town of Roye. The troops were supported by sixteen tanks. The preceding artillery barrage landed too far ahead of the main attack; instead of being 300m in front it was 500m and this gave the German defenders sheltering in the old 1916 trenches time to recover and fire at the advancing Canadians.

The Germans managed to knock out twelve of the sixteen tanks. Although two tanks managed to enter the village of Damery they did so without infantry support because they were pinned down taking cover in the fields and trenches to the west of the town by murderous machine gun and sniper fire. Tanks cannot capture settlements without the backing of infantry. The Canadians could not winkle out the Germans in the old trenches in front of Parvillers-le-Quesnoy and the advance was halted.

To the north, at 10.30 a.m., the Germans launched a counter-attack to recapture the villages of Hallu and Chilly. It was preceded by a heavy artillery barrage. By 1 p.m. they had pushed the Canadians out of Hallu but could not capture Chilly.

## FRENCH TROOPS – DAY FOUR

By 11 August 1918 many of the French troops were exhausted. At 4.30 a.m. French troops recommenced their attack towards the town of Roye but a German counter-attack at Villers-lès-Roye halted the advance. At 11 a.m., to the south, the village of Armancourt was captured but the attempt to seize the village of Dancourt-Popincourt failed. Further south, French troops used the old 1916 trenches to edge nearer to Tilloloy but failed to capture the village.

The most gains in land were to the north and south of the village of Gury. French troops captured Canny-sur-Matz and Gury, and flushed out the German defensive positions around the villages of Mareuil-la-Motte and Elincourt-Sainte-Marguerite.

At 10 p.m. Field Marshal Haig and Marshal Foch agreed to halt operations on the Amiens front.

## CONCLUSION

The British III Corps had fewer tanks than the Australian and Canadian units and the British advance was not as dramatic as that of the tank-supported French, Australian and Canadian forces, which managed to penetrate further into German-held territory. The message was clear: to succeed, the infantry needed the help of massed tanks in a combined arms operation along with closely co-ordinated support of the artillery and air force.

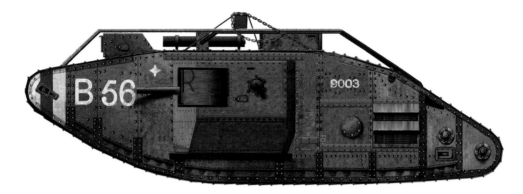

Mark V Male No. 9003 B56 was part of 'C' Company, 2nd Battalion. On 8 August 1918 it saw action when it attacked the enemy defensive lines and reached the Blue Line objective before returning to Allied lines. It was photographed several times as it moved forward from La Motte-en-Santerre. It carried a flag indicating that it may have been used as a command tank. It was back in action on 9 August 1918 but as it attacked it was hit and set on fire. Two of the tank crew were killed instantly; four were wounded but one of them died later of his wounds. The tank was recovered and repaired. On 2 June 1920 it was used by the Russian White Army, 1st Tank Detachment, 1st Tank Division. On 1 January 1921 it was captured by the Russian Red Army.

Tank No. 9376 was a Composite Mark V armed with a 6-pounder gun and a machine gun in its right sponson, and two machine guns in its left. It was given the unit identification number J19 when it was part of 'B' Company, 10th Battalion, Tank Corps. On 8 August 1918, under the command of 2Lt G.A. Price, it attacked and engaged the enemy. It was damaged and had to return to British lines for repairs. On 9 August 1918 it was photographed with other tanks in a field, all covered with straw in an attempt to conceal them from observation by enemy aircraft. It took part in more action on 10 and 23 August 1918 under the same tank commander. On 2 September 1918 it was handed over to the US 301st Battalion. On 29 September 1918, under the command of Lt Vernon, it advanced towards the German lines but ditched in a trench before it got to their defensive Hindenburg Line fortifications.

'Newry' was a Mark V Male No. 9192, believed to have been part of the British tank force that supported the Australian attack east of Amiens between August and September 1918. On 9 August 1918 it was commanded by Sgt Wildman, 14th battalion, 'C' Company. It broke down after crossing the enemy trenches between the first and second objective. It managed to get back to Allied lines and was later sent to Russia.

On 10 August 1918 Female Mark V No. 9260 A6 was photographed during the King's visit to Sautercourt, when it took part in infantry and tank co-operation exercises. It displayed the hand-painted identification number A6 on its sponson. It was fitted with an unditching beam and rails. On 2 September 1918, under the command of 2Lt Lockwood, as part of the 14th Battalion, Tank Corps, it went into battle. It reached and passed the first objective but was hit and burnt out just prior to the second.

German morale was at a low point: just under 30,000 prisoners had been taken during the Battle of Amiens. Foch continued the pressure on the German Army with many minor attacks that became known as the '100-Day Campaign'.

The British launched the Battle of Albert on 21 August 1918, resulting in the recapturing of Bapaume. An attack at Arras started a few days later, on 26 August. In September co-ordinated attacks along the length of the front line resulted in the clearing of the St–Mihiel and Ypres salients and the breach of the Hindenburg Line.

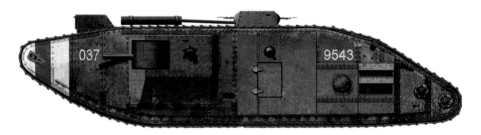

This Mark V* took part in the Battle of Amiens on 8 August 1918, serving in 'B' Company, 15th Battalion, under the command of Lt R.P. Foster. It was photographed in the tank park outside the village of Villers-Bretonneux on 28 June 1919 with the letters HQ painted on the sponson hatch. It was not fitted with the unditching rail and beam. During the battle it crossed no-man's-land but broke down before reaching the Green Line objective. It was repaired and continued the attack reaching all three objectives. It was hit but rallied and returned to Allied lines.

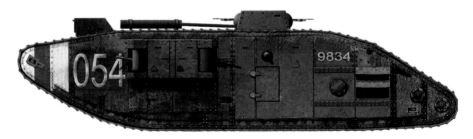

This Mark V* Female No. 9834 called 'Orient Unit number 054 was attached to 15th Battalion, 'C' Company, commanded by 2Lt H. Ayres. It did not have an unditching beam or rail fitted. During the Australian advance near the River Somme in 1918 it was photographed returning to Allied lines behind three other Mark V* tanks, two of which were being towed. Battle reports showed that it had passed the first objective and attacked the third objective from the Red Line second objective. This tank managed to fight its way to the final third objective and returned back to Allied lines.

# AMERICAN TANK BATTLES

American tank crews first trained on the French Renault FT-17 tank in the US. Some volunteered or were assigned to man the British Mark V. This heavy tank training was held at Warham, Norfolk, and Bovington, Dorset.

On 24 August 1918 the men and vehicles of the 301st Battalion, US Tank Corps, docked at Le Havre, France. Around forty-six British-built Mark V and Mark V★ tanks had been loaded on the ship.

The American heavy tank crews were involved in four battles before the First World War ended. The first involved crossing the Hindenburg Line near Le Catelet and Saint-Quentin on 29 September 1918 and the others were on 8, 17 and 23 October 1918.

## 29 SEPTEMBER 1918

The US 301st Battalion had forty tanks in an operational condition in September 1918. They were split into three companies: 'A', 'B' and 'C' Companies.

There were fifteen tanks in 'A' Company: nine Mark V★ Males, two Mark V★ Females and four Mark V Composites.

'B' Company had sixteen tanks: seven Mark V★ Males, two Mark V★ Females, three Mark V Males, one Mark V Female and three Mark V Composites.

'C' Company had sixteen tanks: seven Mark V Males and nine Mark V Composites.

A Composite tank had two machine guns in a side sponson on one side of the vehicle and on the other it had one 6-pounder gun and one machine gun; it was a merger of a Mark V Male and Female and is sometimes called the 'Hermaphrodite' Tank.

Eight supply tanks were also used to transport ammunition and fuel cans. A wireless radio tank was also deployed on the battlefield.

Orders were received that the 301st Battalion was to attack in the area around the villages of Bony and Le Catelet, 20km south of Cambrai. The Hindenburg Line ran north and south of the village of Bony and a second trench system ran south of Le Catelet called the Le Catelet–Nauroy Line.

The tanks were to follow a creeping artillery barrage, one section of five tanks per infantry battalion. Four tanks would be in line with one following behind in reserve ready to take the place of a knocked-out or broken-down vehicle.

They were to go about 100yd ahead of the infantry to clear wire obstacles and destroy the German machine-gun nests and artillery emplacements.

Up until 8 a.m. a smokescreen had effectively hidden the advancing units from the enemy but then the wind died down. The whole battlefield still had a covering of early morning mist, which lasted until 10.50 a.m. The mist caused some navigation problems and some infantry units lost contact with the tanks that were assigned to them.

Two 'A' Company tanks were knocked out when they drove into an old British minefield that had been put down in March 1918 but was not shown on the maps given to the tank commanders.

Three tanks suffered mechanical problems and broke down after crossing the front line, while some became ditched when they fell into old trenches or down the sides of sunken roads. Some were able to get out but a few were stuck and had to be abandoned.

All the tanks came under artillery and machine-gun fire and were shot at by German anti-tank field guns and rifles firing armour-piercing bullets. A number of tank crew were killed and many were injured.

Five of the 'A' Company tanks were hit and two of them were knocked out, one of which caught fire. One of these tanks was No. 9591, which was hit as it drove between the British front line and the starting point. It was recovered and later shipped back to America. It is the only surviving example of a Mark V★ Male tank and is currently kept at the National Armor and Cavalry Restoration Center.

'B' Company tanks had four vehicles break down with mechanical problems. Five tanks were hit by shells; three of these were knocked out.

Three 'C' Company tanks failed to reach the start line in time. One was hit by a shell and had to be abandoned; the two other tanks ditched in trenches. Out of the twelve tanks that crossed the start line, four ditched, three broke down and five were hit and knocked out. One of the five tanks was knocked out just after crossing the start line. Two were hit before they reached the trenches of the Hindenburg Line. The remaining two tanks managed to cross the line but one was hit near the canal tunnel and the other as it returned back to Allied lines.

'C' Company tanks were 1,000yd in front of the regiment, not the agreed 100yd. They came under fire from German guns and were caught in heavy smoke and mist. The visibility got so bad that a few tank commanders dismounted from their tanks and walked in front of them, in the dark, through the muddy abandoned trenches, lines of barbed-wire entanglements and shell holes to guide their tanks.

The 301st Battalion lost three officers and seventeen enlisted men. Fifteen officers and seventy enlisted men were wounded, and seven enlisted men were missing. Although some of the American tanks managed to get through the Hindenburg Line, the final objective, getting past the second trench system Le Catelet–Nauroy Line, was not achieved.

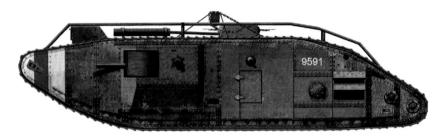

Male Mark V* tanks were armed with two 6-pounder guns and four 0.303in (7.62mm) Hotchkiss air-cooled machine guns. An additional machine gun position had been put in the rear. The Mark V had an improved engine and gearbox, which meant one man could drive and change gears without the help of other crew members. Some had unditching rails and beams fitted. It was issued to the American Expeditionary Force, 'A' Company, 301st Battalion. It saw its only American combat action against the Hindenburg Line, 26 September 1918, where it was knocked out with a single artillery round that pierced the frontal armour of the right sponson. The resulting shattering of the round threw large pieces of shrapnel into the engine. It was repaired, but too late to see further action before the war ended. It was shipped back to America and is currently at the National Cavalry and Armor Museum, Fort Benning, Georgia, where it is painted brown.

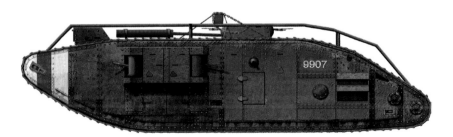

Female Mark V* tank 9907 in service with the US Army and shipped to Camp Mead in the USA to be used as a training tank. It had an unditching rail and beam fitted.

# TANK BANKS

Six tanks were used to raise money for the war effort. They toured the towns and cities of Great Britain from November 1917 until the end of the war to encourage people to buy government war bonds and war savings certificates.

These six Mark IV tanks all had names. They were: No. 113 'Julian'; No. 119 'Old Bill'; No. 130 'Nelson'; No. 137 'Drake'; No. 141 'Egbert' and No. 142 'Iron Ration'. They were called tank banks because the large hatch at the back of the sponson would be opened and used to sell the bonds and certificates. A bank clerk, and in some cases a celebrity, would sit inside the tank and people would queue up by the door to make their transaction.

Posters would be printed and displayed in prominent places a few weeks before a tank's arrival in the city. In some locations they would stay for five days. 'Tanking Hours' would be listed on the poster and within these times the soldiers would let members of the public look inside the vehicle. Demonstrations would be staged so the public could see and hear the tanks drive over temporarily constructed obstacles such as mounds of old brick and rubble.

Banners would be left on the tanks overnight. Some read, 'The Bonds bought here buy bombs and guns and build more tanks to beat the Huns.' Each city and town was given a fundraising target; the amount of money raised was reported in the newspapers. It became quite competitive as one city tried to raise more money that its nearest rival.

Local civic dignitaries, members of parliament and Army officers would stand on top of the tanks and address the crowd to encourage them to hand over their money and buy a bond. Popular singers would stand on top of the tanks and put on a performance. In London's Trafalgar Square singers Beattie and Babs sang songs on top of Mark IV tank 'Nelson' during its appearance between 4 and 9 March 1918.

National War Bonds were introduced by the British government in October 1917. They could be bought by any person, company or organisation; they were interest-bearing and provided a premium payment when cashed in. Five-, seven- and ten-year bonds were available.

In June 1916 War Savings Certificates were issued for the first time. These were aimed at the man and woman in the street. Before decimalisation, twenty shillings made one British pound. A £1 War Savings Certificate could be purchased for just 15 shillings and sixpence. After five years the certificate could be cashed in and the holder would receive twenty shillings. This was a good return for the small investor and was also seen as a patriotic act.

Mark IV No. 130, 'Nelson', was one of six tanks that toured the towns and cities of Great Britain from November 1917 to the end of the war to encourage people to buy government war bonds and war savings certificates.

The tanks would enter the city or town under their own power, normally flanked by a marching regiment of soldiers. Police would line the street to keep the crowds back. The public had only read about tanks in the newspaper and this was the first time most of them would have had an opportunity to see one of these metal monsters. The tank bank tanks were a very popular attraction.

Glasgow set a record for war bond and war savings certificate sales, selling more than £14.5 million – more than London, Manchester and Birmingham combined.

West Hartlepool had come under bombardment from German Navy ships, during which people were killed and houses destroyed. Tank Nelson No. 130 visited the port and although it did not raise as much money as Glasgow, Hartlepool topped the list for the greatest contribution per head of population.

# PRESENTATION TANKS

In 1919 the War Department had an excess of tanks. New, more powerful and efficient models were being developed to replace those that had fought over the battlefields of Belgium and France. The British Treasury decided to present each town and city that had raised money over a certain amount with a now obsolete 'war hero' tank as a way of saying thank you. The task of deciding which town would receive one of these 264 presentation tanks was given to the National War Savings Committee.

After the initial ceremony, many of the tanks were neglected. Left out in the open in parks and on common land, they were exposed to the elements. They deteriorated and became very rusty. During the 1920s and 1930s people wanted to move on from the bad memories of the war years as most people had lost a relative or friend. They wanted a new start and to forget about the bad times, and there was no popular support that insisted the tanks were properly maintained. During the depression the public had more pressing concerns.

West Hartlepool received a presentation tank called 'Egbert' No 141. It was a combat-damaged veteran of the Western Front and a Male tank; these were normally only given to localities that had some connection with tank manufacture or raised a lot of funds. It was placed near the seafront on 29 April 1919, where it remained until 1937 when the local authority ordered its scrapping by a vote of 20–12. The council referred to it as a relic of barbarism.

The presentation tank given to Guildford, Surrey, was cut up on 6 June 1923. It had been placed in a poor location and was often used as an unofficial public lavatory. The council ordered it to be cut up for scrap as it believed it offended those who had lost loved ones in the war, but in reality the high costs of maintaining the tank may have had an impact on the decision.

The town of Goole ordered its tank to be cut up on 11 August 1923. It had been placed near a children's playground and due to a lack of funding by the local council it was not maintained in a safe condition. Children, being children, wanted to play on it but there were rusting sharp edges and it was removed as it was deemed a hazard.

French cities were also gifted presentation tanks. On 25 March 1926, Le Havre in Normandy sold its tank to a scrap metal merchant.

On 12 November 1928 Wrexham Town Council sold its tank for just £10, while Aylesbury Borough Council accepted £22 10s for its tank. It was removed on 13 June 1929 to make way for a bus station. On 26 June 1929 two workmen cutting up the tank with oxyacetylene torches ended up in hospital. Not all the petrol had been drained from the fuel tanks. The fuel exploded, blasting the men through the air.

Yarmouth Town Council only received £12 10s for the scrap value of its tank. It was carted away on 16 August 1929.

Developers of the new London University had a problem: the Holborn presentation tank was on the land where a new building was planned. The local council considered this an ideal opportunity to get rid of the unwanted presentation and it was sold for scrap rather than relocated. The excuse that was given was that it would be too difficult to relocate such a big vehicle.

The money from the sale of the High Wycombe tank went towards setting up a university scholarship in the name of 2Lt Frederick Youens VC. The scholarship would be awarded to a student of the Royal Grammar School, High Wycombe. The tank was cut up for scrap on 17 November 1930.

The Colchester tank was on public display in the town's Castle Park. The local council only received £7 15s when on 6 January 1934 it authorised its removal and cutting up.

The price of scrap metal rose in 1937 to around £3 per ton. The presentation tanks of Hythe, Basingstoke, Hitchin, Carlisle and Bangor were all sold for scrap in that year and most of the councils received more than £40. Middlesbrough's tank was scrapped on 20 November 1939.

A Male Mark IV tank, No. 2322 named 'Damon', saw combat during the Third Battle of Ypres on 20 September 1917. Conditions were awful. It had rained and the battlefield had turned into a morass of mud and water-filled shell craters; no place for nearly 30-ton tanks. They could not find traction and got stuck in the mud. Damon was being driven down a road during an attack when it slid off into a ditch and could not get out. A German artillery observer spotted it and suddenly high-explosive shells rained down on its location. The tank was salvaged and presented to the city of Ypres, where it was placed on display near the railway station. The city was a ruin after the constant shelling but was rebuilt. During the German occupation of the Second World War it was cut up and used for scrap.

Of the many presentation tanks that had been gifted to towns and cities after the war, only two tanks still exist today: 'Daphne', a Mark IV Female tank, given to the people of Gloucester but now housed in the Museum of Lincolnshire Life in Lincoln, and another Mark IV Female tank, home service number 245, in Ashford, Kent.

Ashford's presentation tank was built in 1916, but it is believed it never saw active service. It was presented to the town on 1 August 1919 by Capt. Ferrar of the Army Council in recognition of the splendid response to the National War Savings Appeals. The tank was delivered to Ashford West Railway Station (Off Godinton Road) and driven to St George's Square.

Sadly, in 1929, the back of the tank was removed, as well as all the mechanical workings inside, and an electricity substation was installed inside. However, this probably saved it from being scrapped like so many others. The electricity substation was closed in 1968.

In 1978, and ten years later in 1988, the Royal Electrical and Mechanical Engineers carried out some minor works to the tank, including replacing the guns and painting it olive green. A canopy was also built over the tank to protect it.

In 2005, the council commissioned local engineer Keith Williamson to carry out major refurbishment work. The Tank Museum in Bovington was very helpful

This Mark IV Female presentation tank can be found in St George's Square, Ashford in Kent. It has been placed under a canopy in the centre of the city among the shops. Ashford's tank was built in 1916, but it is believed it never saw active service.

Mark IV Female presentation tank 'Daphne' No. 2743, F3 can be seen in the Museum of Lincolnshire Life in Lincoln. It went into battle on 22 August 1917 but was knocked out by enemy shelling at Bell Vue forward area.

and allowed him access to its tank, also supplying a number of drawings showing the dimensions.

The refurbishment included removing all the rust from inside the tank and repainting it with a rust inhibitor, bracing the sides of the tank (as it has no floor), repairing any cracks in the structure, refabricating a complete back end, which is a complete replica of the original, and repainting.

The tank is a Registered War Memorial (Reference No. 43725). It was rededicated prior to Remembrance Day 2006, in the presence of local MP Damien Green, the British Legion, representatives of the council and the engineers who completed the work.

The Mark IV Female called 'Daphne' at the Museum of Lincolnshire Life in Lincoln was issued to the 12th Company, 'D' Battalion, of the Tank Corps. She was mentioned in regimental diaries as having been involved in the attacks at Passchendaele in August 1917. After the war 'Daphne' was shipped back to England and given to the people of Gloucester.

'Daphne' stood in Gloucester Park from 1919 until the Second World War. She was moved to Hucclecote Airfield and later transported to The Tank Museum in

Bovington and put on display after being restored. As The Tank Museum already had a Mark IV it was decided that she would be lent to the people of Lincoln to be part of their new heritage museum in the mid–1980s.

The wooden plank, called an 'unditching beam', was used to help the tank get out of the mud. It was chained to the unditching rails and worked like snow chains to give the tracks extra grip.

# BIBLIOGRAPHY

Peter Barton, *Arras*

David Bullock, *Armoured Units of the Russian Civil War: Red*

David Bullock, *Armoured Units of the Russian Civil War: White and Allied*

Bryan Cooper, *Ironclads of Cambrai*

Martin Marix Evans, *Passchendaele: The Hollow Victory (Campaign Chronicles)*

David Fletcher OBE, *Tanks and Trenches*

David Fletcher OBE, *British Mark I Tank 1916*

David Fletcher OBE, *British Mark IV Tank*

David Fletcher OBE, *British Mark V Tank*

David Fletcher OBE, *British Tanks 1915–1919*

David Fletcher OBE, *Medium Mark A Whippet*

Brevet-Col J.F.C. Fuller DSO, *Tanks in the Great War 1914–1918*

Major Dennis Gaare, *Edwin M. Wheelock and the Skeleton Tank*

John Glanfield, *The Devil's Chariots: The Origins and Secret Battles of Tanks in the First World War*

Bryn Hammond, *Cambrai 1917: The Myth of the First Great Tank Battle*

David R. Higgins, *Mark IV vs A7V*

Jack Horsfall, *Flèsquieres, Cambrai*

Jack Horsfall, *Cambrai, the Right Hook*

Jack Horsfall, *Bourlon Wood*

Ralph E. Jones, *The Fighting Tanks Since 1916*

Kenneth Macksey, *Tanks Versus Tanks*

Alistair McCluskey, *Amiens 1918*

Chris McNab, *Cambrai 1917*

Michael R. McNorgan, *Great War Tanks in Canadian Service*

F. Mitchell, *Tank Warfare: The Story of Tanks in the Great War*

Olga S. Phillips, Solomon J. Solomon, *A Memoir of Peace and War*

Richard Pullen, *Landships of Lincoln*

Richard Pullen, *Beyond the Green Fields*

Wolfgang Schneider, *German Tanks of World War One*

Jack Sheldon, *The German Army at Cambrai*

A.J. Smithers, *The New Excalibur*

Lt. Col Sir Albert G. Stern, *Tanks 1914–1918, The Log-Book of a Pioneer*

Rainer Strasheim, *Sturmpanzer A7V*

Alexander Turner, *Cambrai 1917: The Birth of Armoured Warfare*

C.H. Wendel, *Standard Catalog of Farm Tractors 1890–1980*

A. Gordon Wilson, *Walter Wilson – Portrait of an Inventor*

F.G. Woolnough, *A Brief History of the Royal Tank Corps*

Steven J. Zaloga, *German Panzers 1914–1918*

Steven J. Zaloga, *French Tanks of World War I*

Steven J. Zaloga, *Early US Armor*

## ORIGINAL DOCUMENTS

RFC Minute 2272.G from General Staff to GOC RFC, 14 March 1918

Cabinet Officer Papers 120/354 August 1940 to September 1942: Tank Nomenclature and Classification

Patent GB126,671 filed 2/2/17 by William Ashbee Tritton

Imperial War Museum

Private Papers of Lt Col L.S. Henshall DSO TD Documents.13825

Henshall papers, IWM 73/126/1 – Papers relating to 5 Company, 'B' Battalion at Cambrai and 4th Battalion in 1918

Private Papers of Major W.H. Thompson Documents.178

Private Papers of E.T. Beale Documents.11960

British Tank gunner Eric Potton 'F' Battalion Tank Corps Tapes IWM London

Tank Brigade War Diary the National Archives Kew

War Diary No.1/A Bttn Tank Corps/A Coy HBMGC 1916–1919

War Diary No. 2/B Bttn Tank Corps/B Coy HBMGC 1916–1919

War Diary No. 3/C Bttn Tank Corps/C Coy HBMGC 1916–1919

War Diary No. 4/D Bttn Tank Corps/D Coy HBMGC 1916–1919

War Diary No. 5/E Bttn Tank Corps/E Coy HBMGC 1916–1919

War Diary No. 6/F Bttn Tank Corps/F Coy HBMGC 1916–1919

War Diary No. 7/G Bttn Tank Corps 1916–1919

War Diary No. 8/H Bttn Tank Corps 1917–1919

War Diary No. 9/1 Bttn Tank Corps 1917–1919

War Diary 1st Brigade Heavy Branch Machine Gun Corps/Tank Corps. PRO WO 95/97

War Diary 2nd Brigade Heavy Branch Machine Gun Corps/Tank Corps. PRO 95

War Diary 3rd Brigade Heavy Branch Machine Gun Corps/Tank Corps. PRO 95/104

War Diary of No. 2 Salvage Corps H.B.M.G.C. July 1917–19. PRO WO 95/96

## US NEWSPAPERS

Man who designed war tractor, former Winonian, never received reward for tank's invention, *The Winona Republican*, 31 June 1942

Winona sees Spider Tank, *The Winona Independent*, 12 Nov 1918

Was former Winonian battle tank inventor? by B. Manderfield, *Winona Sunday News*, 22 Aug 1971

American claims share in Prize of $150,000 for Tank invention, *New York Times*, 28 Nov 1925

## INTERNET SOURCES

www.awm.gov.au
www.chars-francais.net
www.iwm.org.uk
www.landships.info
www.landships.activeboard.com
www.militaryfactory.com

www.nam.ac.uk
maps.nls.uk/ww1/trenches/index.html
www.samilitaryhistory.org/vol145rh.html
www.tank-hunter.com
www.tankmuseum.org
www.tanks-encyclopedia.com

# INDEX

# INDEX